THESE DARK SKIES

THESE DARK SKIES

Reckoning with Identity, Violence,
and Power from Abroad

Arianne Zwartjes

University of Iowa Press | Iowa City

University of Iowa Press, Iowa City 52242
Copyright © 2022 by Arianne Zwartjes
uipress.uiowa.edu

Printed in the United States of America
Text design and typesetting by April Leidig

Printed on acid-free paper

Library of Congress Cataloging-in-Publication Data
Names: Zwartjes, Arianne, author.
Title: These Dark Skies: Reckoning with Identity, Violence, and Power from Abroad / Arianne Zwartjes.
Description: Iowa City: University of Iowa Press, [2022]
Identifiers: LCCN 2021050714 (print) | LCCN 2021050715 (ebook) |
ISBN 9781609388416 (paperback ; acid-free paper) | ISBN 9781609388423 (ebook)
Subjects: LCSH: Zwartjes, Arianne. | Identity (Philosophical concept) | Violence—Social aspects. | Emigration and immigration—Social aspects. | National characteristics—Social aspects. | Social integration. | LCGFT: Essays.
Classification: LCC PS3626.W37 T44 2022 (print) | LCC PS3626.W37 (ebook) |
DDC 814/.6 [B]—dc23/eng/20211112
LC record available at https://lccn.loc.gov/2021050714
LC ebook record available at https://lccn.loc.gov/2021050715

Creativity and imagination, the artist giving birth to something new, propose to us avenues of inquiry and ideas about change that require us to think about how we know the world, how we are in the world, and most important, what in the world is possible. What we will find time and time again, in those turning points and moments where something moves beyond the grip of violence, is the vision and belief that the future is not the slave of the past, and the birth of something new is possible.
—John Paul Lederach, *The Moral Imagination*

Beloveds, I keep trying to speak of loving but all I speak about is acts of war and acts of war and acts of war.
—Juliana Spahr, *This Connection of Everyone with Lungs*

CONTENTS

For Anna
for helping me see farther

PROLOGUE

Months before I started this writing, I was on a train, and we hit a cow standing on the tracks. There was no impact, no thud, just the long sound of splintering bones that went on and on, as though someone had laid out kindling for a fire over an extended stretch of the tracks. There were two young children sitting near me, and when the sound began, their mother's eyes and mine met, wide, over the backs of the seats.

On the way back from that same trip, this time in my own car, as I was driving a twisting, lonely stretch of road through the remote dark of western New Mexico, I came across an accident. Two young men in a small sports car had hit a large black cow, its body all but invisible against the backdrop of night. I pulled over to help and found they were, amazingly, unhurt, though the front of their car was completely smashed. The dark body of the cow lay against the edge of the road, still and bloodlined.

I found myself writing a letter to a friend a few days later that came to foreshadow the entire project:

> Here, violence has been this strange thread wended through everything of late, since the day of splintering cow bones under a train: the dogs' cat-kill in my yard, leaving me horrified and shaken; an owl bloodying a pigeon on the curb in front of my house; some guy in Tucson holding his girlfriend hostage for 16 hours. A. wrote an essay about violence in South Africa, which I read in a cafe and then came home to an echoing midnight gunshot across the street, practically in her backyard. Last night, while leaving a convenience store, I was frozen by CNN images of riot cops clubbing a man over the head in Tahrir Square: first no blood, then suddenly, blood everywhere.

And now a spider is in the process of killing a fly in my kitchen window, and the fly is making this crazy, constant, desperate high-pitched whine which I can hear even from the other room, and which doesn't stop, right on the edge of my ears.

I suppose some of this is the normal, everyday kind of violence that we are mostly inured to or insulated from in our cozy modern society; the kind glossy magazines and IKEA-perfect homes and shrink-wrapped grocery meat keep at bay or render unreal via distance. I watched a TED talk by Chris Abani the other day, and he was talking about having to kill a goat, all Igbo boys have to kill a goat, and how he couldn't do it, he just couldn't, and he cried and cried. His cousin told him, it is always hard, every time, but you cannot let it be *this* hard.

Some of it, though, is a violence related to injustices and human brutalities, and that is harder to puzzle my way through, or understand my relationship to.

I began this book trying to write about violence and connection, which really means it was about what it means to be human, to live with the opposing impulses of Eros and Thanatos; and what it means to be mortal and to live in a body that is subject to violence.

I began it trying to *understand* violence, including mob violence, interpersonal violence, and genocide—and while in some ways this is still that project, I found myself continuously circling back around to questions of the American role in the world's larger violences—systemic violence, institutional violence, violences of inequality, exploitation, and deprivation, as well as of militarization and policing, borders and walls, broad undefined wars, and drones and tear gas and other weaponry.

There are so many ways to define violence, and while along the way I realized that I understand, in many ways, the psychological rationalizations or passions that can lead to some kinds of human violence, I perhaps do not understand the ways in which growing up in a dominator culture—in a culture defined by its own empire and educated toward a complete innocence of that empire's excesses and indifferences and violences—has deeply shaped me and my consciousness, along with my understanding of the world.

In part, this project seeks to examine the inextricable links between my Americanness and my whiteness, the first of which I thought a lot about in my late teens and early twenties, and the second of which I've thought much about in the decades since. It seeks to explore how those identifiers have shaped me and the ways in which I have at times desired to escape or avoid those identities, with their histories and current realities of exploitation.

And it seeks to explore ways I, and others who are both white and American, might move forward through shifting our actions in the world, but also through *understanding ourselves*, for without deep, honest self-awareness, it is impossible to imagine—or avert—the worst things we are each capable of. Those "worst things," in fact, are very often committed in the desperate attempt to escape facing with a clear-eyed gaze what we are—or are capable of. In such evasion it is possible to retain both a comfortable avoidance, along with a helpful amnesia after each "worst thing" is committed, rationalizing away and then indeed forgetting entirely such actions.

And that avoidance is often so very alluring. For example, I can often tell when my wife, Anna, and I are speaking about something truly difficult, because a sort of fuzzy sleepiness washes over me, muffling and dull, pulling me down like a heavy blanket of snow toward escape.

"Acceptance is not the same as apathy; radical acceptance is even, maybe, the first step to finding ways for change," I write in chapter 2, and while in those lines I was talking about accepting the world as it is, I think these words apply just as crucially to knowing ourselves, those of us who are white, who are American, who have been raised on a diet of innocence and plausible denial, of comfortable

ignorance and the complacency of believing our government—and ourselves—
to be good and benevolent forces in the world.

In recent years I have become extremely interested in the field of autotheory,
writers and artists exploring what it means to live in and through the body, to
metabolize theory through lived experience.

I consider this project not so much a work of autotheory as of autopolitics, mix-
ing and interweaving personal narrative with thinking and research on social
constructions of identity, racial constructions, power, and violence.

In my definition of "politics," I lean on the work of Ann Cvetkovich and the
Public Feelings project:

> The personal voice has persisted as an important part of feminist scholar-
> ship, enabled, if not also encouraged, by theory's demand that intellectual
> claims be grounded in necessarily partial and local positionalities. The
> Public Feelings project builds on these lessons and strategies in an effort
> to bring emotional sensibilities to bear on intellectual projects and to con-
> tinue to think about how these projects can further political ones as well.
> As we have learned to think both more modestly and more widely about
> what counts as politics so that it includes, for example, cultural activism,
> academic institutions, and everyday and domestic life, it has become im-
> portant to take seriously the institutions where we live (as opposed to al-
> ways feeling like politics is somewhere else out there).

At any rate, I wish to think about what it means to be both American and white
in this world where both of those identities—together, but also separately—are
so loaded with connotation, myth, and power, and with histories of violence and
resource theft.

I also wish to think about what it means to be a human being in a finite world.
And to think about the power of art—to break us open, to change our thinking,

to teach us things emotively, visually, symbolically, that we cannot otherwise absorb, or will not allow ourselves to feel.

One thing that strikes me as I am finishing this writing is that, more and more, research in science and medicine and psychology is confirming what Buddhists have known for millennia, that the brain is plastic and capable of change; that we are different selves in each moment of our lives, without a concrete, static "self"; that all of us are products of "causes and conditions," shaped by myriad forces from our genetics to our life experiences, not without choice or agency, but without an essentialized "individuality" in the way we usually conceive of it in the US. And that, as human beings and also as one of many species on this planet, we are more interconnected and interdependent than those of us in wealthy, individualistic countries ever tend to think of ourselves as being.

Ultimately, this is a project about art and about violence, but also about hope, and where I find most of my hope is in our human ability to change, our capacity for compassion and equanimity, our capacity for generosity and for self-awareness and for communal thought and connection.

In the words of Juliana Spahr, "How connected we are with everyone. . . . In this everything turning and small being breathed in and out / by everyone with lungs during all the moments."

THESE DARK SKIES

CHAPTER ONE

Choreographies

In the kitchen, Anna's mother is making syrniki, which could be roughly equated with a Russian version of pancakes. In the next room, Anna is reminding me how to pronounce their name: "It has that sound in it that you don't like."

"You mean the sound that makes you laugh at me, every time I try to say it?"

She snorts. "It's not laughter. It's a caring feedback chuckle."

Behind us France 24 news plays on the television, its volume muted. The day before, we'd driven through the tangled summer green of central France, which gave way to tanned earth and fields of lavender and sunflowers as we drew farther south. In the evening we reached the coast, turning east and driving past a string of coastal cities: Marseilles, Cannes, Nice. Arriving finally in Menton, exhausted, we found the address of Anna's mother's apartment, drove around until we found parking we hoped was legitimate, and dragged ourselves and our things inside.

Raimund Hoghe, a German choreographer and dancer whose work I've followed for a few years, is well known in Europe, but less so in the US dance world—aside, perhaps, from his earlier work as a dramaturge for Pina Bausch.

Hoghe's first onstage performance was a solo dance piece in which he tells the story of Joseph Schmidt—a world-famous Jewish tenor who had performed at

Carnegie Hall, and who, fleeing the Nazis, was interned as an illegal refugee in a camp in Switzerland, where he died in 1942.

Hoghe created this piece in the early 90s, when many people, including choreographers and dancers, had died of AIDS. Some of the arguments used in Germany at that time against people with AIDS, Hoghe points out, were the same as those used during the Third Reich.

The day of our long drive south had been Bastille Day, the national day of France. We'd passed strings of fire trucks—large squarish vehicles painted red and neon-yellow—driving in caravans on the highway, and the sounds of fireworks peppered our route. Our trip had been a last-minute one: a week freed up by the cancellation of other plans, we'd hurried to rent a car and begin our drive.

Now, sitting at the breakfast table with Anna as her mother prepares syrniki in the other room, the television screen catches my eye. I watch, confused at first, as a large white truck slowly drives down a promenade, then gains speed. As it nears the more crowded section of the street, it is hurtling down the pavement. People are screaming and running in all directions. It is nighttime, dark out, but the street is well lit. The banners at the bottom of the screen say "Terror truck attack in Nice" and "Lorry plowing through crowd at Bastille Day celebration."

The truck swerves from side to side, targeting as many people as possible. "We could hear the awful thump every time a body hit the front of the vehicle," say a couple who had been watching the festivities from their balcony.

News footage from the early morning shows shell-shocked victims slowly walking between metal barriers, blankets around their shoulders. Others sit, wrapped in gold-foil emergency blankets, echoing photos of refugees in rescue boats landing on the coasts of Italy and Spain.

It takes my brain several minutes to process the TV images of the white truck plunging into the crowd, to grasp that this has just happened, the night before, in a city we drove through, a city just down the coast from where we are now sitting. We are frozen at the little breakfast table, thinking about the roads we traveled along the edge of Nice in last night's darkness.

Anna has already told me that her mother had been planning to attend the fireworks in Nice, but it will take me several more hours before I connect that to what we've just seen, realize her mother would have been at the site of the attack if we hadn't come into town.

This was the early summer of 2016. We'd been living in the Netherlands since the summer before, and it had been a dramatic year, filled with violence and chaos on the international stage. Iraq and Libya were embroiled in war, and Boko Haram, their violence having escalated dramatically over the previous year, had just aligned themselves with the Islamic State. In 2014 ISIS had declared a caliphate stretching from Iraq to Syria, and civilian deaths from airstrikes in Syria were reaching higher levels than ever before. People seeking refuge in Europe—fleeing the swelling proxy war in Syria, as well as the American wars in Afghanistan and Iraq, and largely crossing by boat to Greece—came in unprecedented numbers, topping one million in 2015.

The attack the night before—by the truck driver who ploughed through the crowds in Nice—was one of many violent acts in Europe that year: in early 2015 twelve people had been shot and killed in the offices of *Charlie Hebdo* in Paris, and that fall came the attacks on the Stade de France and Bataclan theater; in early 2016 there were suicide bombings in Zaventem airport and the Maelbeek metro station in Brussels.

The year had been a tumult of upheaval and chaos in places that felt very close to where we were living.

In the summer of 2015, only a few weeks after our wedding, Anna and I arrived in the Netherlands for the first time. Landing at Schiphol in the late evening, we wearily stowed our large suitcases in the storage lockers at the airport and went to a nearby hotel.

The next morning, we took the train from Schiphol to Maastricht, in the southern Netherlands. Anna had been offered a teaching job at an international school in Maastricht, which by complete coincidence is also the city my father's extended family is from. The train lines were under construction, and we had to change trains several times, lugging our four excessively large suitcases stuffed with pillows, sleeping bags, a quilt, and even a small frying pan—we knew our boxes wouldn't arrive for months. It was a hot day, the trains were crowded because of rerouting, and the third train we got on was a stoptrein, a slower train that made more local stops and did not have air conditioning. We were stuck standing in the atrium with a number of other passengers and suitcases, and so we arrived finally in Maastricht, sweaty, exhausted, arms turned to jelly by hauling heavy items up and down the stairs.

Dragging suitcases over cobblestones, we walked the two blocks to the tiny boutique hotel where we planned to spend a mini honeymoon. When we went upstairs to our room, I found that Anna had ordered me flowers: a huge bouquet of orange, red, and yellow blooms filled the whiteness and angularity of the space. The room, with a big white bed and a clawfoot bathtub, was illumined by a sunny dormer window through which we could see the roofs of the city. It was as charming as one could possibly imagine, with the river that divided Maastricht in two flowing nearby.

I've been especially drawn to modern dance in recent years—to the way bodies can move in unexpected ways, twist, jackknife in on themselves; the way the stage becomes a bounded world in which that unexpectedness can play out. All of it embodies something important about the randomness, coincidence, and, at times, chaos the world seems filled with.

One of Raimund Hoghe's most beautiful pieces is called *Sans-titre*, the French equivalent of "Untitled" as the title for a piece of art. Sans-titre can also mean undocumented, without papers.

In the piece, Hoghe performs with Congolese dancer Faustin Linyekula. The two walk from opposite sides of the stage, pass each other, repeat. They stand still, side by side. Hoghe lies flat on the floor, and Linyekula arranges two lines of small, round stones down his back, parallel to his spine.

At one point, Linyekula crawls on all fours, his back lined with small stones, contorting the planes of his back in rhythmic writhing twists.

Hoghe tells the story of coming to the US with his dance-theater troupe to perform. One of their dancers, originally from Nigeria, was denied entrance to the country. We did not replace him, Hoghe says; instead, they made an announcement in the theater of what had happened, and space for the dancer's absence was held by an empty shirt, unworn, on the stage.

A few weeks after our arrival in Maastricht, we'd taken a short trip to Brussels—first to Zaventem airport to meet an arriving friend, then into the city, where we walked beside massive gray stone UN buildings and embassies with guards and high fences, and then into the old city center with its maze of sidewalk cafés and apartments and parks and waffle kiosks.

We stayed in the SoHo of Brussels, in a gray concrete apartment building that was still being renovated. The apartment was a hip studio with a couch and a turntable at one end, a white-quilted bed at the other, and in between a glass-walled bathroom with a walk-in shower. Green plants sat at the base of exposed cement walls. Outside, we could see the roofs and apartments that lined the narrow streets, so European in their angular roofs and small balconies.

Later in the fall, after the Paris Bataclan concert hall and national soccer stadium attacks, and then again after the attacks on Zaventem and the Maelbeek metro station, these streets would be filled with the neon colors of police cars and with soldiers armed with automatic weapons—but when we were there it was just bicycles that lined the sidewalk below us and the occasional person out walking their small dog through the cobbled streets.

———

Anna and I met in New Mexico, but she grew up in the Soviet Union, and then Russia as the communist project fell apart. It was a time of strongmen, thugs, and violent unrest in the country, and some of her childhood stories are mind-boggling to me, such as the time her father came to get her from a school trip to the symphony because there was a coup attempt underway: armed mobs had stormed government buildings and the federal TV broadcasting center, leading to a shutdown of news, and the next morning military tanks began firing on the parliamentary building.

Anna's father was Jewish, most of his family coming from the Pale of Settlement in the region that is now Ukraine, and her mother ethnically Russian; she has an older half-brother whose father is Costa Rican. Eventually, her family was able to get a visa to the US, and they moved to Queens, NY, when she was eleven. Initially, they lived in a Russian neighborhood, but her mother realized Anna would never learn English if they stayed there, so they moved to a more diverse neighborhood, with many Jewish, Korean, and Caribbean families.

Anna prefers outsiderness, she tells me, prefers living in countries where she is explicitly recognized as an outsider, over living in the US, where because she doesn't have an accent, she is expected by Americans—especially white Americans—to act as an insider to a plethora of cultural references she doesn't know, and to a cultural framework she doesn't feel at home in.

———————

I had always loved the dance pieces of Pina Bausch, but my interest in Hoghe's independent work had grown during the time we lived in Europe. His career and artistic interests seemed so aligned with the moment we were living in, full of global conflict—some of which felt quite nearby in relation to where we were living in Europe—and growing nationalism, with a rise in both anti-Semitism and anti-Muslim xenophobia, and with attacks on refugees and other "outsiders" all over Europe, attacks on any kind of perceived difference.

Hoghe regularly and explicitly calls into question the range of what is considered *normal* in his work.

"When I display my own hunchbacked body in my performances, I don't have to say anything to claim 'another' body's right to exist," he says.

In "Dancing the Sublime," Hoghe explains:

> With me, you have this break, this distance: you have what you accept as beauty—the music—and you have the body that doesn't fit what you think.
>
> People . . . can see violence a lot onstage and nudity. But if I just take a shirt off then people say, "We don't want to see this." For me this question of beauty is connected with German history, because the Nazis knew what beauty is, they had special ideas of beauty: which body is beautiful, and which body shouldn't exist.
>
> The Nazis selected Jewish people, people with disabilities, gay people . . . and also bodies like my body. I don't know if I could have existed in the

Third Reich, if I would have been selected. Therefore, I have a very strong reaction to this image of beauty.

"Pier Paolo Pasolini wrote of throwing the body into the fight. These words inspired me to go on stage," writes Hoghe elsewhere.

————————

In 1994, the year Anna and her family moved to Queens, I was a queer white teenager in Maine who'd read a lot of books about the colonial genocide of indigenous communities in North America and spent a lot of time out in nature but who didn't know very much about the world: real cultural difference, national and racial privilege, my own whiteness were all vague concepts to me.

White Americans don't even have *a culture*, I would have scoffed if asked. This was a derisive rather than defensive attitude, but misguided nonetheless.

My eyes opened more to the world when I attended a small school in New Mexico with students from eighty-five different countries, all of whom had undergone a rather grueling process to be selected by their national committees. After graduating from that school, I worked as a carpenter to save enough money to buy a motorcycle and rode it from Seattle to Maine, and then took a bus to central Mexico to learn about sustainable agriculture. In the years following, I studied and lived in China, Taiwan, Thailand, India, Israel, and Costa Rica.

Years later, I returned to that small school in New Mexico to teach, and it was there that I met Anna, who had just moved back to the States after seven years teaching in Cyprus—ours, a random intersection of paths through the world.

When we married, it was up on a hill among the ponderosa pines, a small handful of friends and family sitting on blankets on the ground, and a literature professor friend with a gray suit and a long silver ponytail officiating. After the ceremony, as we were all standing around under the pines drinking champagne we'd hauled up the trail in a cooler, it began to thunder and hail, and we all fled down the hill to seek shelter.

In the spring of our year in Maastricht, Anna and I went to the Theater aan het Vrijthof to see Raimund Hoghe's *Quartet*.

In the first moments of *Quartet*, as the lights come up, a ball rolls out onto the stage. Then another. Another. Another. A man walks out onto the stage. He is very short, his back hunched, his hip on one side protruding. He is wearing high-heeled boots. He throws the balls from a small cloth bag in his hands. They hit the stage, each of them, with a tapping sound. Behind them, the music is sedate.

Another man comes on. His hand dances like a dog chasing fleas. Or a strange bird, tropical and frenetic.

Later, in the middle of the piece, a young dancer in a white shirt is dancing to "On Broadway," angular and jerky with an odd, sexualized jerk of his hips, and it is funny, there are chuckles from the audience. Then the small dancer with the hunched back comes back out, begins kicking the small white balls that are still clustered on the stage, spreading them out until they are an even litter. Then silence. He leaves the stage, it is silent, there is no music, the Broadway guy is still dancing those funny little jerks of his hips, and it all seems less amusing now.

A few days after we first arrived in Maastricht, we'd moved into our apartment, which was—quite literally—round. One of my cousins had generously scouted it out for us the month before and reported that it was in a good location—*but where will you put the couch?* he joked.

We had to get bicycles immediately; we bought them from a British girl who was moving back to the UK, on a small, cobbled side street outside her apartment. They were old, somewhat rusty affairs, classic Dutch workhorses, and they allowed us immediate and delightful mobility around the city.

In those early weeks, we went on several cycling outings to nearby Belgium: riding the bicycle ferry across the Maas, from one riverside café to another, drinking Belgian beers, ordered in French, in the warm glow of the afternoon sun. The flags of Belgium, the Netherlands, and Limburg province flapped and rippled above us in the wind.

In Maastricht, we went to the cafés along the Bassin, the tiny inlet offering docking for many small yachts and houseboats, and ate kaas planke and drank Brand, the local pilsner, before walking back through the city streets to our bicycles. We met my cousin Ron in person for the first time, and his partner, Laetitia, and their small, beautiful child, Joëlle, and they ordered us zuurflees on frites, a local Maastricht specialty.

It was a charming honeymoon to our time living in Europe.

Months later, as we sit in the theater in Maastricht, *Quartet* imbues the space with an operatic stillness. A stillness that wears black.

Quartet raises many questions for me. Why is Hoghe, whose crooked spine already sets him apart, always dressed differently from the other dancers? Would it be disingenuous to ignore his obvious physical difference, to think he shouldn't always be the one set apart, that that's too easy a division? Is it artistically exploitative of the fact that his mere appearance adds idiosyncrasy, adds change, and thus adds energy to the performance? Is the gender-queerness of his various clothing throughout the piece simply another way of setting himself apart, or is it meant to convey other layers of meaning? (Hoghe often plays with gender in his pieces, both through his role and sometimes the roles of other dancers.) If this small dancer with the unusual body was not Raimund Hoghe himself, was not the choreographer of the piece, how much would everything be different? Would it then feel exploitative of him, even mocking, to put him opposite the tall female dancer who is also wearing the highest of heels? Or would it be mocking us, calling attention to the absurdity of our expectations, how narrow the range of what we expect, of what we call normal?

A woman in large black sunglasses enters the stage, which is again littered with small white balls. I have seen this dancer before, in pieces by Bausch. She is very tall and thin and pale, dressed in all black clothing. She never removes her sunglasses.

The stillness breaks as the woman begins to pick up the balls, her energy urgent, even frantic. There are too many to hold; she picks them up futilely, they keep spilling from her hands and bouncing away. It is not physical comedy. She is desperate. This looks to me like life. Hoghe is playing with us: we want so badly for her to succeed, for the balls to be contained. Each time she almost has them, they spill over again.

Finally, she drops her hands, and the balls go everywhere. As she walks offstage, she looks longingly back at them.

———

That on this morning following Bastille Day in July 2016, we are in Menton, visiting my wife's Russian mother who now lives in France—after spending the year in the city in the Netherlands where my extended family lives—leads us to reflection. "It feels like these dance trajectories that are both choreographed and random," Anna muses. "In dance, everyone is pulled and pushed, their trajectories are choreographed by others' trajectories in ways that aren't inherently visible . . . we're all sort of subject to that, this interconnected humanity."

We want so much to have lives that are planned, controlled; to know where we are going. But like this dancer, the balls we try so desperately and so futilely to gather keep spilling out of our control.

Since we arrived in Menton, the conversation between Anna and Kseniya has taken place mostly in Russian, with occasional interjections in French and English, and I am missing most of what is going on. I eventually learn from Anna that the day before, a few of Kseniya's close friends had gone with a Russian priest to visit the Orthodox churches in Nice and to the fireworks there afterward. Kseniya had planned to go with them but at the last minute decided to stay home, unsure what time we would arrive.

Later, Kseniya says to me, in heavily accented English, "My friends were in Nice, and I haven't heard from them this morning. I am very anxious."

Over the next few days, Kseniya worried: she'd still not heard back from her friends; it wasn't like them to not call her back. Sober-faced newscasters told us eighty-four people had been killed, a hundred more injured by the truck and its driver. There were infographics: yellow lines showing where the truck drove along the Promenade des Anglais, where it had turned onto the street by the children's hospital. President Hollande declared three days of national mourning. He declared an extension of the state of emergency that began during the Paris Bataclan shootings eight months before.

Just after we left on our long drive north, Kseniya learned that her friends had all been killed—hit by that truck as it plowed inexorably through the crowds. Only the priest, who had gone back to the car to get something from the trunk, survived.

We could hardly make sense of it, that our last-minute, hastily planned trip— the rental car booked just the day before we left—had saved Anna's mother's life, just three months after Anna's father died from cancer. The coincidental choreography, this continual spillingness of our lives.

At the end of *Quartet*'s first half, the sound of the surf rises in a deafening crescendo. The lights never go down. And the small man appears, again throwing balls, as the tall, elegant woman in sunglasses silently dances herself backward into the shadow of the wings.

CHAPTER TWO

A Wild Blossoming Red

Years ago, before I met Anna, I rode bicycles around southern Spain with a man who had recently become my ex. I am not entirely sure why we decided to take this trip even after breaking up, but both of us wanted to see Spain, and we were good partners in adventure, if not in life.

In embarking on this journey, I was also hoping to write about pilgrimage, about the Camino de Santiago, and about Teilhard de Chardin's paleontological treks through the Gobi. I envisioned our cycling pilgrimage—a series of visits to old Spanish cities with Moorish stone bridges and arches, and to limestone cliffs studded with tufa—as a kind of parallel journey to Marina Abramović's and her long-time partner Ulay's trek from opposite ends of the Great Wall of China.

In their initial conception of the project, Abramović and Ulay would walk from opposite ends of the wall and meet in the middle, to wed. By the time the Chinese government finally approved their permit requests and the project was underway, the pair had separated, and they walked their lonely 1,553-mile journeys from opposite ends to the center to say goodbye.

Earlier in the year of our trip, while visiting New York, I'd seen Abramović sitting in *The Artist Is Present* at MoMA. As part of that retrospective, Abramović sat in a chair, seven hours a day for almost three months, inviting audience members to sit across from her and hold her gaze. The lines to join her stretched for hours.

The Artist Is Present is a sort of expansion on an earlier piece, *Nightsea Crossing*, which Abramović and Ulay performed twenty-two times when they were together.

Of *Nightsea Crossing*, Abramović writes:

> We are sitting motionless at either end of a rectangular table facing each other, our profiles turned to the audience....

> Conditions of the performance.

> During the entire period in which the performance takes place both inside and outside the museum we remain silent and completely abstain from food, only consuming water.

In *Nightsea Crossing*, Ulay once stood up and left Abramović still seated. She recalls:

> Then we had an almost physical fight because he wanted me to give up too because he said it looked ridiculous if I was sitting there alone. And I was thinking that we were working with different time limits and we should show them, we should allow the public to see everything, without embarrassment. But he wanted to draw a line between the private and the public.

My ex and I did go on our cycling trip, and though it was not entirely what I had imagined—a kind of pilgrimage or homage to the ending of our relationship—it was still a mostly charmed trip, despite the wintry Spanish weather. We cycled through the icy rain, and we carried rock-climbing gear in our panniers and went climbing in limestone canyons the December sun hardly touched to warm. We traversed the cliffside iron struts of the narrow, crumbling Camino del Rey, ate churros with chocolate in Granada, and tried to camp in the deep red mud of olive groves. Soon the mud had stained our white tent orange and clogged the brakes of our bicycles, and we resorted to staying in hostels, where we could dry our cycling clothes by the heater overnight. We saw graffiti by El Niño de las Pinturas, cycled through low clouds and among herds of goats standing in the narrow roads.

By the end of that trip, we had found a different way to be present with each other, one that acknowledged the changed connection of our new status.

I used to show my college students documentation from Abramović's early performance pieces. *Rhythm Zero*, often, or *Rhythm 5*. The students were intrigued, often shocked, some of them put off by the nudity, the violence.

In *Rhythm 10*, the first in the series, Abramović is on her knees on a stage, in all black, with an array of knives spread in an arc on the floor in front of her. She takes a knife and stabs the floor in between the fingers of her spread hand as fast as she can. Every time she stabs her bloody hand she changes to a different knife.

In *Rhythm 0*, Abramović is in a closed room for six hours with an audience. On a table are an array of items: grapes, a flashlight, medications, wire, razor blades, makeup and comb, wine, a flute, a Polaroid camera, a rose, a loaded gun. Seventy-two objects. She gave the audience permission to use these items on her body. Her performance notes say, "I am the object. During this period I take full responsibility." By the end of the performance, Abramović stands naked, bleeding where she'd been carved into with rose thorns, her nipples covered with rose petals, her eyes red, and her face streaked with mascara.

When I began to explore her later work—often silent, focusing on the interpersonal gaze, on *presencing*—I understood her initial works in a different light. That going to the body's edge is not unlike becoming fully, baldly, silently present to *what is*. Finding the edge of an audience's discomfort with witnessing nudity, sexuality, pain is not unlike asking them to meet the eyes of the artist for many minutes without breaking.

In one talk, Abramović muses:

> Human beings are always afraid of very simple things. We're afraid of suf-
> fering, we're afraid of pain, we're afraid of mortality. So what I'm doing—
> I'm staging these kinds of fears in front of the audience. I'm using your en-
> ergy [to] push my body as far as I can. And then I liberate myself from these
> fears. And I'm your mirror. If I can do this for myself, you can do it for you.

The ways we try to connect with, to be present to each other are also the ways
we overcome our fear. We bake zucchini bread, offer whiskey, ace wraps, small
notes, a hammer. In such moments of connection, of *usefulness*, our fear of isolation becomes less.

When the relationship with my ex had ended, before our trip to Spain, I felt like
my faith in longevity—my faith in *myself*—was shattered. The sense of isolation
was profound.

———

Years later, when I met Anna, there was a sense of inevitability about our connection, a pull like a tide strong enough to overcome my shaken faith. She had just
moved from Cyprus to New Mexico to teach at the international school where I
worked. I invited her to join me on a backpacking trip to go scout a new area for
my outdoor program, and she told me all about the island nation she'd moved
from: its azure waters and white beaches, its old churches and stony, cobbled villages, the cats that wend their way everywhere.

I knew almost nothing of the country or its history; I had to look Cyprus up on
the map to find its place, nestled in the eastern shoulder of the Mediterranean,
off the coasts of Turkey, Syria, and Lebanon.

I did not know, for example, that Cyprus is home to what is at present the only
divided capital in the world (some sources say "the last divided capital," a statement I find unbearably optimistic).

The Brits practiced their typical divide-and-conquer strategy in Cyprus, fostering tension between the island's Greek and Turkish populations. In 1960 they granted the island independence. Not long after, intercommunal violence erupted between the Turkish Cypriot minority and Greek Cypriot majority, who were essentially the same people, indistinguishable aside from faith. Tens of thousands of people were displaced.

Eventually, Greece and Turkey became involved in the conflict, and Turkey invaded Cyprus, taking over the northern half of the island in a move widely condemned by the international community. Almost two hundred thousand Greek Cypriots left their homes in the north, never to return. Many of those homes were then occupied by Turkish Cypriots, some of whom had been forced out of the south. Turkey has pushed settlers from the Turkish mainland into north Cyprus as well, coercing some of its own people to resettle on the island.

And that is where things still stand today: Turkey unilaterally declaring that the north of the island is an independent state called the Turkish Republic of Northern Cyprus, the rest of the world viewing it as an illegal occupation.

The capital city of Nicosia is drawn through with a Green Line, the UN buffer zone supposedly named after a British general's use of a green china marker to draw the border on his map.

Anna's closest friends in Cyprus, a couple, refuse to visit the north of the island. The husband's father is from the north and was pushed out of his village, his home. None of the family has been back since. To travel there now would require crossing a border they refuse to acknowledge is legitimate.

———

In the summer of 2014, Anna and I decided to travel to Cyprus so she could show me the place that still felt like home to her. We stayed at the house of her friends, who were away on a trip.

When we landed at Larnaca airport in Cyprus in early July, the air shimmered with heat and dust, ringed by turquoise sea.

In the house where we stayed, the dogs slumped on the tile floor and the curtains did ghostly morning dances in the breeze. One of our first nights there, we went out for a stroll, circling the church where Lazarus was buried, when as an old man he died his second death. The white stone of the church glowed in the darkness; the sky, quiet with all its mouths empty.

We visited little hidden beaches all along the south coast, drove into the mountains, and wandered through the old city in Nikosia. Slowly, I began to pick out the sounds made by different Greek letters, watching them on the road signs, the English name for each place written out in white below the yellow Greek words.

I remember my amazement, flying over the wrinkled vastness of the American West, when I first realized I could identify much of it: could point to places I had lived, backpacked, driven through. That it was no longer an unknown stretching vastness that I could fly over and marvel at the mystery of—it was, instead, *known*.

I felt the same way thinking of the several days we'd spent in Istanbul on our way there: sitting by the Bosphorus strait watching the ferries run back and forth; walking about Sultanahmet, the Blue Mosque, with its crown of minarets.

And driving around southern Cyprus, seeing all the minarets on the south side of the island whose forsaken towers stood unadorned—abandoned since the Muslim Turkish Cypriots withdrew to the north—in contrast to the festive Ramadan lights of Istanbul. And walking the streets of Nikosia, where we drank Keo and watched the World Cup, then ate Lebanese mezze inside the Venetian walls of the old city.

These places were no longer blank spots on the world map to me, immense flat mysteries of turquoise or orange or yellow with black lettering.

There, on that contested island, the oleanders mixed with lantana, and the sea lapped with azure tongues. Walk through the old city of Nicosia, and you eventually bump up against the Green Line and its UN peacekeeping soldiers. The buffer zone has swallowed buildings all along its line; now deserted, wrapped with barbed wire, and covered in graffiti, they stare down with dark eyeless windows at the bustle and shops of the old city.

As we explored the edges of the old city, we came across graffiti proclaiming solidarity with Gaza. Unsurprisingly, Greek Cypriots—who feel their land has been invaded by a foreign power that is now bringing in settlers to make the land grab permanent—are very sympathetic toward the Palestinians, who have also been pushed off their land and into smaller and smaller, barely habitable spaces. The settlements in both north Cyprus and the West Bank are considered illegal under international law.

In the weeks before our trip, that tension had escalated, with the kidnapping of several teenagers from the Jewish settlement of Alon Shvut in the occupied West Bank.

Flying to Cyprus, we kept seeing snatches of the TV news in the airport terminals, with CNN's hyperdramatized urgency. The missing Jewish teenagers had been found, killed. Then an Arab teenager went missing. Now, several days later, the news channels in Cyprus show rockets, bombings, Israeli retribution pounding Gazan ground. Sometimes the same images: a woman flees down an alley, screaming. Behind her, a gray cloud rolls down the alley, mushrooming upward. A man carries the body of his six-year-old daughter, in a pink dress, her eyes closed, through the streets in a makeshift funeral procession. "What did she do to deserve this," he tells the camera, his face devastated, gesturing with her small body so her face turns more to us.

In the yard an Italian cypress stood sentinel, flanked by hibiscus: summer was heavy upon us. We were so close, there on that island, to the place where rockets launched nightly over a border, where retaliatory bombs flung back, decimating the night. Just a little stretch of sea between. In the evenings, we sat to eat the same foods: hummus, haloumi, baba ghanoush, kebab, tabouli, cucumber, and pita. What does it mean to live, to be alive—and how is it we keep killing each other on the way to it?

In South Cyprus, graffiti lines the highways: *Turks out of Cyprus!* and *Death to all Turks!* Hard to imagine that in the midst of this highwayed, middle-class, modern Cypriot life, there are aftershocks of war: a UN no-enter zone cutting through the island, locked-up homes that haven't seen their inhabitants since the island was divided.

One night, we were at the sea—still there when dark fell—watching the moon reflect off the water as waves shushed against the sand. Air cooling over our skin, we waded up to our knees in the warm water, feeling the sand suck out from beneath our feet each time a wave came in. A bright round light came up and moved in the sky, farther down the island, and suddenly I was somewhere else— standing in water off the beach of another city: the round light was exactly like the images of night-rockets coming in. I felt we were in the torn fabric, the gaping sag of reality whose wide, shadowed maw suddenly includes the unreality of war. I couldn't shake the feeling—for the rest of the evening found myself looking for the nearest basement, the nearest bomb shelter—I felt that I had stood in that exact place in the dark lapping waters off a city under siege, maybe Beirut, maybe Tel Aviv, both cities full of people who want to live.

The physical feeling of being *there* and not *here* persisted with me all night.

Several mornings later, I woke with the fresh imprints of a dream in my mind: I was huddled in my car, parked on the open top deck of a parking ramp, and being fire-bombed. Live balls of flame were streaking through the air like artillery, like rockets, most barely clearing the garage, aggressively hurling past and arcing down onto a desert landscape. Some of them brushed the car, scratched it with their threat as they streaked by. Wherever they landed they caused huge explosions. I knew if one hit the car it would blow up. I felt I was in Israel, in Palestine, in contested but sacred, beautiful high-desert land. The balls of flame were hot, terrifying, they shrieked as they went screaming by. It seemed all life was ending, that the barren desert itself would crack open with glowing destruction.

I woke with a start and lay in bed watching the sun rise. The sky was light blue, whiter on the horizon, and summer foliage stained the edges green. The windows were open and the air was full of birdsong, trilling and warbling. How, in this one place, could everything be so peaceful, when in another place even the morning light was laced with terror.

It was Ramadan in the midst of all this bombing. In the newspaper, a Palestinian boy lay dead on a table. In Gaza, no one broke fast together; in parks, in public streets, there was only the absence of celebration.

When Anna got up each morning, we watched the news together, moving around the kitchen making breakfast, drinking more coffee. One day, early in our July trip, a flat-faced announcer gave the death toll: Israelis, 0. Palestinians in Gaza, 104.

Israel dropped a bomb into Gaza every four-and-a-half minutes, they said. They'd dropped thousands so far. The Palestinians had fired about 450 rockets, of which the Iron Dome missile defense system destroyed the quarter or more that would have hit close to human targets.

I am not indifferent to the stress of Israelis who fear attacks on their daily lives. No one should have to live in such fear. But neither should anyone, ever, live under the military abuse and extreme economic devastation that the Palestinians have now been experiencing for decades.

Anna switched to the Russian-language news, which I did not understand, but I saw the parading images of that morning's metro crash in Moscow, the long lineup of ambulances parked at the curb.

A week later, the news told us that the death toll had risen to 484 Palestinians, most of them civilians, and twenty Israelis. More than a thousand people in Gaza had been wounded so far.

In the newspaper article I was reading, an Israeli fourteen-year-old asked his mother why the people in Gaza didn't have bomb shelters like they did in Tel Aviv. "They simply weren't able to build them," she responds.

I remembered, as a college student living in Jerusalem, traveling to Ramallah in the West Bank, meeting with people who lived there, seeing their gray, concrete-block homes and dirt roads. They were not allowed to build new houses or to build out, to expand, so with each new generation, they had to build upward, try to create new space. Sometimes Israeli bulldozers came and knocked down the walls of homes the Israelis considered illegal. Across a nearby privacy wall built of neat red brick, we could see the Spanish tile roofs of new Israeli settler homes pushing into the West Bank, their neighborhoods paved with smooth black tarmac, studded with turquoise swimming pools.

The article I was reading went on to discuss the strategies parents were using in Gaza and in Israel to explain what was happening to their children during all this bombardment. *Fireworks* was one of the most common with very small children. *Don't worry, mama, it's just fireworks*, one three-year-old in turn consoled his crying mother.

One father in Gaza, the article noted, had been popping balloons over the crib of his infant to try to get him used to the noise, to try to get him to laugh.

In the mornings, I was the first one up in the house—the iced coffee grew warm before I finished it and a fleece blanket of summer air lay hot against my skin. I sat to meditate and thought about Israel bombing the Gaza strip, about the teenagers from both sides who were killed. I thought about people killing people and how strange it is, how unbelievable—that we're just walking around this world worrying about getting drinking water and going to the store for food and about the thing our neighbor said, and how we are all alike in that, and then suddenly, in the midst of all that, sometimes people are carrying guns or bombing your house. Suddenly, for example, people are shooting from behind birch trees in Ukraine—the same birch trees you might have grown up playing in as a child—wearing T-shirts that look so mundane. So modern.

Or how, in one country, one city, everyone is in the park to break the Ramadan fast in the evening, festively, happily, the birds in the trees making a racket and families on picnic blankets and so on, and in the next country over—just a matter of kilometers, you could easily drive there—no one dares go outside to break their fast together, all the shops are shut, even the birds in the trees are stilled.

Hiking on Mount Olympus in the center of Cyprus, we came across the wall of the old chora fortifications built by the Venetians: five hundred years of rocks whose bodies lay upon each other. Walking the dogs a few nights later we passed under the Roman aqueduct, its tall, shouldered arches a thousand years old. It was almost too much for the mind to imagine: the ancient hands that laid that stone, the water that ran through it.

We are not so different from the people in that past time, whose hands built these structures and whose feet wore sloping paths into the stone. To know that they felt feelings just as individual and powerful as we do is to know, too, that all the people now living in those flat, colored outlines on the map, the mysteries, are also not so different from us. Their brains, too, shrieking in outrage at all this violence; shrieking in disbelief at the nonsensical moment forcing them down an alley, screaming in fear, bombsmoke billowing up behind them.

On our return home from Cyprus, we traveled from Istanbul to Moscow to New York. As we sat on the terrace of our guesthouse in Istanbul, shortly before our flight to Moscow, news came of the Malaysian passenger jet that had crashed just hours before on its flight out of Amsterdam—believed to have been shot down by rebels in eastern Ukraine.

Air space over Ukraine made up the bulk of our flight path between Istanbul and Moscow, and in the cab to the airport I was terrified, my heart in my throat—but once on our 1 a.m. flight, the pilot announced in Russian that the plane would divert entirely around Ukraine.

After landing in New York, we watched interviews with people in Donetsk about the Malaysian airliner crash: people talking about bodies landing in their gardens, coming through the roofs of their houses, bodies only partly clothed after their immense fall, bodies with broken limbs. The horror of this narrative, and the imaginative act of trying to understand what the people in the plane might have gone through, stretch beyond the mind's capacity.

How does the mind deal with horror? is, I suppose, one central question here. The other that I keep coming back to, after seeing the demilitarized zone running right through the middle of the old city in Nikosia, laced and tied with barbed wire; after seeing the brutal destruction of Gaza; or after watching war erupt in modern, middle-class cities in eastern Ukraine—the other question is *why are we, as a species, so prone to violence?*

Or maybe, after all, the more important question is not *why* we keep lapsing, over and over, into violence, but what we do in response, in reaction. That there will always be human violence; that the one thing we can control is how we react.

But I can't help feeling as if there should be something more than that . . . as if stemming violence should be, somehow, within our capacity as a species. Haven't we sent tender, vulnerable human bodies into the hostility of space and brought them back alive again? Haven't we invented a way to send a tiny camera through someone's femoral artery all the way up to their heart, to identify a clot or a blockage? How is it possible that we are still, at the same time, dropping bombs on other human beings, flying planes over them and unleashing drones on them, and sending tanks into their cities and knocking down the walls of their homes, crushing the skin of their bodies beneath concrete, bleeding the blood of their bodies into wild blossoming red.

When asked by an interviewer if she was writing about the siege of Sarajevo, Sontag replied:

> No . . . not yet, and probably not for a long time. . . . I'm not spending time in Sarajevo to write about it. For the moment it's enough for me just to be there as much as I can—to witness, to lament, to offer a model of noncomplicity, to pitch in. The duties of a human being, one who believes in right action, not of a writer.

What I have been thinking about lately has a lot to do with this question of right action, with the duties of being human. It has to do with fear and despair and feeling overwhelmed and trying to make a way through this world; with trying to find hope and faith.

It has a lot to do with living in a world where governments shut down and stop paying their bills, sell their resources off to the highest bidder, and oceans warm up and groundwater is drained and species disappear. With living in a world where my own government's ambitions have always bent toward empire, regardless of the suffering it engenders, a world where power appears endlessly tantalizing. And with trying to understand what it means to be human, what it means to live with integrity and compassion, what it means to try to believe in "right action" in the context of all this apparent destruction.

"Becoming fully, baldly, silently present to *what is*," I wrote in description of Marina Abramović's work, and now I am thinking of what it would mean to truly accept that this is the world we live in: to plainly and flatly accept that violence is a part of its fabric. Acceptance is not the same as apathy; radical acceptance is even, maybe, the first step to finding ways for change. Like sitting across a table from the world as it really is, meeting its eyes, holding its gaze.

Of the potential for transforming conflict and transcending violence, the experienced mediator and professor of conflict studies John Paul Lederach writes that a kind of capacity is required that involves "imagining ourselves in a web of relationships that includes our enemies" and accepting "the mystery of the unknown that lies beyond the too-familiar landscape of violence."

He describes a process of conflict transformation in Carare, Colombia, where "each meeting with each different armed group required careful preparation." What was key, community members reported, "was that they had to find a way to meet the human being, the real person."

So often, the last thing we hear about violent conflicts—not to mention the last thing we think of when we are, ourselves, in some sort of conflict—is the humanity of the individuals involved.

Lederach believes that real solutions to conflict and violence must be envisioned as creative acts, "more akin to the artistic endeavor than the technical process." This does not negate the real value of skill and technique, he says; rather, as human beings we must grow our capacity for imagination—to help us find new paths, ways forward that are "rooted in the challenges of the real world yet capable of giving birth to that which does not yet exist." This seems as true of the massive environmental crisis now facing us as it is of our ongoing tendency toward conflict and violence.

It is for this reason, perhaps, that I find myself turning to art, over and over, for new ways of seeing into human dilemmas that have me mired in a place of profound bewilderment. I want to find new and different ways to be present, in the world and to each other, new ways to imagine solutions to these problems that plague us at a crisis level—and in art and hybridity and the cross-pollination of ideas I see the space for, the capacity for this wild and imaginative kind of thinking.

CHAPTER THREE

The Bent of Light

It is the autumn of 2015 and Anna and I have just recently moved to the little city of Maastricht in the southern Netherlands. At this moment, I am packed into the backseat of a tiny Peugeot with four friends, driving from Maastricht to a Belgian city called Ghent. The landscape speeds by, a string of farm fields and tiny towns.

In Ghent, we wander through cobblestone plazas full of small shops and plan to see the famous painting *Het Lam Gods*—or *Adoration of the Mystic Lamb*, painted in 1432 by the brothers Hubert and Jan van Eyck—currently on display in Sint-Baafskathedraal.

When the cathedral opens in the morning, we cram alongside thirty or so other people into the small side chapel where the painting is housed. Many of them stop by the counter to rent audio-tour handsets, and soon the buzz of digital voices begins to rise and swell around me, indecipherable, unstopping.

I stare up at *Het Lam Gods*. In the top right panel of the painting, depicted in colors so subtle they almost appear black and white, stands Eve. Her posture is in contrast to Adam, who clutches a fig leaf over his genitals and one arm across his chest, and whose downturned face conveys—fear? horror? remorse? Far across the painting, Eve stands indifferently, one hand holding aloft a small fruit, the other carelessly grasping a fig leaf that does not quite cover her groin, though the drape of her arm shadows it.

Her depiction is starkly dissimilar to the wailing, bemoaning grief she is shown with in so many other paintings from around that time. Her face is close to sullen, as she stares downward toward the distance. One feels as if her thoughts are elsewhere and that she is anything but remorseful.

"They had to fall down so that all that saving could happen," one friend exclaims loudly, boisterously, as we walk down the street after leaving the cathedral.

I wonder quietly to myself if that is true, at the defiance I saw on Eve's angled face.

In the Jewish tradition, I read later, the eating of the fruit of the Tree of Knowledge was the moment good and evil became mixed together. Before that, evil did exist but was outside the human psyche. In Kabbalist Judaism, evil feeds on the trapped sparks of holiness in the world, and the two must be separated to cut off evil's life source and make it disappear.

I've never connected with the language of good and evil. I've found them too dichotomous, too pure, when we are all everything, the capacity for everything.

But lately I have been thinking about this concept of evil, about the human impulse to hurt and damage others. Have been imagining that evil, if we are to use that word at all, is for the most part not some kind of cold logic harbored by a malevolent individual but rather the leering angry twist of fear and ignorance into violence. Is more like the incoherent bloodthirst and rage of an angry crowd, the uncontrollable trajectory of energy and fear; more like the vicious mobbing of a vulnerable body, a vulnerable life. It is part of the human passion, and we seem no more able to control or override it now than we were millennia ago.

Back home in Maastricht, the winds are tempestuous. As we were reading Mikhail Bulgakov's *The White Guard* aloud to each other in the evening, curled on the couch with a blanket tucked around our feet, Anna said, "It's different in Russian—the word *blizzard* isn't just weather-channel speak for heavy snow, it has an element of catastrophe in it, of isolation and wolves and starvation."

In the morning the autumn wind still surges with unstoppable ferocity across the landscape. The pods on the trees move like long fingers searching the air. A thick, hairy fly clings to the window and I shudder.

I am listening to a TED talk by Hubertus Knabe, and he is talking about the Stasi, the secret police of East Germany whose modus operandi was to quietly, darkly destroy people's lives from the inside, so that they thought they were crazy or a failure, so that they felt alone and abandoned by everyone they trusted.

Knabe says the Stasi even kept "data" of people's scents. They collected these scents in bottles.

After the wall came down, civilians found rooms full of bottles, lines and lines of glass, each one holding the scent of a human being.

I remember experiencing the dawning awareness that what is most difficult in times of tyranny—and also, I imagine, in moments of disaster or war—is the darkness, the rumors, the mistrust of any news one is receiving, the lack of any clear or reliable information. We are so accustomed, in these times, to having vast information available to us in just a few clicks. But these systems can break down—and do break down in moments of upheaval and catastrophe.

One psychologist outlines four conditions for the generation and transmission of rumors: personal anxiety, general uncertainty, importance of the topic at hand, and—least important in times of heightened threat—credulity. In the absence of clear and reliable information, rumor spreads like fire.

The poet Marie Howe recalls in an interview:

> One of my teachers at Columbia was Joseph Brodsky, who's a Russian poet, a wonderful, amazing poet, who was exiled from the Soviet Union. And he said, "You Americans, you are so naïve. You think evil is going to

come into your houses wearing big black boots. It doesn't come like that. Look at the language. It begins in the language."

In another recounting, a Bosnian Serb woman named Seka Milanovik remembers the way the war began in Bosnia, in the early 1990s:

> The war began with words, but none of us paid any attention. The extremist Serbs and Muslims were misfits, criminals and failures. But soon they held rallies and talked of racial purity, things like that. We dismissed them—until the violence began.

I share this with a friend, and she writes back: accounts from Rwanda just before the genocide are like this too, the way it crept up in the language.

Shortly after this exchange, lying in bed in the morning, fuzzy-brained and trying to drag myself out of deep slumber, I read an article in the *Guardian* about the current atmosphere in Hungary under Viktor Orbán: filled with hatred and fear-mongering. There is a popular website where viewers try to discern whether quotations are from present-day Hungary or from Radio Rwanda on the eve of the 1990s genocide—Hungarian examples include language such as "filthy rats" and "inevitable bloodshed," making it difficult to tell the two apart.

For many years now, I have been obsessed with this question: *how do we know?* How do we know it's coming, identify it earlier, before the violence starts—before it's rolling inexorably forward?

In *War Is a Force That Gives Us Meaning*, Chris Hedges describes the way language was used—manipulated—to create difference between Serbs, Muslims, and Croats in the leadup to the Bosnian war:

> Since there was, in essence, one shared language, [each group] began to distort their own tongue to accommodate the myth of separateness. The

Bosnian Muslims introduced Arabic words and Koranic expressions into the language. The Muslims during the war adopted words like *shahid*, or martyr, from Arabic, dropping the Serbian word *junak* ... [and] the Croats swung the other way, dusting off words from the fifteenth century.

Leaders in that conflict understood the power of language to creep in around the edges. "The nationalist myths stand on such miniscule differences," Hedges continues. "These myths give neighbors the justification to kill those they had gone to school and grown up with."

And so, perhaps, a second question I have been carrying around: even if it were possible to *know*, to see the tipping point, how could enough people be persuaded to act before things moved beyond just language?

A Wordpress site I encountered, dedicated to the Bosnian genocide, hosted article after article, photo after photo of the exhumation of mass graves, of cemeteries, of people grieving.

One article described current efforts to keep memories of that genocide alive:

> Bosniak human rights activists, led by Ms Bakira Hasečić, prevented the nationalist Serb authorities from demolishing a memorial house in which Serb soldiers set on fire sixty-five Bosniak civilians in a 1992 assault on Visegrad.

> In 1992, Ms Bakira Hasečić and her two daughters, aged 13 and 18, were repeatedly gang raped by Serb soldiers. Ms. Hasečić's sister's home was turned into a rape camp by the Serb forces, and she died there after repeated sexual assaults.

If you scrolled further, just below the article there was a photo of a white medical-gloved hand scraping soil away from several human fingers, emerging ghoulishly from the reddish dirt.

In *The Winter Sun*, Fanny Howe writes:

> One of the identifiable factors of a massacre is that the victims can't believe what is happening to them, since they have nothing to do with the idea behind it.
>
> They are not soldiers but civilians in the middle of their hopes.

The mist hangs like a skin over the land this morning, taking away the substance and leaving only a suggestion of the world. Out walking along the edge of the horse pasture, the grass wets my jeans, and spider webs adorn the fence line, coated in tiny silver pools.

When everything is silent and one is left only with the tide of one's own breathing, it is impossible not to ask *whys* of the world.

Scientists know the universe is expanding rather than holding still or contracting, because all the light that comes to us is skewed toward the red end of the spectrum. Anna, who teaches physics, explains this to me in terms of concentric ripples: if whatever created those concentric circles moves in a linear direction, its next touchdown will be closer to one side of the circles, more distant from the other side—making the wavelengths between two "ripples" shorter on one side, longer on the other. In sound, we hear this difference in wavelengths as different pitches (think of the way ambulances sound distinctly different when approaching than when moving away). In light, we see it as different colors. Red is our perception of longer wavelengths, thus the implication that everything in the universe is moving slowly away from us.

Jeanne Theoharis is a professor from Brooklyn College whose student—an American citizen of Pakistani descent—endured three years of pretrial solitary confinement on charges of "conspiracy to provide material support to terrorism" after allowing an acquaintance he didn't know well to stay at his apartment. Of that experience, she writes:

> To one who teaches about civil rights . . . it is humbling to see those rights shredded a few miles from my classroom. Among the hardest things to teach as a historian are the outsized fears, political motivations, and economic interests that rendered good people silent in the face of government repression, civil-rights violations, internment, and redbaiting.

> Courage is costly.

In a recent conversation, Anna commented, "If in Russia you said to someone, *I'm a good person*, they would just laugh at you. There is not this idea that some people are good, but rather that all of us are flawed."

I think about expanding this idea of *good* and *bad* beyond people, to the larger systems or institutions we may have faith in, the beliefs we may hold sacred.

Our tendency to believe in dualities—to think that some systems are good and others are bad—can make us unable to tolerate critiques of what we hold up as essentially *good* and blind us to its flaws. Such binary thinking can lead to inaction: something is either *good* or it's *bad*, inherently, irreparably.

Christian ethicist Reinhold Niebuhr cautioned that the difficult choice we make as adults in a complex world is not between the moral and the immoral but between the immoral and the less immoral.

In practical terms, the choice to do nothing often looks like choosing normalcy over total uncertainty. Little wonder it takes so much to get us to a place of meaningful protest. When we are comfortable, to risk losing it all seems unthinkable.

Of course, sometimes things are simply going to change anyway, though I refer here to the sort of drastic change Westerners have not had to face, not really, since World War II. "When dying regimes collapse, they do so with dizzying speed," writes Hedges.

The ground rejects the roots pushing into it and the hips of the sky splay above.

———

One of my former students writes me a letter. He has just returned to Singapore to do his compulsory military service.

> Dear Ari,
>
> I wanted to give you a quick update on how the army is going. I just returned home after a 7-day field camp out in the "wilderness" here in Singapore—vaguely reminiscent of backpacking, but with the added weight of an assault rifle strapped to my chest.
>
> Instead of cozy sleeping bags, we slept in "shellscrapes" that we dug ourselves—which bore striking resemblance to excavated graves. No sleeping bag, no groundsheet, just full-on skin-to-dirt contact. Our daylight hours were spent performing training exercises: fire movement maneuvers through the jungle, rifle PT, live firing, learning field signs and various airstrike & artillery drills.
>
> I find it difficult to reconcile with the fact that I am being trained to kill another human being. Whilst a certain satisfaction can be derived from watching 700 ball bearings explode out of a grenade at breakneck speed, or the feeling of squeezing a trigger and feeling the kickback of recoil as a round exits your barrel, I definitely don't have it in me to place another

living, breathing human at the receiving end of the above. This is something I will never be able to come to terms with.

I hope things are going well for you & Anna in the Netherlands, and would love to hear an update on life there.

Warmly,
Sohrab

I think of him, and of so many of my other students who have returned home to compulsory military service in their countries.

How many of them will see war in their lives? How many will see political violence, tyranny, despotism—or be asked to act as agents of persecution? How many of all of us, this global network of humans I am now connected to, will directly experience those things in our lifetimes?

The wind moans outside the windows. As I look at the pastoral landscape outside, softly furred with green, the memory of war seems inconceivable. Only the gray sky hangs heavy and has seen all the actions we cannot conceive of. Or prefer to think ourselves incapable of.

"That mass killings and genocides recur on earth does not mean that they are similar," writes Annie Dillard in *For the Time Being*. "Each instance of human, moral evil, and each victim's personal death, possesses its unique history and form."

After the Napoleonic Wars of the early nineteenth century, the bones of the dead were brought from battlefields all over Europe to the port of Hull and ground to powder to fertilize farmers' fields. *Only the dead have seen the end of war*, writes George Santayana.

Searching to understand more about the onset of tyranny, I read an account by war journalist Peter Maass, describing Radovan Karadžić, who was Bosnian Serb president during the Bosnian War in the early 90s and was later convicted of war crimes, including genocide.

Maass writes, "Tyrants don't care if you believe them, they just want you to succumb to doubt. I knew Bosnia well, and I knew that the things Karadžić said were lies, and that these lies were being broadcast worldwide." It's not that people believed his lies, exactly, Maas explains, but nonetheless they muddied the truth, "causing outsiders to stay on the sidelines, and this of course was a great triumph for Karadžić."

> He didn't need to make outsiders believe his version of events; he just needed to make them doubt the truth and sit on their hands.

As a recent article in the *Atlantic* notes, for the most part "modern strongmen seek merely to discredit journalism as an institution" to persuade us that there is no real truth. They know that spreading cynicism is even more effective than spreading lies.

Maass was one of the few American journalists who was able to speak with Slobodan Milošević during his era of power amid the collapse of Yugoslavia. Of his ninety-minute meeting in Milošević's office, he recalls:

> It was as though I pointed to a black wall and asked Milošević what color it was. White, he says. No, I reply, look at it, that wall there, it is black, it is five feet away from us. He looks at it, then at me, and says, The wall is white, my friend, maybe you should have your eyes checked. He does not shout in anger. He sounds concerned for my eyesight. I knew the wall was black. I could see the wall. I had touched the wall. I had watched the workmen paint it black.

On a meditation retreat shortly before we moved to the Netherlands, I dreamed of an empty building painted white, whose floors and walls were awash with blood. A flood of red, splashing up the sides, staining the white plaster. Each room we walked into, more blood. In my dream I didn't know why the blood was there, but that much blood outside a body always connotes profound horror.

———————

Not long after our arrival in the Netherlands, I went to see an exhibit of photos by a French photographer, Alain Laboile.

Walking among Laboile's photographs, in an exhibit called *La Famille*, what one takes away is a sense of things being perpetually in motion. A toddler dribbles milk from a bottle onto the back of a fleeing cat; two more children leap from a downed tree; a girl runs through a field with a knife in her hand.

The father of six children, Laboile's photos capture the moving-picture show of their seemingly wild, magical, dirty, almost feral childhood in the fields, ponds, forests, and old farmhouses of Bordeaux. The children are mostly naked, even as they break the skin of ice on winter puddles with their rubber boots. Naked balancing on a chair to reach into the tall refrigerator. Naked swinging on the curtains. There is a sense that anything goes in this household, so long as it makes a strong image.

A girl holds up a trowel with a dead mole. A four-year-old stands in front of a table with a rooster's dismembered head in a metal cup. Two young girls crouch as though for dear life on an old white door as it slowly sinks below the clear surface of the lake. It is a world full of mud, sand, murky ponds; the farmhouse kitchen is dirty; the house walls are drawn on. One can almost feel the constant movement, play, disaster, the live curiosity of it all.

As I walk through the exhibit, these black-and-white photos full of life and innocence remind me of another collection of black-and-white images I'd looked
at recently, wholly opposite in the reality they portray—photos from a time of
repression and genocide in Cambodia.

The Cambodian photographs—images of men, women, and children—came
from the years the repressive Khmer Rouge regime ruled the country: an era of
genocide in which almost 25 percent of Cambodia's population was killed.

They are individual portraits—mostly all of the upper torso and face, though
taken from many different angles and distances—of prisoners at Tuol Sleng, a
former high school used by the Khmer Rouge as a secret prison in which "at least
14,000 people were tortured to death or sent to killing fields between 1975–79."

Most of the photos are captioned "unidentified prisoner." Some portray young
children. A few of the photos are captioned "postmortem." The majority were
taken just before the execution of each individual.

A *New York Times* article about Nhem En, the chief of six photographers at the
prison, describes him removing the blindfolds of prisoners as they were brought
into Tuol Sleng.

> "I'm just a photographer; I don't know anything," he said he told the newly
> arrived prisoners, as he adjusted the angles of their heads. But he knew, as
> they did not, that every one of them would be killed.

The caption to one photograph reads, "Before killing the prisoners, the Khmer
Rouge photographed, tortured and extracted written confessions from their

victims." Like the Stasi collecting scents, the Khmer Rouge left more than six thousand of these photographs behind when it fled the Vietnamese army.

The photograph I stay with longest shows, in gray tones, the unsmiling face of a little girl, angle slightly off-kilter, with a Mary Jane collar, her bobbed hair tucked behind her ears.

She could have been in one of the Laboile photos, drawing at a table or running through a field in rubber boots. Could have been standing nearby as a small child climbs into a paint can and another girl releases a stream of urine into the grass. She could have been that innocent and that safe.

Those who argue for the existence of evil—that humans are all cruel or savage, selfish, all tipped so easily into the brutality of our underlying nature—often invoke the Stanford prison experiment as evidence.

Of that experiment, Dr. James Doty—a neurosurgeon on the faculty of Stanford Medical School—says: "What it showed was how context and circumstance can actually turn us into . . . a brutal human being, or somebody who has no power. And so this veneer that we have, of being civil, having it together and being strong, can immediately go away."

There are also many experiments showing that people who meditate or who practice gratitude or altruism exhibit significant physiological, neurological, and behavioral changes.

I interpret these divergent, seemingly opposite experiments to show that, in fact, we are far more influenced by the conditions around us than we like to think. What is certain is that our brains are far more plastic than anyone in previous decades believed.

As Doty points out, behavior is contagious.

The science shows that when we see another person act with compassion, with kindness, we are immensely more likely to act with those values ourselves, he says. But the flip side is also true: whoever has read about massacres or genocides knows that violence is also contagious. We all carry the power of this contagion.

I am in the living room, stretching on a yoga mat as I listen to the podcast in which Doty says this, afternoon light spilling in from the tall windows. The dog comes over and nuzzles me impatiently for attention, pushing me off balance.

Doty describes our brain's plasticity using the metaphor of physical exercise: meditation on compassion is a way of growing your muscles for more generosity and altruism.

"Or," he says, "you can do a form of exercise that makes you afraid, that makes you pull away, that makes you think that others are your enemies." Sometimes this is an active choice, but often we don't even realize what we are doing.

The brain will always choose what is familiar over what is unfamiliar. Our daily patterns of thought and feeling—they become the familiar landscape, the default, the go-to in moments of stress or adversity. Seen this way, "good" and "evil" become a matter of daily practice, as well as of circumstance and surrounding.

"We're seeing this," he finishes, "playing out right now in the political arena. We're seeing it playing out in different parts of the world. And my own belief is that it is an understanding of this reality that is ultimately going to define whether our species survives or not."

Outside, some boys are trimming the garden, hacking branches off the overgrown trees.

The novelist Marguerite Duras, who as a member of the French resistance during World War II took part in the torture of collaborators, wrote about the ending of war. "Peace is visible already," she wrote. "It's like a great darkness falling, it's the beginning of forgetting."

"Each generation again responds to war as innocents. Each generation discovers its own disillusionment—often after a terrible price," writes Hedges.

———

In the cool autumn air, Anna and I go for runs on dirt paths amid the corn, its stalks reddened and beginning to bend. Up on the hill, orchards full of ripened apples, woods-lined and open to the sun. It is not clear how one remains a human for all of a life, or even if one does.

During the Vietnam War era, revered and well-loved Buddhist teacher Thich Nhat Hanh visited the US after fleeing his war-torn homeland. What he found, he later recounted, was that the American antiwar protest movement was "full of war." Full of anger, fury, hatred, and bitterness.

Anything we hold sacred can become distorted. Twisted by these human tendencies toward cruelty.

It seems, most of the time, we do not get to know what's coming. We operate, simply, as civilians in the midst of our hopes. And the most we can do in advance is to build our muscles for good instead of for evil, for altruism instead of for fear.

The French author Jacques Lusseyran, who was blind and used a Braille typewriter, recounted his experience in the concentration camp at Buchenwald. He wrote that what you had to do to survive in the camp was to "be engaged, not live for yourself alone."

Never mind how: by prayer if you know how to pray; through another man's warmth which communicates with yours; or simply by no longer being greedy.

By no longer being greedy. It strikes me that "generous" means not only giving things away but a softening of the eyes: a willingness to see kindly. That this extends to everything in the world around us.

Lusseyran ends with two truths from his time in the camp and as a war resister:

The first of these is that joy does not come from outside, for whatever happens to us it is within. The second truth is that light does not come to us from without. Light is in us, even if we have no eyes.

But a third central truth, woven throughout his book, is about connection: "If you can form close human attachments to those around you, you have the possibility of surviving as a human being."

I hear on the news that Maria Ohilebo makes breakfast for immigrants in Greece. She herself came to Greece more than twenty years ago as an emigrant of Nigeria.

Asked why she and others—living in a country struggling under austerity—spend so much of their small salaries buying food to feed this new wave of refugees from Afghanistan and Syria, she says, "Yeah, the time is so bad, but it is when the time is so bad and you can give from what you have, that is when you actually give."

In another interview I listen to, actor and activist Martin Sheen says: "Every time we try to identify God, we are sure to identify what she is certainly not. We don't know what God is. And the genius of God—to dwell where we would least likely look, within the depths of our own being, our own shallowness, our own darkness, our own humanity—that's the genius of God."

The language of god, like the language of good and evil, has never resonated for me. But the way Christian mystics and Jewish Kabbalists imagine god, or what is holy—as sparks of divine illumination, as what is ablaze within us—carries a poetry that is transcendent.

And the idea that all of it—our darkness and our light—is holy, is the material we have to work with in this life, feels more real to the mess and imperfection, the violence and the joy we find all around us. There is a Buddhist teaching that states, "My actions are my only true belongings."

As I roll across the high, arcing bridge over the Maas river, these words echo in my head. As I buy bread in the old Bisshopsmolen bakery by the Jeker canal. As I pedal home on the paths through the fields. *My actions are my only true belongings.*

CHAPTER FOUR

Notes on Bewilderment

I have just received news that, back in the US, my brother's first child has been safely born.

The day before, two American soldiers on the train from Amsterdam to Paris disarmed a gunman ready to wreak havoc. Earlier this year, two brothers broke into the offices of *Charlie Hebdo* in Paris with rifles and killed twelve people; two days later, in a connected attack, a gunman murdered four Jewish shoppers in a Parisian kosher supermarket.

Seated at my desk and looking out the windows of our Maastricht apartment, I watch the clouds settle even more heavily onto the morning. By sudden degrees the room becomes so dark I can hardly see. Only an hour before, there was sun warming the kitchen, but now, it seems almost night.

We are in a moment when such acts of violence still feel "new," before the continued upward spiral that is to come. In only another month or two, the coordinated shootings in the Bataclan theater and several other locations in Paris will happen, killing 130 people. A few months after that, Zaventem airport and a subway in Belgium will be bombed, killing at least thirty-four people and injuring more than 190.

Many analysts believe an underlying factor contributing to these acts of violence is the way a number of European countries—particularly France and Belgium—have ghettoized and isolated immigrants, whom they invited into the country in the first place because they needed their labor.

The sun comes back out, but behind it the sky still growls, glowers; the foliage lights up in glowing green and yellow. I take my dog for a walk in the nearby park; on one of the leaf-littered paths, a woman passes us and, as though I am asleep, I watch my dog lunge at hers, growling. He becomes, in an instant, all muscle and snarling tooth, a beast responding to some signal we humans could not see or perceive, and later I find myself wondering whether some of the shock and horror at these recent large-scale acts of violence is rooted in a lie: that we humans are not as violent as beasts, that our civilized veneer is strong enough to tame us.

In this moment, though, standing in the misty park with a layer of damp, rotting leaves underfoot, I don't know why everything seems so slow, why I couldn't respond faster, and when the woman says "ooh" in a tssking voice and walks away, a red haze of shame rises in my stomach.

Living in a country that is new to me, the tinge of isolation is always present. I take walks in the misty rain past endless Dutch brownstones, two-story brick the same over and over, a familiar life and yet one I feel unsure how to access, interact with. Every time I succeed in hiding behind a "Goede morgen," I feel momentarily safe, unseen in my disguise. I am easily flummoxed, and that begins to feel as if it means something about me. About my *outsiderness*, about my worth. I imagine, over and over, how much harder this would be if I were not English-speaking, US-born, educated, white. If I had not come here out of choice. If I'd come without an income. If I carried with me the trauma of living in a war zone. If the world had not told me over and over again that my life matters, that I am valuable.

———

Making dinner one evening, I turn on the radio as I move around the kitchen in the falling dark, my bare feet padding on the floor. An interview with a well-known author is playing; he says that he writes, always, to ask the question, "Who am I?" Perhaps in effect we are saying the same thing, but I find the question that drives me is less "Who am I?" than the sometimes almost despairing "How shall I live?" What choices do I make in a world of madness, a world with such violence? To acknowledge the suffering, fear, and instability and still make daily choices seems in itself like a kind of madness. Or a deep indifference, a cruelty.

"What I have been thinking about, lately, is bewilderment as a way of entering the day," writes Fanny Howe at the beginning of *The Wedding Dress*. "I have learned about this state of mind from the characters in my fiction—women and children, and even the occasional man, who rushed backwards and forwards within an irreconcilable set of imperatives."

An irreconcilable set of imperatives seems to me as adequate a descriptor of the human state as any.

On my left forearm is a tattoo that says *soften*.

At first, when I drew it, this meant being kinder, more open to others, dropping my fists, allowing my joy to shine out. But now, several years later, I see it is also coming to mean not trying so hard to be in control, not feeling like life is some kind of linear progression with a clear purpose and an organized timeline. And to realize, again and again, that while other people's lives may look really well put together from the outside, mostly they feel just as messy and as full of doubts and questions and uncertainty as mine. That, to echo Marie Howe, *this* is it, this is what we've been waiting for: all the messiness and uncertainty and doubt and questioning *is* the thing.

Years ago, my friend Barbara said to me, "somewhere around thirty I think things start to slip, you start to lose your way." And at the time, because I was around thirty, and because I felt things starting to slip, I appreciated her words. But now, looking back at that conversation and those years, I'm not so sure the slipping stops. Does the idea that we start to slip—and what I'd assumed was an implied cessation of slipping—mean that at some point we step back onto some kind of solid ground?

Recently, I spent an evening talking and drinking wine with an Argentinian friend whom I hadn't seen in almost twenty years. Her life now is largely centered around a fellowship of bible study. She asked whether I believe in God. I paused, shrugged. To me, believing in a merciful god is almost exactly like believing in American exceptionalism, the idea that we are entitled to so many things that the rest of the world is not. Why or how should any of us believe that some kind of godlike figure is watching out for us when s/he did not look out for those in Auschwitz or Rwanda or in the recent decimation in Gaza? And to believe in the alternative, a godlike figure that is indifferent—or worse, tyrannically destructive or punitive—makes it hard to get through the day.

Later, we were speaking of my work, and I told her that I am working on a project about violence, grappling with the question of how humans can commit such atrocities against each other. She nodded and thought for a moment. She said, "In the years since we were young together, I've done some bad things—not terrible things, but bad things. I have come to believe that I am as bad as the worst person, as bad as Milošević, as bad as Hitler. I believe God says there is violence because *you* are violent. There is hatred because *you* hate."

Each morning I read the news about what is unfolding in this world. Here in Europe, so much of the news feels immensely closer, more proximate, than it did in the US—we are not geographically islanded by oceans all around us; we could easily drive or ride a train to the sites of so many of these stories.

In one week in the early fall, there are thousands of refugees waiting, corralled by police, to board trains in Budapest, where the trains have been closed to migrants. They hold tickets to Vienna and other cities farther into Europe. They have no shelter. They have little to eat or drink, and temperatures have been 104° F or more. "We are human too," reads a sign held by one little boy.

A week or two earlier—days after seventy-one migrants' bodies were found suffocated in a refrigeration truck abandoned by its drivers in Austria—another vehicle was found just in time, with twenty-four young teenagers crammed inside, packed on top of one another, the windows barred shut and painted black, the doors welded closed.

In her nuanced and probing book *The Art of Cruelty*, Maggie Nelson at one point examines two art pieces by Ana Mendieta. One piece is a still photo from *Rape Scene*, in which Mendieta "meticulously re-created the aftermath of a rape and murder that took place at the University of Iowa" and invited an unwitting audience to find her, "naked, tied up, her underwear around her ankles, her body smeared with blood and dirt."

The second piece, *People Looking at Blood*, is a photo series of passersby reacting to "a large amount of what appeared to be chunky blood" that Mendieta had spilled "over a doorway and a sidewalk on an Iowa City street." Nelson writes, "Standing in front of *People Looking at Blood* and *Rape Scene* . . . it occurred to me that *People Looking at Blood* is the crueler, albeit the more abstract, of the two." She continues, "It may incite horror, concern, compassion, and revulsion—but it doesn't offer anywhere for these feelings to go. . . . Each pedestrian's only real choice is to walk on by, which looks from the outside—and likely felt, on the inside—like an uncaring abandonment."

Nelson's insight—that we have moments like this all the time, every day, when the world forces us into situations we do not understand and can imagine little helpful action to address—stands out to me as a kindness, a simple gesture of understanding amid the theories of violence and cruelty her book explores.

"There is a Muslim prayer that says, 'Lord, increase my bewilderment,' and this prayer is also mine," writes Fanny Howe later in her book. I grapple with understanding this desire, but I think maybe it is about the way our certainty blinds us—the way our certainty can even *be* a kind of violence, or be at the root of so many other violences. "We keep trying not to embrace our fundamental humanness, because it is so rooted in the uncertainty and vulnerability of being alive," says Anna in one conversation. "But to deny the uncertainty, we have to also deny our own—and other people's—humanity."

Lord, increase my bewilderment. Though to question can be agonizing, it also opens the way to possibility.

"In order to be bewildered, you have to be able to wonder," writes the poet Kaveh Akbar, and perhaps the opposite is also true: to find sources of wonder, we have to open ourselves to the complexity and cloudiness of bewilderment.

I grapple with these ideas on mornings when I feel out of place in this world, lost in its atrocity and overwhelmed. Mornings when it is a struggle to commit words to paper because they claim a certainty I do not feel. When even to speak, to put things into words, feels reductive of the complexity we are immersed in.

And yet I look at the world around me—at social media, at the news—and everyone is speaking so authoritatively, as though they *know* something, as though they truly believe without question. Without bewilderment.

I pretend to be certain too: I ride my bicycle into the center of the city, I walk through the market, selecting vegetables, and to the bakery to buy a loaf of bread. And yet the whole time I am spinning with questions. How does one continue as a writer, think of publishing, in a world where one voice has too often meant another's silencing? How does one relate to any material comforts when they seem to come largely at others' expense?

I am not certain there are ever adequate answers to these questions.

"One definition of the lyric might be that it is a method of searching for something that can't be found," writes Fanny Howe.

———————

In order to be bewildered, you have to be able to wonder. As I pedal my bicycle over the arcing, white pedestrian bridge joining the two sides of Maastricht, I turn these words over and over. I wonder whether I am allowing myself to focus too much on the bewilderment, dwelling in a place of heaviness and cloudiness, not looking hard enough for the moments of joy.

A few days before, visiting the Van Gogh museum in Amsterdam, I'd found myself face to face with the painting *Wheatfield under Thunderclouds*. It was so vibrant and luminous I was momentarily stunned. Even seen from a floor above, the painting glowered and grumbled: clouds scowling down on radiant fields, the storm surly above sunlit green.

The lightness, the color saturation, the richness of the world Van Gogh saw— it glows. Next to the paintings of Daubigny, Millet, and Rembrandt, which seem to depict a life lived in perpetual twilight, Van Gogh's realm is illuminated. Walking through it, I was reminded of a section in Annie Dillard's gorgeous, lyric *For the Time Being*, where she recounts a Kabbalist creation story:

> The creator meant his light to emanate, ultimately, to man. Grace would flow downward through ten holy vessels, like water cascading. Cataclysm—some say creation itself—disrupted this orderly progression. The holy light burst the vessels. The vessels splintered and scattered. Sparks of holiness fell to the depths, and the opaque shards of the broken vessels imprisoned them.

Seeing Van Gogh's paintings in person, it felt as though I was witnessing such sparks, which I imagined illuminating the cracks of those broken vessels, those opaque shards.

Even in his nighttime world, the wheat glows golden.

———

I am still thinking of the glow of Van Gogh's wheat field a few weeks later. Seated at a small café table, I stare out across the cobblestone of the market plaza, so much grayer than anything Van Gogh ever painted.

Across the table from me is a former student, a young Dutch woman who has taken the train down to Maastricht for a visit; she is grappling with the question of why "those people get such benefits" in her country when her father cannot take off work to go to the hospital for health issues. I have been looking every day at pictures of young men, families, running toward razor wire, handing babies over the wire, sitting on park benches with their toddlers in the dark. This is a kind of urgency, of loss, neither she nor I have ever had to face.

It's a false dichotomy, this *us* vs. *them*, I want to tell her. Support for people seeking refuge, seeking asylum, should not also mean that your father cannot go to the hospital.

In 1956 a wave of two hundred thousand people fled Hungary during the Hungarian Revolution. They fled the tanks and the secret police and the hangings and executions. Europe received them sympathetically, even hailed them as heroes, as freedom fighters against communism. Thirty-seven countries came together to take them in; within months many of them had left Austria and been resettled elsewhere, including in the US.

Those refugees followed much the same route that many Syrian, Afghan, Iraqi, and other refugees followed in 2014 and early 2015, crossing from Hungary into Austria. The difference in their reception has been diametric.

Now, sitting with my student in the fall of 2015, many European countries—including Austria and Hungary—are closing their borders to refugees. The Balkan routes through Macedonia, Serbia, Croatia are being shut down with razor wire and guards.

I feel torn between the two pulls of this essay, between witnessing and meditating on the act of witnessing.

After reading the news each morning, I have to go outside into the cool and gusting air, to run with my feet pounding down the paved pathways, feel my breath expand my lungs, feel my anger slowly seep out of me with each exhale until my stomach is not such a hard, tight ball. It is clear that this is a problem with a political solution. It is a problem rooted in decades and centuries of US and European military involvement, foreign and economic policy, and colonial rule. It is a political problem whose cost is human. I feel the outrage and despair, the complicity and apathy, all around me and also in me.

But I want to ask, too, a broader question, not rooted only in this particular moment in time, this particular tragedy. I want to ask about what it means for all of us to live human lives in which some people experience violence and some do not. To live lives in a world full of brutality and horror. About what it means to study violence and hold on to it this way—what one does with the bewilderment, the fear, the anger—though it feels difficult to even make that question explicit in the face of the suffering of those who have recently and directly experienced such violence.

In October 2013, a ship packed with five hundred people fleeing Eritrea via Libya caught fire and sank only a half a mile from the coast of Lampedusa in Italy. Local authorities "had the vessel under surveillance" but did not come to its aid. Three-hundred sixty-six people died on that burning ship, a packed wall of terrified people trapped in its hold as it sank. Mothers clutching children to their chests, young men whose future hopes were small sparks in the darkness.

"Already determined by blood / the earth has eaten its children," writes Josué Guébo in his book-length lyric poem, *Think of Lampedusa*. "The sea does not tell me / what it has done / stretching its tongue / just a few lengths from Lampedusa."

I imagine the voices of the dead speaking to us from the bottom of the sea, a haunting.

There was another ship that left the shores of Libya two years before the catastrophic and brutal sinking of the Lampedusa ship. Carrying seventy-two people fleeing African shores, it went into distress within hours of leaving Tripoli. It made a satellite phone call, it sent out distress signals. It was spotted and even approached by numerous ships, including US and NATO military ships. Nonetheless, it was left to drift on the seas of the Mediterranean for more than two weeks, until only nine of its passengers were still alive.

These deaths carry echoes, what Christina Sharpe calls "the ghosting of transatlantic slavery." The echo of deaths at sea during that earlier era: humans locked in the hold of a sinking ship, people thrown overboard, and those who jumped midsea rather than be subjected to what awaited them. "That word *cargo* repeats," Sharpe writes, "and so do the horrors of the holding, the throwing, the beating."

"Who explains this total loss?" Guébo's poem demands. Who claims responsibility?

In the evenings my wife and I walk on the paths through the fields surrounding Maastricht, and we try to imagine what it was like to be a soldier walking here during World War II. The paths and small dirt roads probably have not changed much, the trees growing around them perhaps even some of the same trees; the fields dotted with horses, sheep, or goats. We imagine skirting through the trees along the small curving roads, up the hillside and into the deep shade and quiet of the forest, never knowing when someone might shoot at you or whether the next village you will surface into is held by friendly forces or foe. Imagine the forest as both menacing and mundane at once; imagine this idyllic and charming countryside beset by artillery, rape, hunger, and burning buildings. We walk as the sun sinks down and turns orange, a glowing orb on the edge of the fields.

In an interview about the Exodus, Torah scholar Avivah Zornberg says: "In cataclysmic moments everything is really going too fast for people to comprehend—so this is human, this bewilderment. Instead of trying to grasp the chaos, to feel like we have a handle on it—we can really only soften to our bewilderment, our disorientation."

Is this just adulthood, I often wonder, this recoiling from the bewildering speed, brutality, and injustice of this world? Or is this really the kind of cataclysmic moment in history it feels like?

We are far away, here in northern Europe, from the increasingly cold sea and cold air that so many desperate parents and children are now trying to cross. Far away, but not so far. The chill in the air sinks here too, but we are dry and we have papers and roofs and food. I read stories from Lesvos, from people who have crossed and from people who bring them sandwiches, bread, anything. I wonder how many of these stories it takes to make someone else care, to make someone want to act.

"Do we believe the individual is precious, or do we not?" Dillard writes in *For the Time Being*. "There are 1,198,500,000 people alive now in China." (She was writing in the late 90s.) "To get a feel for what this means, simply take yourself—in all your singularity, importance, complexity, and love—and multiply by 1,198,500,000. See? Nothing to it."

There is a photo I keep on my desktop. The close-up of a young man, seated, his eyes closed. His hair is short and dark, and he is clean-shaven. His profile is limned with shimmering light, like the sun behind a cloud. His face is calm, almost serene. A second young man leans in, the black thread between his fingers shining like a spiderweb reflecting sunlight. He is sewing the first man's lips shut; a tangle of thread slashes across them already. A single tear runs in its silver track down the seated man's face.

The two men in this photo are trapped in Idomeni, on the northern border of Greece. In recent months there have been several instances of young men in refugee camps sewing their lips shut in protest. Young Iranian men, young Moroccan men, some of them stuck in the camp in Calais, others trapped on the border of Greece and Macedonia, pleading with the world to pay attention.

"We came here to find human rights and we find none," reads a sign held by one young man. Several other young men hold up a sign saying, "Our problem *is not* economical—Iran," highlighting the split in rhetoric describing those seeking asylum from war and physical threat versus those fleeing the violence of extreme poverty or political repression.

The young man's steadfastness, his pain, in the face of such a drastic act, reminds me—every time I look at it—of the desperation and determination underlying the flight of so many people, so many families; the risks they take, up to and including their deaths at sea, to escape the violence and privation of their homelands. It is a moment of singularity, as Annie Dillard puts it, that helps me try to imagine the individual importance of each of the approximately 1.9 million people who have arrived on the shores of the Mediterranean since the start of 2014. And the additional eighteen thousand people who number among the dead and missing. ("As if each corpse in this Mediterranean / was not excessive / on that long nightmare of ocean," Guébo accuses.)

One way we begin that imagining, as Judith Butler notes, is by questioning whose deaths we—those of us who live comfortably in wealthy countries—mourn and whose deaths we largely ignore. Whose lives are considered valuable, and whose are treated as ungrievable: lives that "cannot be mourned because they never counted as a life at all."

It wasn't until the body of three-year-old Alan Kurdi washed ashore that most of the world paid any attention to so many other deaths at sea, so many other people fleeing for their lives.

"The differential distribution of public grieving is a political issue of enormous significance," Butler contends. "Open grieving is bound up with outrage, and outrage in the face of injustice or of unbearable loss has enormous political potential."

It means something to say a name, to detail and recall a life lived, to "publicly display and avow the loss."

I would like this writing to be my expression of open grieving. To begin my actions of open grieving.

To grieve openly is a kind of fierceness. It is to state, *my life is bound with your life*—while not ignoring the ways my life has benefitted at the expense of others' lives, communities, worlds.

"Precariousness," Butler concludes, "implies living socially . . . the fact that one's life is always in some sense in the hands of the other. It implies a dependency on people we know, or barely know, or know not at all."

To grieve openly is to soften to the precarity in our own lives while also looking fiercely into the mirror at how we amplify the precarity in others' lives.

———

Maastricht stretches into autumn, the trees tinged with yellow tips to their branches, as though some kind of dying sun had come too close. Outside the lavender quivers and flexes in the breeze, then bends back.

Bewilderment deepens the spirit, but it can also paralyze. Or we can become lost in its mists, focused only on finding a way out, a way back to solid ground. Once, at a retreat, a teacher told me there's no such thing as *balance*—there's only balanc*ing*.

I keep coming back to the imperfectness of the attempt, the fallibility of this human life. To accept that imperfection, accept our limitations, is a kind of softening also. To embrace those splintered, scattered vessels, the trapped shards of grace and holy light.

There is an old windmill across the street, its face turned to the fields, its walls mossy and stained with time. The house below it has a red tile roof, furred over with ivy. Looking at them, the world is old. Beside it the cars rush by.

"For us, there is only the trying," wrote T. S. Eliot in *The Four Quartets*. "The rest is not our business."

That rest—the paralysis, the hesitation, my desire for certainty—I open my hands to relinquish.

CHAPTER FIVE

Cities of Broken Teeth,
Cities of Dust and Blood

It's funny, Anna said, how when a plane explodes and kills all these people, there's still all this perfectly undamaged luggage that falls to the ground. As she was saying this, the crisp image of a pink suitcase with white polka dots, lying on the dusty roan earth, stared back at us: fallen from the Russian passenger jet that had just exploded over the Sinai.

Her words evoked the vivid memory of watching a Ukrainian family speak to a news reporter on TV the summer before, after the Malaysian passenger jet was shot down over the Ukraine. A body from that plane had fallen through their roof, leaving a large broken area in the ceiling of their kitchen.

After our return from Cyprus and Istanbul—just hours after the Malaysian jet was shot down—I couldn't stop reading about that Malaysian jet crashing, thinking about the people who became bodies that fell out of the sky onto the roofs of other people. About their suitcases: shirts and bras and socks and toothbrushes strewn across the countryside. How all those objects survived the crash so much more intact than the people who had touched them, held them, worn them.

Now I am on another plane, a flight from Amsterdam to Singapore, and as I look at our travel path on the in-flight entertainment screen, I am struck by how many of the places we will fly over are—or have recently been—immersed in deep violence. We will fly over Ukraine, Georgia, eastern Turkey, Iran, Afghanistan, and Pakistan. I wonder how easy or difficult it is to procure surface-to-air missiles. I wonder whether the people on the Malaysian jet had any warning it was coming, or if they were engrossed in their crossword puzzles and onboard movies until the very moment of impact. My stomach is tight with anxiety.

As we fly over Kabul and I watch our inching progress along the flight path, turning it from white to yellow, I think of a Dutch friend who goes back and forth from Maastricht to Kabul, who is down there on the ground below us even now, as we fly overhead. I wonder at the many years she has spent going back and forth, about how it feels each time as the plane descends, landing into such instability. Such a different reality from the calm, undisturbed passivity of northern Europe. I wonder at why she goes, why she chooses to keep going. Or, perhaps, why she comes back? The voluntary alternation between peacetime and war on such a regular, ongoing basis is difficult to imagine.

I am on my way to the Philippines to teach a medical course, and one of the entertainment options on this flight is a Berlitz language-learning program; it teaches basic vocabulary using rudimentary video games. Seeking distraction, I turn it on. As I click over and over on the words *l'hôpital* and *un médecin*, with little cartoon illustrations of a white male doctor and an ER cubicle—accompanied by absurd boinging noises for each correct choice—all I can think of is Kunduz. The evening before, I'd heard several radio interviews with spokespersons from Médecins sans Frontières, whose hospital in Kunduz was recently bombed to ruins by US and Afghan forces. They detailed the destruction found by a preliminary MSF investigation: patients literally burning in their beds, medical personnel gunned down as they fled across the courtyard.

The strike followed a devastating week for the hospital, in which fighting drew nearer, and the ER and ICU were overflowing with patients: doctors, unable to leave, set up makeshift rotations and watched with panic as more and more patients were brought in, watched with exhaustion and despair each time a patient was lost. "The people are being reduced to blood and dust. They are in pieces," said Dr. Osmani, an Afghan doctor who traveled from his own hospital in Kabul to volunteer in Kunduz on weekends and who was killed a few days later in the US bombing of the hospital.

The officially released story about why the bombing happened has changed frequently, but news emerged of erroneous military intelligence suggesting the hospital was being used as a Taliban command center, based on overhead surveillance likely done with unmanned drones.

"Our main question is: How is it that so clearly a civilian structure like that could lose its status as a protected facility?" said Jason Cone, executive director of MSF in the US. "It's a responsibility of the warring parties to be able to distinguish between civilian and military targets."

The MSF had resubmitted the GPS coordinates of the hospital only days before, and the hospital was "among the most brightly lit buildings in Kunduz," with a large white-and-red flag reading "Médecins sans Frontières" across the roof.

That line between civilian and military targets—and between wartime and peace—has been slipping for years, maybe decades. In the 2014 Gaza war, for instance, Israel bombed multiple hospitals in Gaza. The slippage between civilian and military targets by the US has been exacerbated by increasing use of drone attacks and the use of drones to execute targeted assassinations in places we are not officially at war. There have been significant instances of misidentification. One study by a US military advisor with access to classified information found that drone strikes in Afghanistan—despite their supposed precision—caused ten times more civilian casualties than strikes from manned aircraft.

Afghanistan was really the birthplace of the United States' use of armed drones to carry out strikes, the laboratory where we took drones—already used in the Balkans for surveillance—and turned them into killing weapons. In subsequent years, the US has used armed drones for strikes in Pakistan, Afghanistan, Iraq, Yemen, Libya, Somalia, and Syria.

Finished with Berlitz's rudimentary lessons in French, my legs and back stiff from sitting, tired of the recycled air and monotonous hum of the plane, I scroll through the movies. One of them is *Pina*, Wim Wenders's documentary about the incredible German choreographer Pina Bausch.

As it begins, a line of smiling, physically diverse dancers walk unhurriedly across the stage, pantomiming small, absurd gestures, dipping their bodies with each step.

A moment later we see a line of people with shop brooms sweep a perfect square of dirt onto the stage, and a naked woman lies facedown in it, lit only by one diagonal beam of light. She lies still. The slight X of a second beam of light crosses below her feet, near the center of the stage. The woman does not move. She is so still, in the middle of all that dirt.

I realize then that I have accidentally paused the video, held her there so that she is always unmoving, always still.

When I unpause, suddenly there is an army of women, gaunt, in gauzy slips, all moving in the dirt. They lie scattered like dropped handkerchiefs. They stab themselves in the stomach with their own elbows, an army of advancing zombies, dancing jerkily toward us. Their gowns are sweaty, covered with dirt.

"There are situations, of course, that leave you utterly speechless," says Pina. "You just have to hint at them." Their dancing is loose, almost clumsy, as though drunken with grief or despair.

Shortly before leaving for the Philippines, I'd read a report about the US use of drones in Pakistan.

"Drones hover twenty-four hours a day over communities in northwest Pakistan, striking homes, vehicles, and public spaces without warning," the report had said. "Their presence terrorizes men, women, and children, giving rise to anxiety and psychological trauma among civilian communities."

I tried to imagine what that would be like, to always have these mute, impersonal gray slivers hovering in the sky above you, unmanned, ready to dispense death at a second's notice. Tried, and failed. Drones began to populate my dreams, suspended in the air, staring noiselessly. I imagine them now far below us on this airplane, a humming army of deadly mosquitoes.

The presence of those drones, among many other things, has made people in that northwest part of Pakistan—North Waziristan—afraid to congregate, to bring together their governing councils of elders, even to practice normal burial and funeral rites. Afraid to wash and cover their dead, to hold a communal funeral, to recite prayers over the body.

"Proper burial ceremonies and grieving rituals are 'essential to reduc[ing] or prevent[ing] psychological distress' during times of large-scale disaster," the report notes. The inability to grieve as a community, to receive the support of others, to say goodbye, is further wounding to people already living under immense duress.

"Will this be the longest day in history? No one is washing the dead. Let the dead then wash themselves," writes Mahmoud Darwish in *Memory for Forgetfulness*.

I think again of Judith Butler's writing on open grieving, bound up with outrage, and the question of which lives are considered grievable, are allowed to be grieved.

On the screen, a woman holds out her lower arms as though they are cut. The room, a shambles with chairs. The woman is Pina herself. Her chest is a skelter of ribs. Her silk slip hangs from her chest. Beneath it, her breasts are small triangles of flesh.

The plane moves inexorably onward, its progress marked by a monotonous hum. The on-screen map shows our little icon of a jet moving in an arcing trajectory over Afghanistan and Pakistan.

The term *anticipatory anxiety* was used in the report to describe the trauma of constantly waiting for imminent attacks. Uncontrollability, they note, is a key element of this anticipatory anxiety.

In interviews with communities living under drones, people said things like "Before the drone attacks, it was as if everyone was young. After the drone attacks, it is as if everyone is ill. Every person is afraid of the drones."

One humanitarian worker—an American—who was interviewed asked, "Do you remember 9/11 . . . what it felt like right after?

"I was in New York on 9/11," he continued. "I remember people crying in the streets. People were afraid . . . [they] didn't know if there would be another attack. There was tension in the air. This is what it is like. It is a continuous tension, a feeling of continuous uneasiness. We are scared. You wake up with a start to every noise."

It is almost difficult to remember now, but so much of the spreading US warfare—and the widespread use of drones—began with those 9/11 attacks, what Ann Cvetkovich calls "the shadow of September 11 and its ongoing consequences": our invasion of Afghanistan, the declaration of war against Iraq.

Far below us, looking out the windows of the plane, I could see land: tan, dry, and cracked.

A Waziri journalist named Noor Behram, who investigates drone strikes, describes in the report how fearful the children have become: "If you bang a door, they'll scream and drop like something bad is going to happen."

When children grow up in the circumstances of such psychological trauma, it deeply impacts their development: they may be unable to trust others, experience bouts of explosive anger, or periodic emotional breakdowns. Because of a lack of access to mental health care in Waziristan, people have been tied in their houses or locked in rooms alone after breakdowns caused by repeated drone strikes in their community.

": a city of broken teeth / : the thuds of falling / : we have learned to sing a child calm in a bomb shelter / : I am singing to her still," writes Solmaz Sharif in *Look*, her collection of poems built on a scaffolding of phrases from the US Department of Defense dictionary of military terms.

While I was reading the report on drones, I couldn't stop thinking about the enormous US export of war. Of violence, weapons, and destruction. Every time I hear an American express bewilderment or amazement—even now, even after the recent memory of Iraq and Abu Ghraib—that anyone from some other part of the world could have cause to hate us, all I can think about are bombs, drones, minefields, machine guns.

We are flying over ocean now. Far across the gray water, the sun hits the sea and makes a silver line before the horizon.

The language used to talk about the ethics of drone use includes terms such as *dronespace* and *distant intimacy*.

Drones finally completely destroy an element of conventional thinking about war: that combatants share physical vulnerability, that there is an element of reciprocity in the exposure to danger.

They bring a radically asymmetrical relationship, one in which the individual being targeted has no means of response, no ability to exercise autonomy.

In a remarkable November 2017 *New York Times* article, "The Uncounted," Azmat Khan and Anand Gopal report the results of intensive on-the-ground research of civilian deaths from coalition airstrikes in Iraq, finding that over a period of eighteen months, civilian deaths caused by "precision airstrikes" were thirty-one times higher than recorded by the US. They describe the obliteration of the suburban villas of two civilian brothers and their wives and children, which coalition forces reported as the bombing of a car manufacturing factory belonging to Daesh, or ISIS. Almost everyone was killed. "Though the [Razzo family] hadn't known it," the article says, "the burden of proof had been on them to demonstrate to a drone watching from above that they were civilians."

"While the drone operator knows a great deal about the target and holds them in a position of immense vulnerability, the target cannot know anything about their interlocutor," writes John Williams, a researcher of just war theory. Drones will often hover over and surveil targets for days or weeks before calling in a strike, looking exactly and precisely for one person, watching their actions, while that person may have little idea a drone is hovering thousands of feet above.

"You cannot surrender to a Reaper. That is true, of course, for a B-52 bomber, Tomahawk, or MX missile, or a host of other weapons systems. Yet these do not claim the intimacy of drones—the discriminatory precision based on enhanced intelligence gathering and personalized targeting," writes Williams later. "The illusion of proximity—lost through previous technological manifestations—is restored by drones." Distance, intimacy, space.

————

While Trump was in office, the safeguards to try to prevent civilians from being killed by US military drone strikes were "loosened or simply shredded," according to a book on the history of drone warfare. And many other countries are also now making or acquiring drones for military and surveillance use, including Turkey, Russia, China, India, Iran, Britain, France, Iraq, Nigeria, and Pakistan.

Israel, like the US, has been using drones—first for surveillance and then increasingly for armed strikes—for more than thirty years. In Gaza, Israeli drones fire missiles as well as guiding attacks by F-16s and helicopters.

"When you hear the drones, you feel naked and vulnerable," said Hamdi Shaqura, who lives in Gaza City. "The buzz is the sound of death. There is no escape, nowhere is private. It is a reminder that [we are] living completely under Israeli control. They control the borders and the sea and they decide our fates from their position in the sky."

Israel first began the widespread use of drones in the early 1980s, during its invasion and long occupation of southern Lebanon. The 1982 Lebanon war was called "Operation Peace for Galilee" by the Israelis; "the invasion" by the Lebanese. It came to a head with the siege of Beirut in the summer of 1982: the land, air, and sea bombardment that Darwish's *Memory for Forgetfulness* chronicles in poetic yet horrific detail, recounting an "apprehensive silence carrying the weight of metal, under a sun veiled by all the colors of ash."

In the early 2000s, Israel began its use of drones over Gaza, and targeted drone attacks have killed hundreds of Palestinians in ensuing years.

During Operation Cast Lead in 2008, Israel also used drones to practice "roof-knocking": firing small missiles at the roof of a building to warn inhabitants that a larger strike is coming. According to Israel, they provided a ten-minute warning for inhabitants to escape. A United Nations commission found that the tactic was not effective: it did not give residents sufficient time to flee and led to chaos and panic.

During college I lived in the heart of downtown Jerusalem, at the intersection of Jaffa and King George streets. I loved it—I was so charmed by Jerusalem's old city, with its ancient stone walls and its Muslim, Armenian, Christian, and Jewish Quarters; by the street markets full of spices, olives, hummus; by the way everything would close down in the early afternoon on Fridays, and students and businessmen alike would be hustling through the streets with bouquets of flowers to get home in time for Shabbat candle-lighting. I loved sharing the Passover Seder dinner with old family friends who were Israeli, loved the ceremony and the food and the way the old cultures blended together. I remember the way the light refracted, the sacredness of the high desert.

And at the same time, I knew from high school friends who were Israeli Arabs and Palestinians how complicated the reality was. At some point in the semester, we traveled to Ramallah and Bethlehem in the West Bank and saw the degree to which Palestinians were increasingly displaced and confined. We visited ancient olive groves that were in danger of being cut down, drove down the rough dirt roads past unpainted cinder block homes, saw the border wall and the groups of teenaged Israeli soldiers with their green uniforms and standard-issue assault rifles. And we saw the fancy new housing developments, with smooth blacktop streets and red roofs and swimming pools, that were illegal Jewish settlements encroaching onto Palestinian land.

I remember feeling deeply bewildered by how Jewish Israelis—a people who had, so recently, experienced immense violence and atrocity, even the very denial of their right to exist—could in essence turn around and commit similar oppression and denial on another people, claiming the land of that other people as though they'd never even existed, bulldozing their villages into dirt, exiling them from their homes, and ghettoizing them so profoundly.

In early March 2018, Israel began using drones to drop tear gas on Palestinian protesters in Gaza and the West Bank. A potent crowd-control technology, tear gas causes burning of the eyes and skin, gagging, and panic; it has also led to permanent blinding and caused numerous deaths around the world.

In the Aida refugee camp outside Bethlehem, into which many displaced Palestinians have been pushed, tear gas deployment occurs at least monthly and often multiple times a week, leading a 2018 report from Berkeley's School of Law to describe Aida residents as likely the most tear gas–exposed population in the world.

The report notes that tear gas exposure in the camp was "widespread, frequent, and indiscriminate" and that its use was primarily unprovoked. Aida residents described the use of tear gas "not as a defensive weapon to protect against riots or defend public safety, but rather as an offensive weapon." One person interviewed said, "they use it when they are bored, when they want to provoke a clash, or when they want to get into the camp." And nowhere is safe—tear gas seeps through closed windows, into kitchens, bedrooms, school classrooms. People in the camp reported tear gas lingering as long as three days in their homes and schools. Those interviewed said that with every exposure, "they felt like they were choking and couldn't breathe. 'Every time, I feel like I'm going to die. You don't know that you will survive. It's like hell every time,'" said one interviewee. "It doesn't just go away, I can't see or work or think all day."

Mothers described children picking up littered tear gas cannisters from the street and being accidentally gassed—the spent cannisters so plentiful that it is hard to clean them all up.

In October 2015, an Israeli border patrol officer drove through the streets of the Aida camp in a patrol vehicle, issuing a warning in Arabic through a loudspeaker. "People of Aida refugee camp, we are the occupation forces. You throw stones and we will hit you with gas until you all die. The children, the youth and the old people, you will all die. We do not want to leave any of you alive."

In the video of this moment, his patrol vehicle moves through dark streets, backlit by streetlamps; its headlights define its silhouette. The voice on the speaker is loud, insistent, repetitive. It reverberates off the close concrete walls.

People in Aida are deeply concerned that the tear gas now being used on them is "dramatically more potent, longer lasting, and dangerous" than earlier compositions. "While tear gas is usually composed of a mixture of synthetic or naturally occurring gases, including pepper spray, 'the specific chemical utilized by the [Israeli security forces] in recent years is unknown,'" notes an article in *Al Jazeera*. "This is not tear gas, it is poison," said one camp resident.

During the May 2018 Great March of Return—six weeks of protest by Gazans against their displacement and blockade—a series of weekly protests were attended by more than ten thousand people in predominantly nonviolent protest. Israel used drones to dispense tear gas on the crowds, even dropping tear gas cannisters in an area with vehicles clearly marked "Press" and on a tent of women and children more than a third of a mile from the border. Eight hundred people were treated for gas inhalation. One photo shows a man standing in front of rising clouds of gas, eyes closed and face grimacing in pain, holding aloft a tennis racket he was using to return tear gas cannisters fired by Israeli soldiers.

The drones being used to drop tear gas can carry six cannisters and can drop them individually, in clusters, or all at once. Israel is one of the leading countries in the world in developing drone technology, among other weaponry. According to Major Assaf Shaish, who in 2018 was head of the Israel Defense Force's drone department, the IDF is now developing technology for the use of drone swarms—which could push back protesters or be used for attack missions—and "suicide drones" equipped with grenades.

In recent decades, Israel has tested numerous new technologies of war on the Gazan population, from white phosphorus to "butterfly bullets" and DIME bombs, which hurl miniature particles throughout the patients' organs, causing damage that is almost impossible to fix. Many of these weapons have been devastating in their toll on human life.

One Israeli human rights lawyer, who tracks the export of weapons, notes that Israel has used conflicts in the past to "showcase its weaponry with the intention of selling it on." Israel, like the US, has been criticized for selling weapons to governments with poor human rights records—including, in the case of Israel, to the Malaysian government during its recent bloody ethnic cleansing of the Rohingya minority. And the US government has been a major funder of Israel's weapons development, providing billions of dollars in the past five decades for military assistance and missile defense funding, making Israel the largest cumulative recipient of US foreign aid since World War II.

Now, Israeli weapons companies are actively partnering with the US Department of Homeland Security to bring similar surveillance and technologies of low-intensity warfare to the US borderlands. Like Gaza, the US borderland is quickly becoming a zone stripped of constitutional rights.

In 2016, Palestinian artist and filmmaker Khaled Jarrar journeyed along the US-Mexico border, observing similarities between the border wall there and the wall between Israel and Palestine. He created an installation that locals are calling *Khaled's Ladder*; taking metal from the border wall, he constructed a ladder and planted it upright in open space near the wall in Tijuana. This was his first trip to the US after being prevented by Israeli soldiers from leaving the West Bank to attend an exhibition featuring his work at the New Museum in New York, despite his having obtained a visa. When Jarrar was invited to the US for this border journey, he was in the middle of working on a film about Syrian refugees. He'd obtained the same false papers that many of the refugees were using and walked with them on their journey from Greece to Germany.

I heard Jarrar speak at the University of Arizona, where I'd gone to graduate school and taught English for years. We sat in a cool, air-conditioned conference room with floor-to-ceiling glass walls. He was presenting, together with Jewish artist Robert Yerachmiel Sniderman, on art and images of the occupation.

Gaza has been a laboratory for weapons testing, for both Israel and the US, Jarrar said in his presentation. Some of the weapons tested on Gazans were developed right here at the University of Arizona, which has extensive defense and home-land security research programs.

He showed us an excerpt of an old video, from the late eighties or early nineties, about the settlement of Israel. Israeli strategy toward Palestinians became known as "break the bone" strategy, the video narrator said in a soothing voice.

The "break the bone strategy," I find when I look it up later, is a literal term: dur-ing the first intifada which started in 1987, Yitzak Rabin directly ordered soldiers to break the bones of Palestinian protesters.

Though Rabin eventually shifted from military suppression to attempts at a dip-lomatic solution, he was assassinated before the "two-state solution" could be finalized in the Oslo Accords. The right-wing government that took power after his death shifted course, back to military suppression, back to ongoing Israeli incursion into and settlement of the West Bank. A recent US State Department map shows Palestinian populations in the occupied West Bank in white against a green Israeli background, and I am shocked to see the degree to which the once contiguous territory has been moth-eaten, broken up by illegal Israeli settle-ments—an immense degree of change even since I lived in Jerusalem twenty years ago. The Palestinian populations now are a scattering of broken teeth.

Jarrar says: "As Palestinians, we cannot know our landscape. We are separated . . . the occupation prevents us from knowing one another. We are alien in our own land. Our imaginations are proscribed, imprisoned."

A close friend, an American writer who just returned from a research trip in Egypt, Jordan, Israel, and the West Bank, described her time in Egypt and Jordan as joyful, beautiful, expansive. In contrast, she said, in Israel everything felt so heavy, predetermined, walls and barbed wire fence everywhere. She took the buses that mostly Palestinians and Israeli Arabs use, and they were constantly being stopped at checkpoints, forced out into the broiling sun, into caged-in areas, while the bus was searched by twenty-year-old Israeli soldiers with machine guns. At one point, she thought: "If we have to stand here any longer in this cage in the hot sun, I am going to lose it, lose my shit entirely. And if I feel this way, after a week or two weeks or three of this treatment, how do people here stand it? Even the old women were angry, furious, you could see it in their faces, and if you're making even the old women hate you . . . ," her voice trailed off.

Israel has become distorted, built itself into a cage by caging in the people it has displaced. James Baldwin described racism in the US in similar terms: "No one has pointed out yet with any force that if I am not a man here, you are not a man here. You cannot lynch me and keep me in ghettos without becoming something monstrous yourselves."

––––––––

In early 2019, Michael Rakowitz, an American artist of Jewish Iraqi heritage, withdrew from the 2019 Whitney Biennial. He withdrew after it became known that Warren Kanders, the vice chair of the Whitney's board, was the owner of Safariland, a manufacturer whose tear gas and other munitions have been employed against asylum seekers at the US-Mexico border; against protestors everywhere from Standing Rock, Ferguson, and Oakland to Puerto Rico and Egypt; and against journalists and civilians in Gaza and the West Bank.

"For me, this was a material evidence of the way in which there's a not-so invisible line that connects the museum, here in New York, to spaces like the border wall, and Palestine, and Istanbul, and Kurdistan, and everywhere," Rakowitz explains. "When I was at MIT a few years ago there was a scientist who told me that, in science, when you want to know how a system works, you introduce a coloring agent . . . and so the gas was this incredible agent that made very visible and very, very clear the way in which the power structures had been drawn."

"In the end," Rakowitz said, "I remembered the tear-gas cannisters that I saw at Dar Jacir, at Emily Jacir and Anne-Marie Jacir's [artist's] residency in Bethlehem. . . . This beautiful house that their ancestor built is right there at the border wall, and it's where demonstrations [are held] against the Israeli army, and it's where those tear gas cannisters end up, in the garden. So instead of picking flowers, they're gathering the tear-gas cannisters. And these things for me are a very physical and visual symbol of bodies that are being evacuated from the world, either through death or through displacement."

When asked why he does work in Palestine, Rakowitz responds, "To say that art doesn't have a place in these cities under siege is a further dehumanization of the people that live there, and a spectacularization of this violent image that we have of [such] places."

"But I also have some very real historical and autobiographical connection to that place," he continues. "It comes from my grandparents being Arab Jews from Baghdad who were there for millennia, and suffering the heartbreak of having to leave when nationalist programs in the Middle East made it impossible for them to stay there. I grew up in a house where all the food was Iraqi, and the music at family functions was classic Iraqi songs. It's not that there's not a difference between a place like Ramallah and Baghdad, but there is [also] quite a lot of connection. . . . And I believe that our liberation and our struggle for that liberation is intertwined."

⸻

Belgian-Iraqi choreographer Mokhalled Rasem was born and trained in Baghdad and now directs at the Toneelhuis in Antwerp. During the war that resulted from the US invasion of Iraq, he fled to Belgium as a refugee, waiting five years to receive his papers there.

In 2015 Anna and I went to see one of his performances, "Body Revolution," at the Theater aan het Vrijthof in Maastricht, climbing several sets of stairs to the smallest dance theater on the top floor. In it, three men dance, silently, in front of a screen with projections of destroyed buildings.

"'Body Revolution' is about violence, and what violence does to a person. How violence develops into fear, [and] fear stays in the body," Rasem said in 2015. It explores the responses of those who have fled, who have made it to safety, to seeing the violence still transpiring at home.

As the lights go down, the audience tapers into silence.

White sheets hang behind the dance space; a projection on them slowly pans to a scene of wrecked buildings, gray and black and abandoned. Instantly, I am carried back to Darwish's lyric, *Memory for Forgetfulness*, in which he describes the vacuum bomb dropped on Beirut by Israel: "It creates an immense emptiness . . . sucking the building down and turning it into a buried graveyard. And there, below . . . the residents of the building keep the varied forms of their final, choking gestures. They turn into statues made of flesh with not enough life for a farewell."

On the stage, more scenes of destruction, the demolished plaster white and beige. The dancers begin to emerge, cloaked in white and beige, from amid the wreckage. Their bodies are swathed like mummies. The buildings projected behind them are falling through.

The three dancers slowly unwrap themselves, their dark beards and hair become visible, their faces, their bodies in loose white clothes. They look through us, they look beyond.

We see them through a projection of shattered glass, webbed as though many heads had hit it at once. Two beautiful old sofas, ornate and antique, line a room; beside them a wall of plaster blown in.

One of the most devastating aspects of US drone strikes, in Iraq and northwestern Pakistan and elsewhere, is "double tap," the policy of carrying out multiple strikes in succession, so that those who come to assist those injured or buried in the rubble are putting their own lives at risk. Such a cynical move on the part of the aggressor undercuts one of the only glimmers of light in times of war: the willingness of people to help and care for each other.

The dancers, standing, hold each other tenderly.

"In this show the body screams without a voice . . . and breaks without words," writes Mokhalled Rasem.

The men dance silently, without any sound, while images of them appear projected on the screens behind them: sitting calmly amid the plaster dust and wreckage. It is an eerie disembodiment: the bodies dancing, their shadow selves sitting still just behind them on the screen.

In front of the screen, the actual dancers dive to the ground. Over and over their bodies hit the floor. Seated near the stage, I can feel the impact they make when they hit.

One of the men's projections sits quietly atop layers of collapsed concrete, floors and ceilings and roofs in rubble, smoking a cigarette.

The projections begin to transition, changing from images of bombing in Iraq and Syria into images of other conflicts, other eras—scenes of war, of police brutality, of attack. At first it feels too much: crude, heavy-handed. But after a while, as I watch the violence and agony of their bodies jackknifing in the projections, it begins to seem to me like something else: a way of declaring that the tragedy and violence now being imposed on their homeland has its place in a long history, a deliberate claiming of space and recognition in the historical register. A way of acknowledging that so many of these conflicts—like the technologies of war used in them—are interwoven, connected by webs of power and profit.

As the piece ends, the last dancer left on stage retreats back into the stone and plaster now projected on the screen. His white clothing blends with the white of the rubble. He slowly, almost imperceptibly, disappears into the screen, through it, one limb at a time.

Only his face left now, he stares out over us: glassy, vacant, surrounded by the collapsed landscape.

CHAPTER SIX

The Psychology of Violence

Late November now, I am returned from my teaching trip in the Philippines and sitting at a window on the top floor of AZM, the large teaching hospital in Maastricht. I am here with a friend, who, as I sit at this window, is having a catheter inserted through his femoral artery up to his heart, where they will try to use a small balloon-like implement to clear obstructions from the arteries feeding blood and oxygen to the muscles of his heart, and then they will try to place small wire mesh tubes called stents into those arteries to keep them open. My friend is young, in his forties, and he has a baby due in just a week, his first child. He is from India and his fiancée is from Macedonia; my wife is from Russia and I am from the US; and now we all live here, in this small Dutch city on the Maas, far from our families and our larger support networks.

The hospital staff are wonderful; they switch to English cheerily when they come to speak with us, and they crack jokes with the doctors and with my friend. The hospital is large and light and has a high airy open space in the center where musicians sometimes sit to play Beethoven and Brahms.

From where I sit, I can see the green parks lining the bicycle paths and the trees, brown and bare, standing behind.

Far to the south, boats are carrying groups of people from Turkey to Greece, from the countries they have worked so very, very hard to leave, often at the risk of their lives, their bodies, everything they had known or built until now. It is hard to believe that this is happening, as I look out over a parking deck of cars that look so small from here, that maneuver and nose their way through the rows; cars that in only a day's time could drive the highways south through Germany and into Austria and then Slovenia and Bosnia, Serbia, Macedonia, and after twenty hours—the equivalent of driving from Boston to Orlando—could be in Greece, where thousands of people are washing up on the island shores each day, hoping against hope that they won't be sent back into war or extremism, into situations and conditions that put their lives at risk.

We are here, in this large light airy hospital, trusting that they will take care of us, of my friend's body, that they will be respectful, try to help him—even as foreigners, with a certain degree of added vulnerability and uncertainty. There is a chasm between the way that some people can trust that others in society will take care of their body, be respectful of their body, try to save it, and the ways that, for others, that's so far from the reality—for so many people at this very moment, who are even now risking their bodies and their safety and their lives on boats shoving off into rough, cold seas, headed for Greece or Italy or Spain. A chasm based primarily on money, but also on documents and language and borders and on the whole idea of nationalism and nation-states.

I arrived at the hospital early this morning, locked my bicycle in the bicycle-parking garage, met my friend in the lobby, and walked with him up through the floors of the hospital to this ward, where he was asked to put on a gown and to lie on the bed and wait to be wheeled downstairs. Several hours later, they took him down to surgery, and now I am waiting and hoping, and texting updates to his fiancée, who is also waiting, anxiously, at home.

As I wait, I open my laptop and begin the process of renewing my American EMT license online. Looking around on the National Registry of Emergency Medical Technicians site, I come across a document from the Department of Homeland Security called "Active Shooter and Complex Attack Resources."

This gets my attention. A set of bombings and mass shootings have just taken place in Paris: three suicide bombings outside the Stade de France during an international soccer match, a shooting at a 1,500-person rock concert in the

Bataclan theater, and a third group of attackers firing on and then bombing crowded street cafés and restaurants. One hundred thirty people were killed.

Just ten months before, in January 2015, were the shootings in the *Charlie Hebdo* offices and at a Jewish supermarket in Paris.

Suddenly, western Europe feels tense, and vulnerable in a way that I imagine most Americans and Europeans are not used to feeling vulnerable. I try to imagine what it would feel like to be on duty as an EMT, called to respond to a bombing or a mass shooting, and can only envision a blurry tumult of panic and chaos.

The beginning of the DHS document reads:

> As the recent events in Paris so tragically demonstrate, we continue to face ongoing threats in an uncertain world. Active shooter events, the use of improvised explosive devices (IEDs), and the threat of complex attacks like those seen in Beslan, Russia; Mumbai, India; and now, Paris, France must be considered as at least plausible, if not probable.
>
> A pre-planned, integrated response by all first responder disciplines is required to maximize effectiveness and improve the survivability of those injured in such attacks. Some of the considered actions may seem contrary to those responders indoctrinated in the time-honored doctrine of "scene safety trumps all."

That last line catches my eye. "It is no longer acceptable," a second document clarifies, "to stage and wait for casualties to be brought out to the perimeter."

I am somewhat shocked to see this—this one short, clinical sentence represents a massive change. As medical personnel, we have been instructed over and over to wait until the scene is safe—until law enforcement or firefighters have mitigated any safety hazards and cleared us to enter. I think of the Boston Marathon bombing that took place two years before, in 2013, and what it would have been like to enter that disaster scene. Rumors of more bombs, yet unexploded, abounded. The stress, tension, and fear must have been almost paralyzing.

Instead of staging and waiting at the perimeter, a joint committee formed to create a national policy to "enhance survivability from mass-casualty shooting events" now recommends that medical responders be trained in tactical combat casualty care and that they work directly with law enforcement, ditching the old policy of "surround and contain" for "a more modern and aggressive response." It does not specify what this response should entail.

The DHS document provides links to resources with titles such as "See Something, Do Something: Improving Survival—Strategies to Enhance Survival in Active Shooter and Intentional Mass Casualty Events" and "Active Shooter Study: Quick Reference Guide." Such dry, technical language for something so terrifying: another human picking up arms or planting explosives to deliberately hurt and destroy the human beings around them.

In the joint committee report, there is an acronym for responses to shootings or "intentional mass-casualty incidents": THREAT. These letters signify the most important early steps in a response to an incident of this kind:

> Threat suppression
> Hemorrhage control
> Rapid
> Extrication to safety
> Assessment by medical providers
> Transport to definitive care

"The most significant preventable cause of death in the prehospital environment is external hemorrhage," an adjoining article notes. In other words, major bleeds kill people. The new emphasis: stop the bleeding.

And, the report recommends: "Hemostatic dressings and tourniquets may be needed to effectively stop bleeding . . . all police officers and any concerned citizens [should] carry a hemostatic dressing, a tourniquet, and gloves."

We now live in a moment in which everyday citizens are being encouraged to carry tourniquets and blood-clotting bandages, I think, taking a deep breath. This applies both to the US and to the northwestern Europe I am now living in, though in somewhat different ways.

> Bleeding control bags should be accessible in public places as determined by a local needs assessment. Potential sites for bleeding control bags include shopping malls, museums, hospitals, schools, theaters, sports venues, transportation centers (such as airports, bus depots, and train stations), and facilities with limited or delayed access.

> Contents of the bleeding control bags should include the following:

> > Pressure bandages
> > Safe and effective hemostatic dressings
> > Effective tourniquets
> > Personal protective gloves

"It is no longer sufficient to 'see something, say something,'" the report concludes. "Immediate responders must now 'see something, do something.'"

"Unfortunately, the time has come when intentional civilian mass-casualty incidents require a military-like response," concludes another source.

Intentional civilian mass-casualty incidents. Such clinical language for such violent actions, shocking because of how they seem to come so out of the blue. I think about what it means to believe you're secure, safe, and yet to face this kind of unpredictable violence. About how, in a way, it brings those of us who tend to think of ourselves as safe—think of our lives as relatively predictable or controllable—closer to the reality of unpredictability, hazard, and violence so many other people face daily: some of them in our own communities, some of them in other parts of this globe we all share, and many of them, at this moment, seeking sanctuary on the shores of Europe, fleeing war zones such as Syria and Iraq and Afghanistan, or fleeing persecution from gangs and governments.

I think about how we so infrequently make that connection, how those of us who regularly feel "safe" don't allow that connection to push us toward empathy. Don't allow it to make us feel *compelled*, like we have some responsibility, some obligation as humans to act.

I think of the idea of *expected deaths* versus *unexpected deaths*: 130 were killed in the Paris attacks, and that sounds like a lot because our society presents them as people not subject to death, not objects to be acted upon by death. And yet when we hear of a boat capsizing in the Mediterranean and of 150 people killed or three hundred people who have drowned in the sea—they are so often spoken of and thought of as people who *are* subject to death, who are at risk in ways many of us in wealthier countries don't identify with, ways that feel far from the risks we think we ourselves face.

There is a certain tension between feeling the expectation that your body will be taken care of, will be safe, and the way events such as mass-casualty shootings illustrate that anyone can be unexpectedly vulnerable. And yet, as Anna said to me the other day, the way the discourse around active shooter events goes, it doesn't ever point out, "you expected to feel safe, but then you weren't—and how can you take that as a basis of connection with other people who have also found themselves unsafe?" It doesn't ever make a link to the ways in which people who lived in a stable country gradually found themselves living in a war zone; to the way people fleeing had hopes for safety and protection and then found themselves in a camp surrounded by razor wire, or found themselves at gunpoint boarding an overloaded boat in the dark on rough seas. It doesn't ask how can we as a society process this experience of an active shooter event in a way that leads to empathy and connection?

The original guidelines for EMTs and paramedics emphasized scene safety above all else—a professionalized response, a distinction between the dangerous zone where "bad shit happened to some bodies" and the protected zone for other, safe bodies. In a way, the paradigm shift in thinking in these new guidelines is more honest about what it means to be human, acknowledging that we're all in this together.

I keep thinking of the practice of "double tap" by the US in Pakistan, Afghanistan, Yemen, Libya, and Iraq: those multiple drone strikes in succession, destroying not only the military target but killing or maiming those who have responded to help. Of what that does, what it means, for the human urge to respond, to help.

"Compared to the stress soldiers experience in combat, facing aggression and hatred in our fellow citizens is an experience of an entirely different magnitude," writes Dave Grossman in *On Killing: The Psychological Cost of Learning to Kill in War and Society*.

And, Grossman notes, the *Diagnostic and Statistical Manual of Mental Disorders*, that central authority of the psychiatry world, states that posttraumatic stress responses "may be especially severe or long lasting when the stressor is of human design (e.g., torture, rape)."

"We want desperately to be liked, loved, and in control of our lives; and intentional, overt, *human* hostility and aggression—more than anything else in life—assaults our self-image, our sense of control, our sense of the world as a meaningful and comprehensible place, and, ultimately, our mental and physical health," concludes Grossman.

In his 2007 performance piece *Domestic Tension*, Iraqi-born artist Wafaa Bilal lived in a gallery space for thirty days, livestreaming himself 24/7, and inviting audience members to chat with him online. Viewers also had the option of choosing to shoot Bilal with a paintball gun set up in the center of the studio and controlled virtually.

The piece commented on the realities faced by the Iraqi people in a country torn apart by multiple wars but also sought to "highlight the violence and racism of US culture after 9/11" and to "grapple with the trauma of [the artist's] experiences under Saddam Hussein's regime, during the Gulf War attacks, and surviving years of Sunni-Shia brutalities," according to Bilal.

The gallery room contained a bed, a lamp, and a potted plant. There was a coffee table he could use as a desk. There was also a plexiglass screen the artist used to shield himself from the paintball bullets.

In one striking photo from the project, Bilal crouches at the end of the gallery space, wearing heavy black safety goggles and facing the gun. It is mounted on a gray metal worktable in the right foreground and is pointed at him, the black eye of the camera lit up on top. The walls of the space are dripping in gold, ochre, rich yellows.

Over the course of the thirty-day exhibit, more than sixty-five thousand paintball bullets were fired at Bilal in this living space. Though the gun was configured so that there was a short delay between each round, one viewer figured out how to hack it so that it would "fire on repeat, blowing a hole through Bilal's plexiglass screen," according to arts organization Rhizome. Though online the piece had a video-game-like aspect, anyone who actually visited the gallery in person "had a visceral experience of its brutality: the barrage of gunfire and the fumes from the slimy paint led many to describe it as a war zone."

Living in the gallery space, under the scrutiny of the camera and the constant presence of the gun, Bilal found his PTSD symptoms resurfacing. His childhood in Iraq was "defined by the horrific rule of Saddam Hussein, two wars, a bloody uprising, and time spent interned in chaotic refugee camps in Kuwait and Saudi Arabia," and at the time he put on *Domestic Tension*, he was "still processing his grief over the loss of his father and his brother Haji"—his brother killed at a US checkpoint in 2005.

In early video blogs from the piece, Bilal speaks about how difficult each day has been; the direct hits he's taken to his arm, his chest; the ways in which he can't allow his body to slow down, to feel safe. The screen is hazy from a thin smear of yellow paint. "Who do you think is shooting?" he asks one friend who visits the gallery space. "I wonder if violence becomes just a way of filling your time, when you have nothing better to do" she ponders, when he tells her the shooting slows during lunch and dinner time.

By the later days of the video blog, Bilal is tense, almost haggard. Bullet shots snap and echo in the background, again and again, the sound ricocheting around the bare room. He keeps his goggles on, speaks of the health impacts of living under these conditions of tension and unease. It feels hostile, aggressive, angry, and mean; I am stressed out just from watching the video. "I just wanted to be closer to my family back home, mentally and physically . . . but also to show, they are living under extreme conditions," he says to the camera. "Breathing is becoming heavier and heavier every day. . . . I don't know if it contributes to the anxiety . . . but paint fumes are thick . . . the air is not circulating." He gives us a tour of the room: a landscape of cracked and bubbled paint, the walls dripping with it, the plant drowning in its yellow coating. People are firing constantly, he tells us, it's worse than ever. More than four thousand shots were fired today. The gun empties quickly, and he has to fill it every twenty minutes at the current rate of shooting. I try to imagine the heaviness and dread of this task, replenishing the gun's hopper with the yellow, marble-sized projectiles that are menacing his every moment.

In *Domestic Tension*, Bilal faces human hostility and aggression without end. The piece reflects not only the suffering and war—or warlike conditions—suffered by Iraqis over decades but also, he says, "the difficulties and joys of the American immigrant experience."

"We may think we are surviving," Bilal writes in his book about this interactive performance, "but as I . . . twist and turn through sleepless nights, flailing between worlds of comfort and conflict, hope and despair, I wonder."

Near the final day, the room is a ruin of saffron, a wrecked landscape, destroyed items strewn and caked in yellow dust like a bombed building.

As I watch the video footage from *Domestic Tension*, I think of my own fears: what I would do, who I would become—but also, how unprotected I would feel—if society were to descend into instability and nihilist violence. I feel so vulnerable and unprepared for something like that to happen, I tell Anna, like I'd just get steamrolled by all the hypermasculine, bullying, violent elements of society.

When she and I talk about this, Anna says she thinks it's an illusion of the wealthy, to think that you could be independent and self-reliant and *prepared* for that sort of thing. "That's why we need to not treat people in conflict zones as though it's really their fault that they're in trouble," she says. "That's an illusion, but one that actually works very well to keep other people, other countries from acting."

See something, do something, all those US reports and policy documents on active shooter events say. And yet, for anyone living under the threat of double-tap drone strikes, exactly the opposite is true. Some humanitarian aid organizations have implemented a six-hour mandatory delay before responding. "A mode of collective paralysis," one researcher calls the effects of such double strikes.

Outside the windows of this hospital room, the wind pulls the tree branches into tremors and shudders. A couple on bicycles waits for the light to change. The air swirls around them in late autumn gusts.

A bit later that winter, I would find myself drinking a beer with my friend John, a Marine Corps veteran, in an über-hip bar in Reykjavik. John is also an EMT, and we were there to teach a medical course during the darkest days of winter.

We began talking about the changes in the EMS world—about active shooters and mass killings, about the imperative element of immediate bystander response—and segued into talking about bystander syndrome. John said, "All those studies report that people are less likely to help when there are lots of other people around because everyone expects someone else to act—I've always been skeptical of that explanation because it's not based in evidence, it's just a guess about why no one acts."

I nodded. It has always seemed to me as if on some level it's about conformity—you look around and no one else is acting—and also about *embarrassment*, because if you act, everyone else in this big crowd will be watching you risk making a fool of yourself.

John told me, "When I taught a medical course in Pune, India, last year, my students there told me, 'The absolute last thing anyone here would do, if they saw someone get hit by a car, would be to go toward that person and offer help. Because in this country, we all know that either the police are going to come and arrest anyone they can find to arrest, or a mob is going to form and beat or kill whomever they perceive as being associated with the incident.' So when someone gets injured or there's some kind of incident there, everyone around just starts backing away, putting as much distance as they can between themselves and the person who's hurt."

I think of that story often as I teach students about scene safety and responding to the scene of an accident. Of the tension between *see something, do something* and the actual reluctance of many or most bystanders to get involved, even without the threat of double strike. And of the terrifyingly quick descent into mob violence as a way of discharging fear, anger, or grief. Of what it must feel like to be so alone in one's injury, seemingly abandoned by everyone nearby.

I have always found big crowds, huge groups of people, both bewildering and somewhat terrifying—large sports events, parades—the anonymity of them, the chance of becoming trapped, the way group "moods" can shift and cohere so quickly.

In seeking to better understand how people descend into acts of individual violence or into mob violence—and I'm aware as I write these words that even our language points to our cultural conceptions of violence as something outside ourselves, something we "descend into" but then recover from, rise back out of, rise above, back to our "true" selves—I keep coming across the work of Stanford sociologist Mark Granovetter.

One essay published in the late seventies, "Threshold Models of Collective Behavior," seeks to understand how people can at times act in ways they normally would not—for example, during a riot. In Granovetter's words, it explores how "collective outcomes can seem paradoxical—that is, intuitively inconsistent with the intentions of the individuals who generate them." His argument is that everyone has a different threshold—think of it as a barrier to entry.

If we take, for example, the question of joining a riot, some people have a barrier to entry that is a 0 out of 100; these are "people who will riot even when no one else does," Granovetter explains. "These are the 'instigators.'" Think of them as gleeful hurlers of bricks. Other people are more reluctant to join. Each person has their own threshold: whether they need to see ten people or two hundred people participating in the riot before they will join in. Some people—presumably quite few—have a 100 percent threshold; that is, they will never join the riot, no matter how many others do.

I find myself wondering about the threshold to entry for those who fired the gun on Bilal: did it feel like a video game to them, or did they just enjoy the opportunity to fire on another human being, someone they perhaps saw as less human than them?

Granovetter's model of threshold-based behavior, particularly in the context of rioting, prompted me to return to a book I'd read years before; published in the 1990s, it was written by an Indian psychoanalyst, Sudhir Kakar. The book, *The*

Colors of Violence: Cultural Identities, Religion, and Violence, seeks to understand the psychological landscape of the communities participating in the decades of Hindu-Muslim riots in India—and the leaders instigating those riots.

Finished now with the process of registering to recertify my EMT license, still seated in this white, sterile hospital room awaiting my friend—and feeling very conscious of the irony of reading about active shooter events, mass casualties, and mob violence while seated in a sterile, "safe" hospital; conscious of the great distance between coming to a hospital for a "controlled, predictable" surgical procedure and finding oneself in the midst of unpredictable acts of violence, whether war or public shootings—I pull out Kakar's book, and after one more glance out at the gray skies, begin reading.

Early in the book, in his exploration of social factors underlying the riots, Kakar notes, "There is now empirical evidence to suggest that the greater the legitimization of violence in some approved areas of life, the more is the likelihood that force will also be used in other spheres where it may not be approved."

That idea makes sense to me, but what I have struggled to understand is why—or how—it is that when seemingly calm, rational people get into a group setting, their outlook and actions can shift so fundamentally to xenophobia, anger, even violence. The answer to this must partially rest on Granovetter's thinking on thresholds, but also, it has always seemed to me, it has much to do with our sense of identity. From a psychological perspective, Kakar seems to agree:

> The group can have [a profound effect] on the consolidation of a person's "sense of identity" and in increasing the cohesiveness of the self. Even in individual psychotherapy, we often see that it is not unusual for patients in a state of self-fragmentation to achieve a firmer and more cohesive sense of self upon joining an organized group.

> The Nazis are not the only group who turned quasi-derelict individuals into efficiently functioning ones by providing them the framework of a convincing world image and the use of new cultural symbols and group

emblems.... As Ernest Wolf perceptively observes, "It seems a social identity can support a crumbling self the way a scaffolding can support a crumbling building."

Chris Hedges, too, concurs with this thinking. In *War Is a Force That Gives
Us Meaning,* he writes: "Lurking beneath the surface of every society, including
ours, is the passionate yearning for a nationalist cause that exalts us.... It reduces
and at times erases the anxiety of individual consciousness."

The *anxiety of individual consciousness.* What a phrase, to sum up all our neuroses
and fears and insecurities, this overwhelmingness of human existence.

And, as Kakar points out, such social identities—often these days rooted in
nationalism—are at the mercy of current events, fluid and subject to change,
even while they enhance the individual sense of "self-sameness and continuity
in time and space."

This psychological grasping for a sense of self-sameness, of continuity in time
and space, strikes me because it points the same direction as Buddhist beliefs
about conditionality and no-self, that while we are constantly seeking ways to
make ourselves feel that we are stable and secure and rooted, there is in fact a
fundamental inconstancy to this thing we call self. Constant change, constant
insecurity.

An orderly comes in to straighten the room; there is still no word on how my
friend's procedure is going. Outside, the trees stick their skeletal arms toward
the sky, and the tiny cars keep nosing around the parking ramp in tiny squares.

"What happens in the period of tension is that individuals increasingly think
of themselves as Hindus or Muslims," Kakar writes. This can be thought of

as increased group salience. In these moments, "an individual thinks and be-haves in conformity with the stereotypical characteristics of the category of 'Hindu' (or 'Muslim') rather than according to his or her individual personality dispositions."

During periods of tension, hate and rage toward external targets heightens: "Since the enemy is also a reservoir of our own unwanted selves and negative feel-ings, it is important it be kept at a psychological distance," notes Kakar. "Con-sciously, the enemy should never be like us."

Because of this, "even minor differences between 'us' and 'them' are exaggerated as unbridgeable chasms . . . which evoke stronger hostility and hate than do wide disparities."

The diminishment of a person based on a sense of them as "other," on perceptions of the body they were born into or some other aspect of their self, is the denial of the richness of a human being—what Teju Cole describes as "the incontest-able fundamentals of a person: pleasure, sorrow, love, humor, and grief, and the complexity of the interior landscape that sustains those feelings."

Philosopher Emmanuel Levinas, notes Maggie Nelson, "proposes that the per-ceived precariousness of an Other simultaneously provokes in us the urge to pro-tect him and the temptation to kill him."

"All of us," Grossman writes in *On Killing*, "would like to believe that we would not participate in atrocities. That we could deny our friends and leaders and even turn our weapons on them if need be. But there are profound pro-cesses involved that prevent such confrontation of peers and leaders in atrocity circumstance."

I think of this when I think of the idea of bystander syndrome, of the studies that have been done—that we all want to believe we would act, when so much evidence seems to suggest we would not.

John Gray comments on our contemporary Western view of progress, our idea that we are evolving into more and more enlightened and civilized beings, growing away from our violent animal selves.

Older views of the world, held by most major religions and most peoples before modern times, observed that while our knowledge, learning, and innovation may grow cumulatively, "advances in ethics and politics are erratic, discontinuous and easily lost," he writes. Instead of evolving away from war, "peace and freedom alternate with war and tyranny, eras of increasing wealth with periods of economic collapse. Instead of becoming ever stronger and more widely spread, civilisation remains inherently fragile and regularly succumbs to barbarism."

This belief is almost intolerable to many Westerners now, I think, the idea that we are not securely in the end zone, not safely sailing beyond the darker eras of the past. That at any moment—and quite outside the control of any individual to prevent—we could swing back into atrocity, into chaos, and the immense vulnerability and fear that would follow.

For those of us who have experienced mostly safety, mostly stability in our lives, so much of how we look at others' violence or others' experience of violence has to do with our own fear. The fear that what has happened *there* can also happen here.

Maggie Nelson explores this thought from a lens of projecting our vulnerability onto others, writing that in those moments when the Other ceases to be the repository of our projected vulnerability, "the radical precariousness in which we all share jumps into focus and becomes everyone's burden to bear."

It is a precariousness that many Westerners seem hell-bent on denying.

I think again of the shootings and bombings that have just occurred in Paris, of Wafaa Bilal living under the constant rotation and clicking of the gun. I think of the many images of gutted, bombed out buildings that played on the white screen behind the dancers in Mokhalled Rasem's *Body Revolution*, the dance piece that Anna and I saw in Maastricht.

In one of them, two dancers stand mummified in front of the screen. Behind them rise three stories of gutted, crumbling concrete, so destroyed that it looks like dripping, melting flesh. Like something that was alive, now rotting.

The sun is trying to battle its way through, and across the river, the hill of Sint Pieter pokes up from the trees, the old fort atop it visible above the cliffs, above the cement factory, above the brown trees with just a slight fur of green remaining. Bicycles float along the pathways; a steady stream of people walk the glass halls of the hospital building below me, entering and exiting out onto the roof of the car park, driving their tiny, toy-looking cars that nose their way in and out of parking spots, and above all this the gray sky, hanging low, allowing peeks of washed-out blue behind it, and a desperate, faded sunshine making its attempts at presence.

My friend has not come back up yet, and I am beginning to feel afraid. For those fragile, lacy arteries wrapping his heart, for his pregnant partner, for his soon-to-be daughter. I sit in his hospital room and I wait, facing the glass, the car park, the bicycles and the trees. The gray of the afternoon has settled in.

When my friend John and I were teaching that dark, midwinter medical course in Reykjavik, we visited Thingvellir, site of the first Viking congress, held in

930 CE. The snow was pelting us blind, and we more or less ran through the cleft in the rock that drifting continental plates are slowly and irrevocably pulling open. But for a moment, the wind dropped and the snow stopped and stillness broke through. A wing of light angled down over the afternoon and the slate-colored lake and the thick gray air. In the distance, a wide plume of steam rose from some geothermal vent or other. It seemed too barren even for a congress of Vikings, for human habitation, like some prehistoric landscape not yet softened by plant life or the accumulation of soil.

The guesthouse we were staying in had a bookshelf in the common room, and I stumbled across *Facing the Extreme: Moral Life in the Concentration Camps* by French Bulgarian moral philosopher Tzvetan Todorov. In it, Todorov interviews survivors of Nazi concentration camps and Soviet gulags, as well as guards and commanders of the camps.

At one point, in a chapter about the fragmentation of self that can occur in such brutal, traumatic settings, he writes that Auschwitz survivors "repeatedly point to one trait that was common to all camp guards, . . . behavioral inconsistency. "A person could help one prisoner and, without batting an eyelash, send another to his death." This, according to Todorov, is "the 'social schizophrenia' specific to totalitarian regimes."

This idea of inconsistency and irrationality is so much easier to square with my understanding of humans, of human behavior and the human mind and heart, that it is almost reassuring, less frightening somehow than a fixed concept of cold, clinical evil.

That fragmentation of self we are susceptible to feels more realistic, more *human*, fraught as we are with fallibilities and fears. "The bones of the soul are like a thousand tiny fishbones," said my therapist once: "they have a hundred cracks upon a hundred cracks upon a hundred cracks." Another psychoanalyst, D. W. Winnicott, describes such fragmentation as "falling forever and ever," as disintegrating, falling to pieces. Kakar writes of the need of egoically fragile strongmen to consolidate their sense of self, to create coherency through external structures such as the Nazi youth. *Self* is a slippery thing. The *I* drags bottom and some-times never catches; it fails to cohere. As Primo Levi observes, "Compassion and brutality can coexist in the same individual and in the same moment, despite all logic." This is a paradox of human existence: the fracturing and fractured self, temporally bound, ever-changing.

John Paul Lederach, in his thinking on conflict studies and mediation, argues that while justifications for violence come from so many sources, so many angles, "the moral imagination that rises beyond violence has but two: taking personal responsibility and acknowledging relational mutuality."

That sense of relational mutuality, of human connection, is core to who we are as social animals. When we teach stress first aid in our medical courses— techniques to help medical responders reduce the stress injuries patients may ex-perience during moments of acute medical trauma—we teach them to emphasize connection and calm. To say things like, "You're safe now. You're safe here." To help the patient bring their awareness into the present moment—which can sig-nal their nervous system to tell the body all is clear—by listening to the sounds around them or feeling the texture of the ground beneath their hands. To em-phasize a sense of human connection by asking them about themselves or helping them speak with someone they love.

I feel my body connect with the chair I am sitting in, with the cool surface of the desk beneath my forearms. My feet rest fully on the floor, hospital tiles sparkling white with cleanliness. I can feel that I am safe, and with that feeling comes a little twinge, high up under my ribs, with the knowledge that so many people cannot feel that sense of safety in this moment—is that twinge shame, guilt? Or grief? I cannot say for certain. I think of drills I have done as a teacher, practic-ing what we would do if there were an active shooter in the building—drills that were surprisingly terrifying, that made me realize how hard it would be to keep someone armed out of my classroom, to keep the students and myself safe. Of how quiet the room is in that moment, with all of us huddled on the floor, against the wall, just waiting. I think of Bilal's saying he couldn't get his body to slow down, couldn't feel safe, when at all moments the camera and the gun watched his every movement. Of how alone he was in that room, with only outside eyes upon him.

My friend finally comes out of surgery and is wheeled back into the hospital room where I have been waiting for him. He is groggy and in some degree of pain, and his arms and legs are marked up with purple ink. The procedure has not been entirely successful, they tell us, and he will have to undergo another, more serious surgery. He can wait until after his baby daughter is born, the doctor says, but then he will need open-heart surgery to address the problem.

The trees outside stand silent witness. Late November's brown has fully arrived, the hills no longer dusted with a firelike tinge. Still, the ground is littered with the leaves' fallen crust. The horses run in the fields, and it is as though their hooves are being pushed up out of the earth. Rebounding. The winds have arrived and everywhere the air is moving. The horses, too, moving in circles, manes and tails running out behind them.

As I walk the dog through the fields in the morning, the geese let out cries when we pass by, fattening themselves in the recently shorn fields, searching out the fallen kernels of dried corn. Overhead, they are a mélange of brown, black, and white, ruddy and orange-footed. They are a particular constellation of noise.

CHAPTER SEVEN

Blood Sugar

as if we're not all in this together
—Kara Walker

Everything was misty, pastel, and cold when I walked out through the Maastricht fields in the early winter morning. Small patches of fog hung over the fields; the trees lined the edges in brown and purple, and the hills rose, a paler brown, to the other side. Even with a dazzling sun breaking through the low clouds, the landscape was muted, soft around the edges. Only the small field of koolzad—canola, bright green and flecked with small yellow flowers—reflected the vivid world Van Gogh painted, and I thought, Willem Witsen, whose work I do not love, in fact got it right. So where did Van Gogh find that brilliant, electric world he painted his way into?

Researchers say that a significant factor in the development and wealth of northwestern Europe was the deep bed of loess-rich topsoil that parts of the continent lucked their way into, allowing farming to scale up sufficiently to support armies.

In *For the Time Being*, Annie Dillard writes:

> The Chinese empire grew from the loess soil. Loess deposits in China are the deepest soils in the world. The fertile loess plains around Xi'an are thick layers—up to four hundred feet thick—of fine windblown sand and rock flour. The deposits run to fine textures: they absorb water and feed minerals to plants' roots. All you have to do is irrigate. Irrigation requires

that many people cooperate; it requires civilization. The Chinese have been irrigating this region for twenty-three centuries.

Each winter, the city of San Antonio, where my parents now live, experiences several weeks of dust haze that is actually wind-blown sand from northern Africa. An entire landmass transmogrifying itself, shifting slowly through the air.

Another immense factor, of course, in the enrichment and wealth development of western Europe was colonialism. Wealth built from the soil—and labor— of other lands, other peoples.

In Amsterdam recently, I was walking through the exhibits at the Rijks-museum—the major national museum of arts and history in the Netherlands— and suddenly came upon a wall of faces. White plaster heads in lifelike detail, mounted in a grid set forward from the wall, they cast a river of shadows behind them.

In 1910, Dr. Kleiweg de Zwaan went to Sumatra to take facial casts of Nias Is-landers. He covered their faces with plaster and brought the masks home. Now in the Rijksmuseum in Amsterdam you can see a wall lined with the reproductions of these men's faces: eyes squinted, mouths shut against intrusion. This is one kind of research. He lacked the imagination to see that they were also people, just like him.

In the late summer, not too long after we'd moved to Maastricht, Anna began work at her new international school. One afternoon, she brought home the previous year's yearbook, and we sat on the couch, paging through it. Sunlight streamed in the floor-to-ceiling windows of the apartment.

We'd met and previously worked at a sort of sister school in the US and were flipping through the pages, commenting on a few students we knew as cousins or siblings of students we'd taught the year before, when we stumbled across an entire page of small children posing gleefully with what was clearly a white adult in blackface. Thick red lips, face completely blackened, a dark curly wig atop. Our hands stuttered to a stop.

The comments below the photos said that the blackface character is known as Zwarte Piet, or Black Pete. I looked at the faces of the kids of color in that classroom photo, my stomach squeezing, wondering how they felt when they first saw this person, clownishly made up as a caricature of someone who might look like them.

As we began to adjust to life in the Netherlands and the summer dropped into autumn—the air crisper, the light lengthening to golden—we asked everyone we met about Zwarte Piet. Who is this character? What's up with the blackface? In effect, what we were really trying to ask was, how is it possible that such a celebration still exists in the Europe of today?

There were a confusing array of answers.

People told us that Zwarte Piet is the mischievous accomplice to Sinterklaas, or Saint Nicholas. That Sinterklaas was based on a Turk, but now the children are told he comes from Spain. And that Zwarte Piet was based on an enslaved North African man that the Turk bought and freed, but these days he's based on a Moor from Spain. Or maybe his darkened skin comes from climbing through chimneys, and he's not of African descent at all.

They told us that Zwarte Piet and Sinterklaas sail around from Spain to deliver gifts to all the children of the Netherlands; that Zwarte Piet brings candy and can be seen jumping around on rooftops and looking in on families through the chimneys. He's playful and mischievous and all the children love him—except they're also warned that if they're bad, he'll catch them up in his jute sack and take them back to Spain. Still, many people told us, it's not a harmful tradition—he is such a source of joy and delight to the children.

As the inconsistencies in the story emerged, they belied that sense of innocent joy. The multiple strands of the narrative—that Zwarte Piet provided delight, but also warning; that either you have a white person in blackface, or you have someone with coal on their face—could be partially the result of culture change over time, but they also seemed to reveal an underlying discomfort with the narrative, however much people sought to deny it.

I began to do some research about Zwarte Piet. I learned that he was supposedly the servant of Sinterklaas (Saint Nicholas), that white-bearded white man atop the white horse in his bishop-like robes and headpiece. Saint Nicholas of Smyrna came from what is now Turkey, but his relics were later moved to Spain.

In 1850, a children's storybook published in Amsterdam—*Sint Nikolaas en Zijn Knecht* (Saint Nicholas and his servant)—first documented the character of Zwarte Piet. The book, by primary school teacher Jan Schenkman, became so popular that it stayed in print until 1950.

Zwarte Piet spoke broken Dutch, wore gold hoop earrings, and performed absurd antics for the entertainment of the children. He eventually proliferated into a crowd of Piets who accompany Sinterklaas each year. "While some say that their darkness comes from climbing through chimneys (as did the Italian immigrant chimneysweeps of the nineteenth century)," writes one scholar, "their likeness to Al Jolson is hard to miss."

Around the same time that Schenkman's book was first published, minstrel shows were hitting their peak popularity on the other side of the Atlantic.

Minstrelsy began to emerge in the US around the 1820s and waned in popularity by 1900, though film performances by white actors in blackface have persisted much longer (in the case of the extremely popular Al Jolson, for example, Hollywood produced *The Jazz Singer* in 1927, and a slew of movies from more recent decades feature white characters in blackface, or brownface or yellowface, giving lie to the idea that this is an issue of the past).

When the performance of blackface started in America, it started in the North, not in the South as many of us might imagine. It started, in part, because white people in the northern states were curious about the "exotic" plantation life and about the people of African descent they had little direct experience with. White performers blackened their faces with burnt cork and performed grossly caricatured Black characters who were enslaved in the south. They spoke in an exaggerated Black vernacular, portraying bumbling, childishly unintelligent country bumpkins who were frequently compared to animals and who were, almost always, the butt of the joke.

And America exported our practice of blackface: in the early to mid-nineteenth century, minstrel troupes from the US traveled to Europe and to many other parts of the world. In the UK, especially, the idea of blackface took a deep hold on the imagination of the (presumably mostly white) British public.

This all started well before Schenkman wrote his 1850 book introducing Zwarte Piet, so one might feasibly imagine that the minstrel troupes of America influenced the origins of what has now become a widespread Dutch performance of blackface.

Many scholars believe the Zwarte Piet figure has its roots in the chained devil figure that accompanied Saint Nicholas in medieval iconography—a permutation of the pagan demon Krampus, who can still be seen in terrifying regalia at winter celebrations in the mountain regions of Austria, Germany, Slovenia, Italy, and Croatia.

Though this aspect of the story has softened somewhat over time, Zwarte Piet was initially used to ensure good behavior by striking fear into the hearts of children—he was often shown carrying a birch stick with which to frighten or punish any misbehavers. As one professor at the University of Maastricht explained, Dutch children know that Zwarte Piet "hands out sweets and gifts from his big bag . . . [but] the children also know that once the big bag runs empty, Zwarte Piet fills it with all the children who have been 'naughty' in the past year, and takes them away with him—back to Spain!"

For those of us from the US, it is impossible to read about this aspect of Zwarte Piet's role without hearing echoes. The association of Black men with fear—and the use of that fear to justify atrocities—is not a new concept.

———

In the seventeenth century, the Dutch—including perhaps some of my own direct ancestors—played a major role in the trafficking of people from western Africa, with Dutch ships abducting them into ruthlessly packed holds to sail across the Atlantic. The Dutch gained control of Suriname—tucked between Guyana and Brazil on the northeast coast of South America—where sugar was the primary industry, one that demanded a high input of physical labor and one which in many ways drove the trade in human beings.

In "The Price of Sugar," Edwidge Danticat writes:

> Midway through Candide, Voltaire's famously naive protagonist enters Dutch-controlled 18th-century Suriname, where he encounters "a negro stretched upon the ground . . . the poor man had lost his left leg and his right hand."

> "Good God!" exclaims Candide, who proceeds to ask the man why he's in such terrible shape.

"When we work at the sugar-canes," the man answers, "and the mill snatches hold of a finger, they cut off the hand; and when we attempt to run away, they cut off the leg. . . . This is the price at which you eat sugar in Europe."

"We still," Danticat notes, "eat sugar at a similar price. And not just in Europe, but all over the world." The sugar industry from South Africa to the Americas and the Caribbean still relies on cheap, exploited labor—migrant labor, child labor, sometimes even forced labor. In Central America, one report found that laborers worked twelve hours a day, all seven days of the week, and three-quarters reported workplace injuries, mostly with machetes. The pay was insufficient for adults to support a family, forcing children into the fields as well.

On our way to Turkey and Cyprus in 2014, Anna and I spent a few days in Brooklyn with some old friends. We went to the old Domino Sugar refinery to see artist Kara Walker's installation: "A Subtlety or the Marvelous Sugar Baby an Homage to the unpaid and overworked Artisans who have refined our Sweet tastes from the cane fields to the Kitchens of the New World on the Occasion of the demolition of the Domino Sugar Refining Plant."

The installation was open for only nine weekends, and a line to enter wound around the entire long New York block. Inside the warehouse was Sugar Baby, a colossal sphinx figure made of white sugar. Her goddess-like face, that of a Black woman wearing an Aunt Jemina–style kerchief, stared blank-eyed out over the warehouse interior.

Around her, the dark walls of the warehouse were sticky with the brown residue of decades of sugar-making. Our shoes stuck to the floor as we walked. The sweet, heavy smell of molasses, thick in the air, dripped from the rusty ceiling. The approach to Sugar Baby was scattered with round-cheeked brown-sugar boys, carrying large baskets in their arms: five-foot-tall enlargements of ceramic figurines

Walker found online. In the summer heat, some were melting; broken chunks of the collapsed had been thrown into the sugary fluid in others' baskets.

By the 1800s, the Domino Sugar factory was processing more than half the sugar consumed in the US. In a video interview with Creative Time, Walker says, "I wanted to make a piece that would sort of complement [the Domino Sugar factory,] echo it, and hopefully would contain these assorted meanings about imperialism, about slavery, about a slave trade that traded sugar for bodies and bodies for sugar."

"I think that's one of the reasons I chose a sphinx, because it's emblematic of a ruin, and it's living in this ruin that's about to come down."

While searching for more information about the history of Zwarte Piet, I stumbled across an old photo of Josephine Baker on a 1957 visit to the Netherlands, meeting Sinterklaas and a blackface Zwarte Piet. I tried to image her reaction, which is not clear from the carefully schooled smile on her face, and could only come up with a sense of horror. Though I searched and searched, I could not find anything else written about this moment.

Before moving to the Netherlands, I had imagined the racialized landscape of Europe dividing primarily along lines drawn by Islamophobia (which is certainly partially true), so to find this striking visual remnant of Europe's colonial and slave-owning past still being vibrantly and gleefully celebrated was a shock.

And yet, as James Baldwin noted acerbically in 1953, "Europe's black possessions remained—and do remain—in Europe's colonies, at which remove they represented no threat whatever to European identity. If they posed any problem at all for the European conscience, it was a problem which remained comfortingly abstract: in effect, the black man, as a *man*, did not exist for Europe."

I remembered comments from two of my Belgian students at a previous international school, when we were analyzing racialized narratives in US literature. "We never talk about these things in Europe," one of them said. The other student, who had emigrated from India to Belgium, nodded: "They do exist, but no one really talks about them, it's all just . . . kept quiet and polite."

Though in some ways this abstraction and silence has diminished substantially in the several years since Anna and I lived in Maastricht—with more voices making it into the mainstream, identifying and speaking out about race and racism in Europe—the dominant narrative in both Europe and the US still has such a long way to go toward fully acknowledging our nations' racialized landscapes, and the damages they have wrought.

In another interview about her installation at the Domino Sugar refinery, Walker comments:

> There's this insane amount of pressure, heat, centrifugal force, and manpower necessary to bleach the sugar. Not to bleach it, exactly, but to turn it from its natural brown to white state. . . . The project presented an opportunity to invert this paradigm and maybe call into question the desire for the refined—to ask what is lost in the process of refining. This is a testament and monument to the quest for whiteness, the quest for whatever that means.

And in "Unpour," author and performer Shailja Patel writes: "It takes bones to get sugar white. Thousands of pounds of cow bones burned to bone char are used to bleach sugar in processing plants."

"Basically, it was blood sugar," Walker says. "Like we talk about blood diamonds today, there were pamphlets saying this sugar has blood on its hands."

One of the most striking scenes of a recent documentary film opens in an art gallery. We see loaves of sugar being placed on the floor, some of them cracked through the middle, others intact. They are twelve inches tall, hand-shaped like clay, firm cones of sugar in a palette of whites and light browns. In the background, a woman's voice keens in song.

As the cones add up on the floor, a voice tells us: "These sugar loaves were baked in Amsterdam. The raw sugar was transported from the colonies to the Amsterdam harbor. Amsterdam was among the biggest refined sugar producers."

We pan into the speaker. "I found out that sugar and blood are inextricably connected," says Patricia Kaersenhout, a Dutch visual artist of Afro-Surinamese descent. She is standing in a white-walled gallery, holding aloft an IV bag full of red liquid. As she speaks, she affixes it onto an IV pole above the loaves of sugar.

"During the slave period, enslaved people were forced to cut down sugarcane. The sugarcanes were pressed in large crushers. Production continued around the clock to meet the huge demand for sugar, and the enslaved people had to feed the cane into the crushers. And sometimes their fingers got caught, and ended up in the raw sugar.

"There would be someone with an axe at the ready and the moment somebody got caught in the crusher, they would cut off their arm, so the blood mixed with the raw sugar."

As she speaks, blood drips from the tubing onto the bullet-shaped loaves of white sugar standing on the gallery floor.

"Today, the Suikerbakkersteeg alley still reminds us of these sugar bakers."

The documentary film in which this scene takes place is called *Amsterdam, Traces of Sugar*; it is beautifully filmed and disquieting.

At its opening, we watch two white Dutch men working on the rigging of bells in a belltower. The wires for the bells are a maze, an intricacy. Below them, an old worn wooden floor, a trapdoor, a window.

"The Dutch sold an estimated 600,000 African people or more into slavery," a voice matter-of-factly narrates. "These people were kept as slaves in Brazil, Suriname, Curacao, and other Caribbean islands. They were regarded as merchandise rather than human beings. Working on the plantations, they produced coffee, cocoa, cotton, tobacco, and sugar. . . . In those days, the Netherlands were an economic world power."

The bells ring. Our view travels up the bell tower, then outside: narrow, gabled Amsterdam row houses, a typical gray wintry sky. Below the gold-numbered clock on the bell tower is a year: 1620.

"Ignoring part of your history feels like part of your dignity is being taken away," says artist Kaersenhout elsewhere in the film, speaking in Dutch, her slender dreadlocks falling around her face as she speaks. "I would like to make this history visible, so I can give back this dignity."

In an online tour of the Rijksmuseum, viewers can move around in a circle to view the immense underground stores of art, stored on grilled panels that hang in tight rows—like shelves in a research library that can be pulled out into the aisle. Each grill holds perhaps ten or twenty paintings.

"Revenue from the goods produced with slave labor funded much of The Netherlands' Golden Age in the 17th century, a period renowned for its artistic, literary, scientific, and philosophical achievements," write the authors of "Whitewashed Slavery Past?"

In another room is a golden sleigh and a wealth of antique furniture pieces made of teak or other tropical hardwoods, some gilded with decorative gold. One chess set, carved in ivory, contains figures mounted on elephants. It is difficult to look at these pieces without seeing them as stained with colonial history: spoils of an era of oppression and extraction that fueled the Dutch Golden Age.

"Without a postcolonial discourse or better education in history," the article's authors note, "white Dutch people are often ignorant of why they have Surinamese, African, and/or Antillean neighbors in The Netherlands. They often perceive black people as poorly educated and reluctant to work, as if they have come to The Netherlands to feed off of its wealth. Few know of the historical labor relations between their own ancestors and those of the black community in producing this wealth."

For a time, in the busy-ness and stress of adapting to a new country, I forgot about Zwarte Piet. September and October passed in a blur of cycling around the city, errands, dog walks, and travel for work.

One afternoon in early November, the sun slanting gold through the windows, I sat at our kitchen table, opening the mail. On the other side of the street, horses in a pasture chased each other in brief sprints across the velvet green. I flipped briefly, aimlessly, though the junk mail—and froze at the Christmas section in the middle of the Kruidvat catalogue.

Paper plates and cups were dotted with white Sinterklaases and Zwarte Piets with black or brown faces, their lips red, the whites of their eyes outlining large black pupils.

A holiday Playmobil set contained Sinterklaas—white-bearded and regal on a white horse, with tall gold staff and red miter—with a brown Zwarte Piet beside him, holding aloft a birch stick and carrying a sack of gifts.

On a third page of the catalog, among the holiday candies, was a bag of clownlike chocolates that could have come straight from an 1850s minstrel show poster:

dark chocolate faces with round white eyes, big red lips, and large icing loops of curly hair.

I thought of the sugar used to make those chocolates, of the history of enslaved people's labor to extract that sugar, and the deep irony of these holiday sweets still embodying that exploitation. I thought of what it means to see such blatantly dehumanizing holiday candies, decorations, and celebrations today—what blind spots, myths, and self-delusions they might make visible.

Dutch academic Gloria Wekker points to one such myth: the commonly held Dutch perception of the Netherlands as a highly egalitarian society. "This is not the case," she argues. "Race and ethnicity really make a difference in people's lives here. If you point this out, you are likely to be called a killjoy, or even to be called a racist yourself." And Wekker refers to the work of Philomena Essed, which has generated "public attention, turmoil, and rage" by arguing "that the Netherlands is as deeply and as structurally racist as the United States."

In one academic paper I read, cultural historian Nancy Jouwe pointed out that the Netherlands has seen a shift in racist attitudes, from "anti-Black to anti-Muslim (and back to anti-black)," but that the underlying problem remains the same: the presence of institutional racism, alongside the general denial of its existence. And all of this is taking place in the context of Europe becoming "increasingly hostile to cultural 'Others,' making it very hard for European 'Others' to maintain or gain a sense of place."

As I read this, I couldn't help flashing through some of the images that had been in the European news in the past year: images of boats overturning and the bodies of those who had drowned, washing up on beaches.

Images of massive, terrifying, human-made fires crackling in the dead of night at asylum buildings—those buildings that finally offered some refuge, after so much dark rough ocean and then stifling heat, after waiting for trains and sleeping on benches and being put in overcrowded camps. Buildings that offered refuge to those who had survived the arduous journey north, after surviving the years of bombings and mass executions and chaos and loss in their homeland.

When the film *Amsterdam, Traces of Sugar* comes back to Kaersenhout, she is holding a piece of her artwork, a history book she has altered. "I cut out parts from the book, like the word, 'guilt' (*schuld*) here, referring to this particular chapter." On the page large letters have been carved away from the page: **SChuLd.**

"Next I cross out all these lines, because part of my history is being denied in this book. This is about the Golden Age, with a picture of Michiel de Ruyter," the widely celebrated seventeenth-century Dutch admiral.

All the lines of text in this section of the book are blacked out, like an erasure poem, with no words left behind to speak.

"I cut away all these texts and also cut away their eyes to symbolize people being blind to their own history." She points to a painting of a white man, a gap like a blindfold sliced from the page. "History is also a matter of cause and effect. Enslaving and oppressing people for years and years is bound to have consequences."

The film cuts away, and for a moment we see tropical vegetation, the old cogs of a sugar crusher, grown over with bamboo or sugarcane.

It cuts again, and we see Kaersenhout at a table in the Rijksmuseum library, carving pages away, erasing them with whiteout. Behind her, the shelves and shelves of old, leather-bound tomes rise in a three-story wall, a monument to history, the wood pillars that hold them gilded with gold.

Words from earlier in the film echo in our ears:

> You cannot say "it's time to move on" . . . if you fail to acknowledge fully what has happened. The impact that it had for generations and still has today. And that this is a shared history.

Walking my dog that afternoon, the day grown cloudy, gray, and blustering, I saw a Zwarte Piet doll hanging in a house's front door below a heart-shaped wooden sign with hand-painted letters: *Love never takes a holiday.* The doll was crafted in Raggedy Ann style, black cloth sewn into a round head, lips of red felt lips, white lining the eyes. He leaned sideways, grinning, his black yarn hair in knots around his head.

That evening, biking to meet Anna for dinner, I began to see them everywhere, in shop displays, apartment windows, hanging in the doors of houses: Zwarte Piet dolls propped up and grimacing, skulking in every corner. It felt suddenly as if there were an angry undertone to all the festivity, ready to stab out at any dissenter in the flash of a moment.

There has been a growing anti–Zwarte Piet movement within the Netherlands, and the push for change has not been calmly or kindly received. While some progress has been made, particularly in recent years, there have also been death threats sent to those who object to the tradition and threats of assassination against protest organizers.

Reading about this, I thought back to the inconsistencies in the Zwarte Piet story: the way they revealed some degree of discomfort or cognitive dissonance, no matter how much people denied it.

Underlying such aggressive backlash, there must be a repressed unease: if you know on some level a thing is wrong, but you want it anyway, then you've backed yourself into a corner in terms of maintaining your self-image. You're going to double down, to dig your heels in and become vicious in claiming it's not wrong—because if it were wrong, then *you* would also be wrong, your integrity corrupted, your self-regard broken. Better to maintain the delusion of innocence and good.

When the popular Dutch department store Hema stated on social media that they would remove the Black models dressed as "Piets" from their window displays, their employees were threatened and harassed. The woman who requested that Hema remove the models received thousands of threats in just a few days, expressing hopes that she would be raped, advising her to jump in front of a train, or—most evocative of Europe's painful past—to crawl through the chimney of a crematory.

The very basic fact, Wekker observes, is that the Netherlands was a colonial empire for almost four hundred years. How can we possibly think, she asks, "that we have been an empire for four hundred years, yet that it wouldn't have left any traces, in our history, in our language, in the way we think about ourselves and the Other? There is a tension between those two things that is untenable."

Or, in the words of Dutch scholar Markus Balkenhol, "Much like other former colonial powers, . . . the Netherlands suppresses an awareness of colonial continuities in present European societies." More specifically, Balkenhol depicts the Dutch as viewing their country as a nation of freedom and tolerance while cultivating amnesia about the racial violence of its colonial past.

This term, *colonial continuities*, should be in all our vocabularies, I think when I read it.

Like the Netherlands, the US has not dealt with—has hardly even acknowledged, really—our colonial and slave labor–based past. And like the Netherlands, the US also suffers from amnesia about our history—despite the fact that the "colonial continuities" of that past keep rearing their heads.

The celebration of Zwarte Piet is highly visible and provokes a deeply visceral reaction in many people from outside the Netherlands—but in the US at this very moment, a wave of states are passing laws to further disenfranchise voters of color, protect statues that commemorate slaveholders, and ban the teaching of critical race theory—ban ever teaching students that America "has done bad things." There is a widespread desire to say, "what's past is past," and ignore the ongoing costs of that history, those colonial continuities.

And yet, as Saidiya Hartman asserts:

> If slavery persists as an issue in the political life of black America, it is not because of an antiquarian obsession with bygone days or the burden of a too-long memory, but because black lives are still imperiled and devalued by a racial calculus and a political arithmetic that were entrenched centuries ago. This is the afterlife of slavery—skewed life chances, limited access to health and education, premature death, incarceration, and impoverishment.

It is impossible to look at the holiday tradition of Zwarte Piet without thinking of the individuals whose lives have been brutalized in horrifying ways over hundreds of years in the Americas. Of the Dutch West India Company's domination of the shipping trade in human beings, from West Africa to plantations in the American South—or to Dutch plantations in Suriname. Or of the colonial exploitation—of coffee, sugar, tea, human labor—that produced the great wealth of northwestern Europe and the United States.

A wealth that most likely my ancestors benefitted from directly. Which perhaps your ancestors, too, if they were white, benefitted from. Certainly any of us who have means in the societies built on the labor exploited through slavery; any of us who have inherited advantages, have benefitted from that wealth. Any of us who have visited an art museum, who have attended a big university, who have invested our savings into banks that pay interest or into the stock market, or who have been able to buy property, have benefitted from structures and institutions built with wealth from those brutalities and exploitations.

Those of us who are white tend to imagine white supremacy as an explicitly violent, hostile force; to picture it through images of groups of white men carrying torches, chanting white nationalist slogans of hatred. But as Paul Lipsitz writes in *The Possessive Investment in Whiteness*:

> White supremacy is usually less a matter of direct, referential, and snarling contempt than a system for protecting the privilege of whites by denying communities of color opportunities for asset accumulation and upward mobility. Whiteness is invested in, like property, but it is also a means of accumulating property and keeping it from others.

The practice of Zwarte Piet does not target me directly, but nonetheless it includes me—in a whiteness I do not want to contribute to, be a part of, and yet one I have benefitted from all my life.

A few days later, a Sunday, we went into the center of this little city to wander the Christmas market, and there were the live Zwarte Piets themselves, standing in the shopping area, handing out flyers with their makeup-blackened hands. I danced away from them in deep discomfort as we walked by, unsure where to put my gaze.

I thought of the glowing phone conversations I had with Aisha in the late summer, just after we'd arrived, when I was charmed by the arching bridges over the Maas and the narrow cobblestone streets and summery street cafés, words spilling out as I tried to paint the pictures for her, hoping she would come visit.

I would feel ashamed if she visited now, my whiteness implicating me in this malevolent thing, this caricature of her Blackness—and ashamed, too, of my ability to ignore it if I chose, my relationship to this place tarnished but not broken.

———————

Almost every person of color I spoke with in the Netherlands expressed a dread of the late autumn season. Almost all of them had been called Zwarte Piet, at least once, by other school children or by their peers or coworkers.

In an appearance on the Dutch talk show *Pauw*, Dutch Guianese actress Sylvana Simons said: "I wish I could explain how my entire life I and many others have had to maneuver the public domain from September through December. I recently spoke to a friend of mine [who] has an Afro and went to a party. She said: 'I'm not going to wear red lipstick and gold earrings because we all know what happens next.'"

Simons continued: "I'm here at the table to tell you about pain. It may be a pain you cannot feel and a pain that you cannot understand, but I am telling you about it. . . . You wave it away and turn it into something like 'yes, but you must have been wearing strange clothing [when someone called you Zwarte Piet].'"

She was the only person of color at that talk show table—or anywhere in the roomful of studio audience as far as it was possible to see—and I thought how intimidating it must be to sit at that table in that very white room and to speak out publicly on this topic, especially when others have been so aggressively threatened and harassed in response.

This was early December. December 6 would arrive and be gone, and with it, Sinterklaas and Zwarte Piet would disappear back to Spain for another year, to be replaced by Christmas crèches and evergreen boughs. But for the moment, the festivities were in full swing.

It made me feel sad, out wandering through the glittering, holiday-bedecked, bustling streets filled with the excitement of white people. The little Black faces tucked into corners of displays, suspended from the ceilings of department stores, or hanging in shop windows felt like constant reminders to any person of color who walked by: *You are an outsider. This is not for you.*

This is where I ended the essay when I first wrote it. But looking back at it now, I see with that ending I was still trying to write this on the behalf of others, as though racism is something that does not affect me directly, damage me personally, is not mine to have to grapple with.

What did seeing those little Black doll faces tucked into displays and shop windows say to *me*—that I am an insider to something I don't want to be inside of, something that brings me shame? Why did *I* feel sad, walking past them? Was it because seeing them is a reminder of my fears that this ugly objectification of others by the forces of whiteness has shaped me, is inside me, and will drive a wedge between me and people I love? That my friends who are not white will simply tire of dealing with the ugliness and untrustworthiness of whiteness in our society and cast me off aside along with it? Or that the gap will be too great, the work of crossing it not worth the effort to maintain our friendship—I know this thought especially brings me great grief.

I am aware that as I try to write my way further into this, my writing voice feels awkward, unpolished, unsophisticated, because as white Americans we so infrequently practice talking not just about our whiteness but about our feelings about our whiteness: our fears, insecurities, and shame. I find myself wanting to edit out all the personal mess, to avoid the awkwardness and vulnerability of it, to avoid the exposure.

The Zwarte Piet dolls are evidence of a conflict, a sense of ugliness in the midst of all the celebratory holiday bustle, a kind of violence that most of the people around me seemed only too happy to ignore, to remain indifferent to or even unaware of. They reminded me of something in myself that scares me, that I carry within myself the blithe indifference and carelessness that have, at both a systems level and an interpersonal level, been profoundly damaging to other people for centuries now.

And perhaps—even more indicting—that I carry inside myself a subtle willingness to tolerate a system I can see is flawed, distorted, damaging, but that makes me reasonably comfortable.

What do you do when you come to terms with the fact that you have done something unforgiveable? As a people, if not as an individual?

I think one answer lies in relinquishing the pretense that we're all innocent and "good" in our well-meaningness. Lies in acknowledging how difficult it is, and how scary and how painful, to really open our eyes to everything that is happening in this world—and how much we contribute to it or are a part of it or benefit from it.

We can't move forward until we truly feel our own fear and pain. In the words of somatic therapist and racial trauma expert Resmaa Menakem, who writes that white Americans must confront our own need for foundational healing:

> Healing trauma involves recognizing, accepting, and moving through pain—clean pain. It often means facing what you don't want to face— what you have been reflexively avoiding or fleeing. By walking into that pain, experiencing it fully, and moving through it, you metabolize it and put an end to it. [You also] build your capacity for further growth.

> Clean pain is about choosing integrity over fear. It is about letting go of what is familiar but harmful, finding the best parts of yourself, and making a leap—with no guarantee of safety or praise. This healing does not happen in your head. It happens in your body.

James Baldwin has argued that white Americans are perpetually infantilized, stuck in a state of helpless dependence by our refusal to look clearly at the traumas we have enacted, the brutalities we have perpetuated. That our capacity for further growth is stunted, shut down by our unwillingness to accept what we have done. In one interview, he said: "It doesn't matter any longer what you do to me. You can put me in jail. You can kill me. By the time I was seventeen, you have done everything that you could do to me. The problem now is—how're you going to save yourselves?"

That clean pain that Menakem writes of is a break with the self-image of innocence we so stubbornly cling to, a break with the historical amnesia that allows such complacency and self-congratulation for our goodness, both in the Netherlands and in the US—a self-congratulation that takes form in the mythology of the "tolerant, worldly Dutch" and in the American sense of ourselves and our government as more evolved, benevolently superior, and "helping" the rest of the world develop democracy and social rights. These are myths that blind us to ourselves, to our history, and that scab over and avoid what Menakem calls our "dirty pain." If we want to grow up, to heal—truly, to *save* ourselves—the route through ruthless honesty, through a clear-eyed gaze at the things we most fear facing, through clean pain, seems the only way forward.

In one of the most beautiful and haunting scenes of *Amsterdam, Traces of Sugar*, Kaersenhout walks into the towering Oude Kerk in the center of Amsterdam.

"A black man was entombed there who had been made a slave, but whose freedom was bought," her voice tells us. "He was a direct ancestor of mine who shares the last name as my mother. So it's very special being there, seeing [his] gravestone." She walks through the high vaulted nave of the church, her boot heels clicking and echoing on the marble floor.

"I go there often, I've been there many times," she continues, "and now that I've found out . . . one of my ancestors lies buried in the Oude Kerk . . . it feels so special for me to be there."

As she speaks, her hands move white eggs from a small box into a wooden bowl.

"I know he's not there anymore but his spirit is still present. I once went there with my niece and we both felt his presence." As she speaks the camera pans over the flat stone, embedded in the floor of the church. Its dark face is engraved with letters: Jacob Matroos Beeldsnyder. *Geboren in Paramaribo, Suriname. Overleden binnen Amsterdam, 27 September 1817.*

"We shared this moment of stillness."

Carefully, gently, she begins to place eggs from the bowl onto the dark stone, one by one. The eggs turn over and roll across the stone and, finally, come to rest. Behind her, light spills in the high windows and down the towering white columns.

The camera pulls away. The entire black gravestone comes into sight, white eggs lying upon it in small clusters.

CHAPTER EIGHT

Strangers in the Village

In the daytime, the steep hillsides glowed yellow-green with grasses, moisture steaming off them in the morning sun. Each evening, a thick mist settled down the valleys and over the small Austrian towns, erasing the Alps around us. It was December, and Anna and I were staying in a tiny mountain village akin to the one where James Baldwin once spent a few winters writing, on the Swiss side of these Alps.

Upon deciding to travel to the unseasonably snowless Alps for our winter break, we learned it was cheaper to rent a car in Germany than in the Netherlands, so we found a Hertz office in Aachen, a city about thirty minutes from Maastricht.

Arriving in Aachen to pick up the rental car, we realized neither of our phones—with their Dutch SIM cards—worked in Germany, and we'd forgotten to download the map for offline use. We took the bus, then a taxi, filled out the paperwork, and suddenly we had this car.

We'd only been to Aachen once before, to walk around the center of the city near the cathedral. Now it was dark, and we were on the outskirts of the city with nothing open nearby; the car rental place was about to close, and they had no map to give us. It was also the first time either of us had driven a car since our arrival in Europe. I got behind the wheel and discovered the small SUV—a manual transmission, like most European cars—had seven gears, in a different configuration from the US's typical six.

This is how it went from there:

Me (*driving out of the car rental parking lot and onto the six-lane road, the
    car stalling and restarting automatically*): Did we just stall? Why did we
    just stall? . . . Is the middle lane a bus lane?!
Car: Achtung! Dies ist eine Busspur. Spurwechsel sofort!
Anna: Bus lane! Bus lane!
(*I swerve into the right lane.*)
Anna: But we need to go left here!
Car (*loudly*): Holen Sie sich auf der linken Spur. Gehen Sie in 100 Metern
    links ab.

And that was how it continued. I proceeded to stall three more times—the engine was quiet as only new German engines can be, and the car had auto restart,
making it only faintly evident that I was even stalling—before I finally realized
that I was in third, not first.

We turned right, and I drove us in circles around Aachen, only half understanding some of the road signs, while Anna desperately scrolled through the car's
computer settings, trying to figure out how to change the navigator's language
to English.

We eventually made it home that evening, through a combination of sheer luck
and Anna's navigational skills. But the next morning, just after leaving Maastricht, we found ourselves surrounded by corn fields, turning onto increasingly
smaller roads, until we were driving down a dirt road in the countryside—
despite the navigator acting as if we were on a highway—when Anna figured out
that the GPS had switched into "demo" mode and taken us kilometers off course.

After that blunder-filled start, we eventually made our peace with the German-
speaking navigator, who as it turned out did not have an English-language
mode—and by "we," I really mean Anna, who is incredibly adept at making sense
of spoken words in new languages.

We drove all the way from Maastricht to the Austrian Tirol that day, skirting around Frankfurt and Munich to reach the small region called Kaiserwinkl, the mecca of cross-country skiers. The towns of Kössen and Reit-im-Winkl were unusually snowless, and there is little stranger than spending time in a built-up ski town that is empty: empty shops, empty restaurants, empty sidewalks. An odd sensation, walking through a normally bustling ski village that is all but devoid of visitors; walking into restaurants full only of empty tables, where the hosts rush with relief to seat you.

This warm winter, this strange snowlessness all over Europe, I kept thinking, is but a pale shadow of the global climate unsettlement we've wrought. Though this is economically devastating to people here, there is a safety net. All is still beautiful green grass and sunshine, not the devastated landscape of a flood or a typhoon, nothing destroying their sturdy Tirolian homes or forcing them to flee. Something I read recently called the climate emergency the greatest inequality issue that exists today.

The towns in the Kaiserwinkl region were really small villages, with towering wooden Tirolian houses and plentiful dairy cows. These villages made me think of a conversation I'd had recently with my friend Kris, who had moved to Germany around the same time Anna and I moved to Maastricht.

"What strikes me about northern Europe," he'd said, "is the incredible homogeneity of the people, of the culture."

"And out of that homogeneity, the immense sense of conformity and complacency," I'd added—it struck me frequently, cycling around Maastricht or walking the dog through placid neighborhoods full of crisp white, modern row-houses with Buddha statues in the gardens, or seeing people enjoying an afternoon beer on a garden terrace or cobblestone street sidewalk bar, that it all seemed so pleasant and charming, serene but docile. This impression of complacency stood out more and more over the course of the year, seemed to underlie so much of the resistance and anger toward the growing wave of immigrants from Syria, Afghanistan, Iraq, and farther afield.

Before we moved to Maastricht, I really believed people in Europe were somehow more culturally enlightened than people in the US. But it turns out people are just people. They are complex and contradictory, welcoming or cruel or driven by fear and bias.

An article I read around this time talked about European history, about how eventually nation-states were drawn up that put all the same-seeming people together. Europe hasn't really ever recovered from that homogeneity and provinciality.

Despite the warm weather and snowlessness, we found we were able to Nordic ski on a one-kilometer strip of snow trucked in from wherever it had been stored and preserved and then laid into a looping track by a giant grooming machine. We skied every day, and then we walked through the village and drank glühwein at little stands in a cobblestone town square.

The rest of the time, we entertained ourselves with hikes and beer, ate spätzle and knödels until we couldn't move, and read and read. I was reading Baldwin's *Notes of a Native Son*, which includes several essays from his time in Europe.

In one essay, "Stranger in the Village," he writes of the small Swiss village of Leukerbad, which he visited one summer to stay in his lover's family chalet and then returned for two winters to write. I imagined, as I read, how similar that village was to the little towns on the Austrian side of the Alps: to Kössen or Ebbs, where we stayed.

Of his time in the village of Leukerbad, Baldwin writes: "From all available evidence no black man had ever set foot in this tiny Swiss village before I came. . . .

I remain as much a stranger today as I was the first day I arrived, and the children shout Neger! Neger! as I walk along the streets."

> All of the physical characteristics of the Negro which had caused me, in America, a very different and almost forgotten pain were nothing less than miraculous—or infernal—in the eyes of the village people. . . . If I sat in the sun for more than five minutes some daring creature was certain to come along and gingerly put his fingers on my hair, as though he were afraid of an electric shock, or put his hand on my hand, astonished that the color did not rub off. . . . In all of this, in which . . . there [was] no element of intentional unkindness, there was yet no suggestion that I was human.

One day, Anna and I took a break from skiing laps around the loop of snow to walk into a little café nearby for hot cocoa. In the corner, behind our seat, was a bewildering thing, a sort of strange Black doll, hung on the wall. It seemed vaguely African in style, and yet there was nothing else in the décor of the rather homely European café to explain its presence. Thinking of Baldwin's writing, I felt it staring at us: a marker of the uninterrupted whiteness of the place—and of us.

For the most part, we moved through the villages—villages in some ways inscrutable to us, as they perhaps were to Baldwin—fairly inconspicuously.

My body, mostly invisible, as we traveled through Austria and the Netherlands—a white body, a cis-gendered female body—generally invisible and safe in ways Anna isn't, with her short-cropped hair and boyish style of dress: invisible as queer until Anna is beside me, her gender-presentation revealing us. Otherwise—and even still—in provincial Austria and Germany, we passed. She passed for American, not Russian. We passed as generally conforming and white, as not radical, not anticapitalist. We dressed the part—comfortable, nondescript, outdoorsy clothes, looking more or less like any other tourist.

It is a normative invisibility that creates comfort, a sense of safety—most of the time. There was an edge of discomfort for me, always, entering small towns, going to the pub at night, surrounded by straight couples and straight men. A sense that violence might be lurking beneath the surface, unseen or unexpected, the unfamiliarity of the place making us unable to identify it—just as when we've traveled to rural areas in the US. That Anna and I, made alien in their eyes by our queerness, might be perceived as a threat—a threat to their comfort, to their identity, and thus also, somehow, to their safety.

I think about the time in my twenties when I was doing antiracist community organizing in New York City—riding my motorcycle from Brooklyn to Washington Heights with my friend Shana on the back, sitting in town hall gatherings in an old school building in Alphabet City, teaching workshops on intersectionality (though we called it intersecting oppressions then) and on white privilege and institutionalized white supremacy, learning so uncomfortably and so massively about my own whiteness and privilege, including from the several older mentors of our group who had been Black Panthers decades before, and from devouring books by Angela Davis and Eldridge Cleaver and Malcolm X and Frantz Fanon and Tim Wise. One of the things I observed most distinctly at that time and that has always stayed with me was that almost all the white people doing that work were either Jewish or queer, often both, as well as mostly female. I understood this to indicate that if you have never experienced what it is to gain awareness of yourself as a self—and then to find that that self is in some way seen as distasteful, less than, other—then empathy is, apparently, incredibly difficult to access. Or incredibly easy to ignore.

When I read a piece by Helen Klonaris in *The Racial Imaginary*, her clear articulation of this principle jumped out at me: "As a first-generation Greek Bahamian woman who is also queer . . . my differences, however subtle, have provided enough friction and energy to have made walking around in the story of white supremacy complicated and uncomfortable."

My own frictions—my queerness, my reluctance to conform to gendered expectations—have also made this complicated and uncomfortable. A part of me is driven by a need to please that presses me to conform—but it is always bumping up against my unruly desires, and my nonconforming appetite for adventure, for living a wide range of experiences and cultures.

In *The Racial Imaginary*, Jess Row, author of *White Flights*, writes, "I think that a great deal of the psychic pain I have experienced in my life has to do with anxiety—largely unconscious anxiety—over maintaining my status as a privileged human being."

Earlier years of my life, even decades, seem lived with a sense of irreverence and experimentation that—I knew even then—was born of great privilege. I could choose to be broke, always strapped for money, because I knew there was a safety net beneath me if things got dire. There was also a desire—and a freedom—not to conform to the narratives of gender and the mainstream. I worked as a cabinetmaker, as a carpenter framing houses, on a chainsaw crew, as a hiking guide, teaching GED classes and performance poetry. I rode a motorcycle, worked many, many restaurant jobs, had a community full of activists and artists. I felt connected, relevant, critical-thinking.

Lately, though, I feel beset by anxiety. Part of this is politics: capitalism, neoliberalism, and militarization—the brutalizing structures of greed and misogyny and racism and the damage they inflict on so many people. Part of it is getting older and *feeling* older: less fit, less connected, less easily relevant (how did I have *time* for all the social and artistic things I did in my twenties and thirties?). Part of it is stress over wanting to raise a child and being forty and married to a woman and thinking about risk and cost and sperm donors and the medicalization of fertility. Part of it is feeling overwhelmed at what seems like the blitzing speed of cultural commentary (how do I find time to *keep up*? I don't, and then I feel anxious about that, too); the overwhelming stream of Twitter commentary, which I both value profoundly for the ways it confronts me about my whiteness—frequently making me squirm at the thought of something I've said and what it may have revealed about my blind spots—*and* can only bear to pay attention to about once a month. And part of it is anxiety over work, wanting work that is both satisfying and pays enough to allow me to save money in an adult way that I eschewed in younger years. But also, it is an anxiety that is a culmination of all those things and that is inextricably entrenched in whiteness in ways I am still trying to pick apart and understand.

I think also it is an anxiety rooted in fear, a fear that drives some of the worst excesses of whiteness, of Americanness: desperation to avoid pain, but also to avoid losing status; that sense of self as alone rather than as interconnected. This, to me, is what Jess Row means when he speaks of his anxiety over maintaining his status as a privileged human being.

Elsewhere, Row writes, "I take it for granted that part of my background and my psychology is racist, that my psyche has been shaped by the lifelong experience of privilege in ways that I will never fully understand." This, he notes, is only "an entry point and a provocation" to do the ongoing work of self-exploration and accountability—in his case, he notes, "through writing, through Buddhist practice, and through therapy."

When I contemplate where this anxiety comes from—or what I am grappling with on a sort of spiritual level—one thing I think about is direct violence, the intentional physical damage inflicted by one person upon another person, and my own fears of experiencing that.

I also think about what it means to live in a world where there is such immense violence, both systemic and militaristic, in which my country is deeply complicit, making any material comfort or safety I enjoy in my life also deeply complicit.

I also think about guns, and about gun owners, especially in a part of the US I love—the West and the Southwest—and small towns near the mountains, which I also love but find terrifying at the same time. And about the burning hate of some white people, the burning hate of some men, for everyone they see as Other, which sometimes includes me, and to whom I am sometimes invisible—particularly with my tattoos covered and without my wife or other friends by my side. I think about how, in those moments, I'm just a straightish-looking white woman in boots getting a wink from the cowboy in the feedstore while I'm picking up dogfood, or knowing when I drive by the sheriff's car that the EMT sticker on the back of my car marks me as acceptable, even an insider. This is a different iteration of passing, but not entirely unlike the way in which Anna and I moved through the small mountain villages in Austria.

———

In *I Am Not Your Negro*, in video footage of a speech he gave, Baldwin states flatly: "The story of the Negro in America is the story of America. It is not a pretty story."

Later on, his gaze meets ours, serious, pinning us to his words. "But"—and here he touches his brow, and then his lips, quiet—"the future of the Negro in this country is precisely as dark or as bright as the future of the country. It is entirely up to the American people whether or not they are going to face and deal with and embrace the stranger they have maligned so long."

Two summers ago, Anna and I went to Cyprus and felt deeply our proximity to a Gaza suffering from heavy bombardment and deprivation. Now, a year and a half later, the two of us and our dog are squeezed into this tiny studio apartment in the Austrian Alps, where we have come seeking the little snow that can be found anywhere in Europe this warm winter. Warm, but not warm enough for the thousands of people piling onto—and if they're lucky, wetly off of—boats as part of their hazardous journey away from the violence of Syria, Afghanistan, Iraq. In the evenings, I obsessively read first-person narratives of those who have crossed, news articles, Facebook posts from a person I know who is in Lesvos volunteering. On TV we watch buildings burning from acts of hate-filled arson, protesting their arrival.

While there are many people who have welcomed the asylum seekers, so much of Europe—or at least a highly visible contingent—is reacting violently to these families and individuals arriving on its shores: an influx of the Stranger whom they fear will change the homogeneity and complacency of their provincial lives.

On our drive from Maastricht down to the Alps, curving through the rolling cropland of central Germany, we passed a number of roadblocks. Most of them were on the other side of the highway as we drove south—checkpoints where German police looked in cars and searched lorries—reminiscent of those I was so familiar with from living in the US borderlands of southern Arizona. Lines of stopped traffic backed up for miles.

On a day trip down to Innsbruck a few days later, I saw "Welcome, refugees," painted large on a wall in English. But for the most part, this swell of newcomers was largely invisible in the places we traveled, or was hinted at only by roadblocks and evening news.

I read about huge protests in some towns where there was a proposed resettlement of refugees. In the Dutch town of Enschede, for example, where a center to host six hundred refugees was supposed to be built, someone dumped twelve butchered pigs' heads—a pointed message to the sanctuary seekers, clearly presumed to be Muslim.

One of the heads with its long, pink snout was wedged in a fence, barbed wire arcing over it. Another lay on its side on a boulder, eyes closed in a repose belied by the blood on its jaw and snout. The rest of the heads were scattered, bloodless, in the thick mud; their necks ravaged, their ears aloft amid the carnage.

Photos of the heads, taken at night, were posted on Twitter with the line *Welcome to the hell that is Eschmarkerveld.*

A few weeks before that, a civil servant with the Enschede city council was stabbed six times by an unknown assailant close to this same field. Two days before, six people had been arrested during a march protesting the planned asylum center, several of them for giving Nazi salutes.

In 2015 there were more than a thousand attacks on refugee housing in Germany, ranging from swastika graffiti to arson. In one, a local firefighter disabled the smoke alarm and then set fire to a home for asylum seekers. In another, a man threw a grenade into an arrival center. Similarly, in Sweden there were multiple acts of arson—more than a dozen in just one month. Things became so bad that in Munkedal, in southern Sweden, refugees began to take turns patrolling around their new shelter at night, in subzero temperatures, using only the light of their cellphones to guide them through the darkness.

"What white people have to do is try to find out, in their own hearts, why it was necessary to have a nigger in the first place," said Baldwin in other footage from *I Am Not Your Negro*. "Because I am not a nigger. I'm a man. But if you think I'm a nigger, it means you need it. And the question you must ask yourself, the white population of this country has got to ask itself . . . , you've got to find out why."

In *The Racial Imaginary*, describing the qualities of whiteness, American playwright Casey Llewellyn writes: "We feel alienated from other people. We are scared and angry. We worry if we said the right thing or the wrong thing. . . . We are afraid, rigid. We hurt the people we love. . . . We are treated like people when others aren't. Our language exploits. We exploit ourselves. We get drunk. . . . We don't accept ourselves. We don't accept anyone else. Someone says, I need you, and we build a wall. We are suspicious. We think, what keeps me back? We think, we need to arm ourselves."

To me, American whiteness is laden with distrust. It is status conscious and perfectionistic. It is always being cool, logical, and in control. It is constant comparison and passive-aggressive competitiveness, hidden behind the niceties of polite, upbeat positivity. It feels frequently unsafe to me, and yet when I am in it, I go into conformity mode: play along, put on a good face, smile a lot. Keep my guard up. Act professional, calm, friendly, and avoid conflict at all costs.

I think of the way I tend to react to new people, new situations, with suspicion. I warm up quickly, usually, but my initial reaction is always wary. I've always thought this had to do with being an introvert. But I see now that most likely it has to do with whiteness too—the way white people often react to each other, initially, with either suspicion or competitiveness.

I think, too, about the ways that white Americans, when they randomly encounter each other abroad or at a party or gathering with predominantly people of color, will often noticeably avoid each other. Is it suspicion, or the desire to avoid that mirror of ourselves, to be the only white people there, the "good white ones" who have escaped the confines of our problematic whiteness or Americanness?

Llewellyn's greatest fear around race, she writes later, "is that race can really keep us from each other." I reflect on this often in my thinking about whiteness: how it has shaped me, how it impacts my relationships with my friends of color, and also how it affects my relationship with Anna, who both reads as white and yet was not shaped in the school of American whiteness.

When we talk about what constitutes whiteness, Anna observes that she has a kind of whiteness that on the surface protects her—for example, against being profiled and pulled over while driving. But once she is actually interacting directly with power structures, some of that privilege is diminished, both by her cultural affect and by her name, which cops and airport authorities tend to look at and see an Other.

There are many times when I feel my own whiteness is oppressive toward Anna, but it is difficult for me to tease out: when am I, as a partner, validly expressing something that is difficult for me, and when am I trying to mold her to the norms of WASPish white Americanness, to tame her, whip her into shape? I know that I sometimes push her to conform out of my own discomfort, my desire for us both to blend in—to act *nice*, to phrase things politely, to not make waves or create conflict. To not create friction where things are supposed to be smooth by pointing out the unspoken or by being blunt and unsmiling or by advocating for herself instead of acting grateful.

She and I talk about this often, especially in the context of American norms of positivity, because I am often worried about people reading her—and, indeed, I sometimes read her—as being "too negative," coming across as complaining or focusing on what is bad.

Anna has explained to me that in Russian culture this is how one connects meaningfully with other people; that in fact she mistrusts many interactions and friendships with white Americans because of our "enforced positivity"; that she never feels she is truly connecting; that we never open up and trust each other with the grittier truths of our reality.

"Where is the human connection in all this shallow conversation?" she says to me at one point. "I feel like a tree cut off at the roots, like I can't get any nourishment in this society."

She often thinks, in fact, that Americans just aren't truly letting her into their circles, that they must be having those vulnerable, honest conversations frequently with each other and just not allowing her to be part of them—the kinds of conversations where people get angry or cry together, or just the same kinds of conversation she witnesses all the time, but without its feeling as if everyone's guard is always up, she tells me.

A real conversation, Anna says, would just be more honest and open, without its feeling as if there's a constant subtext, or as if certain things are "off limits" to say—"like if we're playing a board game and your dad is being domineering, it wouldn't be shocking or rude to just point that out—and it also wouldn't be a value judgement that he's a bad person or that he's not deserving of love. It would just be what it seemed at face value."

My family is the first white family she has really interacted with so closely, she tells me. And for a long time, she thought they were just unkind: not interacting in a deeply present and honest way with each other, never telling each other what they really think of them. But then she began to realize that this was common to a particular kind of Americanness, the white waspy kind.

We frequently talk about styles of communication, how Americans—white Americans, at least—are fairly conflict averse and don't even like to disagree in conversation, are always softening and hiding our disagreement with politeness. Whereas for Russians, having a conversation does not mean agreeing with each other; to the contrary, the ultimate sign of respect is to listen carefully and offer critical feedback by explaining why you disagree. Anna has had to learn to censor herself, she tells me, because if she does this with American friends, they become offended, and the friendship becomes strained.

If I were to listen to translations of Russian podcasts for example, she tells me, I would frequently hear people who are friends and colleagues saying directly to each other, "No, you're wrong"—whereas in the US, we mostly only hear those words on talk shows, from guests invited with the explicit design of having conflict with each other, creating an "ooooh" sense of "they're having a fight."

This is one of the many reasons I love discussing the world, and our lives, with Anna: through her eyes, what I have taken for granted as normal in my life becomes strange, scrutinized, explored.

But also she helps me more clearly see myself, in ways that are often profoundly and viscerally uncomfortable and challenging. Including asking me—as partners should—to be more vulnerable and more emotionally open, something I struggle with even in these essays, where my constant tendency is to use research and a clinical voice to avoid being vulnerable. And asking me to look at the areas where I hold shame, where I lash out if poked.

When I think about all the ways I have pushed her to conform, to not stick out— to not be too curt or too honest, to not be too vulnerable or too open—it makes me feel monstrous, and so sad, for the ways I have introduced her to a kind of self-consciousness she hadn't cultivated before. And it makes me feel sad because I want to be a parent, and I don't want to do that same thing to our child.

Not long ago, at a family gathering, my parents had invited over another family they'd met on an airplane and had made a nice connection with. My mother introduced Anna—my wife of six years at that point—to them as "my friend," and I was so stunned, I just froze—unforgivably, I didn't say a single word.

Helen Klonaris also writes of whiteness: "I learn that silence is a way of refusing to see. Of willful ignorance." I think of silence and how, when confronted with the very most difficult conversations with Anna, the ones that most clearly outline how my actions have been selfish or have directly othered her, or where I have failed to break the silence to speak up on her behalf—the ones that push me most clearly into a place of cognitive dissonance, of having to see something I don't want to see—my brain becomes hazy and sluggish, almost like I am deeply sleepy. This happens infrequently, but it has been repeated enough times now that I can identify it, realize it is a self-protective mechanism—self-protective in the moment, but also for the future, where my memories of the conversation will be hazy, cloudy, and difficult to recall, to examine.

I do not like this haziness, but I have not yet figured out how to sidestep it other than to write down everything that is said, so that later and in a clearer frame of mind I cannot avoid it.

In a recent conversation, Anna said: "How can I know you really value me, if you're not actively pushing back against the things you don't like about whiteness, about your family culture? You say you value me—but then you don't speak out against the things that actively devalue me or my differences, . . . so how can I see that you really value *me*, even as much as, or more than, you value conforming to and obeying the dictates of family culture or waspy white culture?"

She is speaking of things such as working all the time without boundaries, choosing politeness over conflict, not saying how you feel, quietly judging others, keeping up appearances, not being vulnerable, not being emotionally "messy" or angry, never saying no.

She is requesting a kind of disruption of the status quo I had no idea I feared so much, resisted so deeply. I know this is how white supremacy has perpetuated itself for so long, and yet I am still surprised to find, in myself, the degree to which it feels difficult to move against.

———

Just before leaving the Alps to return to the Netherlands, in the little German-Austrian border town of Reit im Winkl, we are drinking hot chocolates in the café of an inn when Anna leans forward and says, "All the servers here are speaking Russian."

"You should talk to them," I say. "Ask them why they all speak Russian."

"No *way*," she says. "They think no one understands them." I shrug, so?

Later, when we are getting the bill, I ask our server, "Why do so many of you speak Russian?"

"Oh, the hotel is owned by a Russian," she replies. Anna elbows me on the way out; "thanks a *lot*," she hisses.

"What's wrong with asking?"

"I don't want us to get ourselves killed," she says.

"*What?* Why? How could asking possibly get us killed?"

She shrugs. "Rich Russian, owns a hotel in Europe . . . you don't want to mess with that."

This feels like hyperbole to me, until I think about how revealing her as a Russian speaker might implicate her in having overheard something I was oblivious to. I think of Russian movies she and I have watched, depicting the power grabs and instability of the 90s in that new country: because no one had work (and even the few who did weren't actually getting paid), many people in Moscow got involved in some degree of organized crime, the death rate of young men was incredibly high, and violence was rampant. Anna's mother, when she sold their Moscow apartment as they were moving to the US, was terrified that the buyers would simply have her killed instead of paying her for it.

Later, on the drive back home to Maastricht, we are standing in line for Burger King at a highway stop outside Frankfurt. I comment on the sneakers of a guy in front of me, white Nike Airs with high ankles and Velcro. "We really have returned to the 80s," I say, and Anna says, "What do you mean? I never saw the 80s."

What she means is she never saw the 80s in the West. I forget, sometimes, that she grew up in a Soviet city rich with classical music, rigorous education in literature and the arts, and gorgeous, marble-walled subway stations set deep below the city—but very little in the way of consumer choice, outlandish fashion, or David Bowie.

"Nouns are magical to an immigrant," writes Bhanu Kapil, and I remember Anna telling me about how the street names of her teenage years—after they'd moved from Moscow to Queens, NY—slowly began to have meaning to her.

Still, occasionally, we'll be talking or she'll see a word somewhere and laugh— "*this* is what that street is named for?"—as it morphs from an abstract to a particular.

A few days after our arrival back in the Netherlands, we have to return the rental car to Aachen. This time we remember to download the maps before going. Anna snickers every time I say the address of the Hertz office, on Jülicher Strasse.

After having rented a car for a week, our sense of the scale of things here in the Netherlands has changed. Driving from Maastricht to a little city a half hour away seemed like an errand rather than a journey. And driving from our apartment through the Maastricht city center, onto the highway, all the way through Germany to Austria—and then back—has shifted my perception of the landscape in western Europe. Everything seemed so industrial, so gray. Germany, so *Midwestern*.

We realize that living without a car, getting around our city only by bicycle and the bus, getting to farther away cities by train, has enhanced our sense of the exoticism and charm of "living in Europe." Our experience was part real, part magical invention of a romanticized European life: cycling to the bakery and the shops, walking to the small grocery store near our house, taking the train when we needed to travel. We never saw the big box stores, the industrial areas along highways, the policing or asylum centers. The Europe we were living in was small and local; cobblestoned, charming, and inviting.

This was the opposite of the experience the one million people who had arrived on Mediterranean shores in 2015 were having: they, too, came seeking an inviting European life—or at least an escape from the dystopic realities unfolding in their homelands—and were met with attitudes ranging from welcome to indifference to violence, with angry graffiti, protests, and burning buildings.

———

In *I Am Not Your Negro*, Baldwin muses: "What can we do? . . . The tragedy is that most of the people who say they care about it, do not care. What they care about is their safety and their profits."

Elsewhere, ever the grim optimist, he says: "I do not believe the twentieth-century myth that we are all helpless, that it's out of our hands. It's only out of our hands if we don't want to pick it up."

We are back in Maastricht now, and I am back at my desk. The cold and gray have sunk down on us once more: spring in December turns to January winter. The tiny white flowers that had begun to bloom in gardens shut their faces to the chill.

I also do not believe—or do not want to believe—that it is out of our hands. But I struggle with knowing how to pick it up, am haunted by the fear— growing into knowledge—that to truly pick it up means we have to stop, to *re-fuse*, to allow total disruption to enter our lives as it has entered the lives of so many other people without their willing it.

At ten in the morning, the day is as gray and heavy as twilight, and sheets of rain smash into the glass of the windows. Wind pulls the trees into dark, spiny contortions of themselves. The old windmill, only a few hundred meters away, is fuzzy and indistinct in all this water.

CHAPTER NINE

A World Without Lines

Outside Sint Jans church in Maastricht, the day catapults between sunny and glowering. The strange pastel of spring has begun to touch the ground, here and there, with bits of daffodil and crocus, a sort of yellow and purple confetti attesting to some spreading crust of newness. When we biked into the city center from our apartment on the outskirts, the pavement was wet and sordid, and an abandoned pair of men's leather shoes sat neatly beside the bicycle path, soaked with rain. A braggadocio wind swore in bursts of fury, trying to tear the sides from the buildings; now it too has gone still.

I am late, rushing to lock my bike on the hill beside the back of the church, trying to find where to enter the building. Here to meet Anna and her coworkers for a conference—designed and run by the students at their international school—I slide into a seat just in time to hear a student speaker describe the theme of the conference, "Where Do We Draw the Line?"

We are in the center of Maastricht, in a very old church: Sint Janskerk, which stands next to the massive Basilica of Sint Servaas. Sint Jans's distinctive red tower looms over Vrijthof Square, where religious heretics—circles of early Protestants, practicing in secret within a Catholic society—were once put to death. The large cobblestone plaza is now bordered with restaurants and sidewalk cafés. When the Dutch ruled to practice religious tolerance in 1632, Sint Jan's was given across the line to those former heretics, the Protestants, to hold their services in.

Inside, the ceiling is crossed by arches of white stone, the pillars on each side of the nave a darker gray.

"Imagine a world without lines," the student says. "Imagine no lines of floor and walls, no pillars, no vaulted ceiling, no edges to this space."

A pulpit of amber wood ascends one side of the chamber, and the windows are long, glowing slices in the wall.

"Imagine a world with no political lines, no borders between countries, where all people are free to move where they will."

He draws a deep breath. "Another question about lines is who should get to draw them." Drawing lines, after all, is the very embodiment of power.

In 1992 the Treaty of Maastricht was signed by twelve countries: Belgium, Denmark, France, Germany, Greece, Ireland, Italy, Luxembourg, Netherlands, Portugal, Spain, and the United Kingdom. The treaty brought the EU into existence. After a century of internecine slaughter and war over national borders, it emphasized unity and de-emphasized borders, creating a kind of pan-European citizenship.

And yet, as we sat in that church for a conference about lines—in the very city where the Treaty of Maastricht was signed, erasing the lines of Europe—the emphasis on borders was rearing its head, rising again.

Belgium had just announced new border checks for those entering from France—almost unthinkable in the western Europe of today, akin to establishing a border check between New York and Connecticut in the US.

Austria, Slovenia, and Macedonia had also tightened their borders, preventing migrants from moving through the "Balkan corridor." People seeking asylum in Europe were stuck sitting next to train tracks, in front of tents, on the ground, waiting to be told when they could move and where they would be pushed to. In Athens, the numbers of people swelled, still coming in from the sea but with nowhere to go.

I shifted on the hard wooden bench of the church. Art historian Henry Thomas was now speaking. He described a series of different artworks and asked the students, "Is this art? Where is the line?"

Thomas showed us photos of Mark Quinn's *Self.* Made in 1991, it is a death mask of the artist's own face, mimicking the death masks historically made from wax or plaster, and more recently, from latex. The piece began a series: Quinn now makes a new bust every five years, in an ongoing act of self-portraiture.

In photographs of the piece, it is patchy and textured, mottled a deep red and purplish black.

The mask, in fact, has been made from Quinn's blood and frozen. Nine pints of blood go into each mask, the same amount of blood as is in a human. To make the masks, Quinn banks blood over time before starting his work.

In an interview, Quinn says: "In a funny way I think 'Self,' the frozen head series, is about the impossibility of immortality. This is an artwork on life support. If you unplug it, it turns to a pool of blood. It can only exist in a culture where looking after art is a priority. It's unlikely to survive revolutions, wars and social upheaval."

A few years after this conference in the church in Maastricht, another piece involving blood would be exhibited in Belgium: Andrei Molodkin's *Young Blood*, part of a 2019 show called *Black Horizon*.

A photo of his piece shows a large glass panel marbled with blood inside. Squared off letters full of red liquid spell out BURN THE TEMPLE. Next to the panel, two IV bags and drip tubes hang on a metal stand, partially filled with blood.

Molodkin asked those who attended the show to donate blood, which he would preserve in medical refrigerators and then, using industrial compressors, would pump into tubes. The blood in the tubes spells out phrases from songs that he has found on government blacklists throughout Europe.

Two other glass frames contain letters spelling out COP SHOT JUST FOR KICKS and OFFICER I'VE DONE NOTHING. Lights are trained on the glass panels, projecting the letters and the marbled, liquid blood bubbling through them onto the wall in enlarged form.

Many of the lyrics, Molodkin says, came from drill music, which originates in communities of south Chicago and now London that are beset with gang violence and whose lyrics graphically invoke violence. Molodkin sees the censorship of this music as clear evidence of a power structure that would rather crack down on the violence suggested in music lyrics than acknowledge the extreme poverty, violence, and oppression from which the drill generation draws its material.

The other artist in the show, Erik Bulatov, a Soviet-born conceptual artist, is displaying a towering sculpture of the words "Everything's not so scary" in Russian, "intended to encourage visitors to reject propaganda and censorship."

Molodkin said the *Black Horizon* show was inspired by the ways in which an "open world . . . without censorship, [without] strong nationalist feeling, where religion wasn't dictating its own laws" had begun "to close in front of our eyes." We are watching a slow loss of faith in the European project—as memories of the horrors of a twentieth-century Europe split by violent war fade and are replaced by a swelling nationalism.

As we sit here in this ancient church in the center of Maastricht, we are only three hours away from a huge camp outside Calais in France, full of people hoping to find a way to cross into the UK. Young men keep getting killed on the highway there, trying to enter the tunnel, trying to jump onto a lorry, to find a way through.

The camp in Calais is known as the "Jungle," and in the weeks before this "Where Do We Draw the Line" conference, the French government began to bulldoze the camp. Thousands of migrants and refugees were living there, most fleeing violence in the Middle East and North Africa—they'd built makeshift schools, theaters, churches, mosques, restaurants, women's and children's centers, even small shops—and most hoped to get to the UK, where many had family or friends already living.

A remarkable photo series in the *Guardian* shows the interior of makeshift shanties in the Calais camp. "The home of Sami," the captions read, "The home of Adam," "The home of Hushan Osman Alzubair." The photos—of homes often constructed of plywood or wood crates, with blankets lining walls and roofs—show beds, side tables, clothes neatly hung on walls, language dictionaries, decks of cards, tea sets. In one, several sets of men's shoes are tucked beneath a bed built of scrap wood; in another, a pair of black-and-white sneakers sits tidily by the door beside a white rug and a coffee table.

In March 2016, the French government decided to shut the Jungle down. Residents of the camp protested, leading the police to wade in with riot gear and fire tear gas on camp residents. One striking photo of the operation to clear the camp shows two robotic-looking police in full black riot gear, with helmets and leg armor and shields and gas masks. They are walking between two plywood shanties wrapped in white plastic, the words LIEU DE VIE (place of life) spray-painted in black on their walls. On top of each white-wrapped box, young men in black sweatshirts sit, bandanas or hoods partially covering their faces. Behind all of it, the sky is a thick gray despondency.

In *Lande: The Calais "Jungle" and Beyond*, published in conjunction with a 2019 exhibition at the Pitt Rivers Museum, Oxford archeologists Sarah Mallet and Dan Hicks record artefacts, artworks, teargas cannisters, and other remnants recovered from the camp in Calais, left behind by displaced people from Syria, Afghanistan, Sudan, Eritrea, and elsewhere.

Hicks points to lines drawn across the landscape, to the "use of the environment as a kind of weapon against the weak. The alteration, the building of fences, physical violence and threats, the tactics of trying to keep people away from Calais." Mallet and Hicks's book notes that the degree of wall building occurring globally—from the southwestern US to Norway, Israel, and India—is both unprecedented in human history and highly militarized, creating increasingly large groups of human beings who are labeled illegal.

According to a *Guardian* article on the exhibition, Hicks argues that "it is no coincidence that most of the people who came to the camp, all desperate to get across the Channel, were from parts of the world that came under a British sphere of influence or protection in the late 19th and early 20th centuries. The origins [of this displacement] go back centuries, right back to that time when England lost Calais—and slowly embarked on acquiring an empire."

I have been teaching and studying some bits of colonial history over the past few years, and I am more and more convinced of the need to better understand our history—colonial history, the history of imperialism—and the ways it underlies everything, every single power dynamic and system and institution we might find ourselves critical of today.

In *Frames of War*, Judith Butler distinguishes between "'precariousness,' a general condition shared by all forms of life due to our physical liability, and "precarity," which is human-created and subjects specific groups of people to "state violence or neglect." With these terms, Butler aims "to emphasize our mutual dependency while acknowledging the ways in which . . . geopolitical forces make some lives more vulnerable than others," according to Holly Brown.

And in considering the decisions made by "European governments to conduct airstrikes on Syria in the wake of Paris," notes Brown, "we can perceive how modern warfare is dependent on the aim of maximizing precariousness for specific, ungrievable groups while (allegedly) minimizing precariousness for others."

I've been looking at photos of the shelters in Calais—only a few hours' drive away from where we are living in Maastricht—being demolished. "We are not terrorists," reads one hand-lettered sign, "so please don't destroy our homes." The collapsed shelters reveal bedding, clothing, belongings that people couldn't carry with them.

Some of the photos reveal shelters ablaze, fiery skeletons against the dark countenance of night.

Three weeks after the conference at Sint Janskerk in Maastricht, Anna and I took the train to the nearby city of Liège for the afternoon. We sat in a tiny Belgian bistro, short white candles burning on all the tables; behind the counter with its row of wooden stools, wine bottles lined the shelves, and white tiles stretched to the ceiling. Across a small wooden café table from me, Anna sipped at a beer. Large windows opened onto the sunny streets, their sills adorned with jars of multicolored tulips.

But for the electric lights and fancy espresso machine, one could imagine a quaint café like this existing a hundred years ago, its Belgian patrons reading newspapers as they sipped their coffees. It was the early spring of 2016, however, and out on the street military cops in dark blue-and-black uniforms and heavy boots walked in pairs, assault rifles across their chests.

Arriving from Maastricht and stepping out of the station, we were immediately in another world. Coming from the white-bread, affluent-but-provincial feel of the southern Netherlands, where conformity can feel oppressive, Liège—though

its streets are lined with tall, monotone gray stone buildings—was a rich eddy
of human cultures, styles, and languages. Around us walked Moroccan women
in headscarves and stylish clothes, Congolese women with lilting accents, and
teenagers of all stripes excitedly rushing out of school. As we ambled along the
blocks from the train station to the city center, passing hair salons with brightly
colored extensions and ads for braiding in their windows, Anna—who grew up
partly in immigrant neighborhoods in Queens—remarked, "You always know
you're in a neighborhood with lots of immigrants when you start to see Lyca
Mobile advertisements . . . they kind of suck domestically, but they have good
rates for international calls."

As we'd approached the city center, though, we discovered this other way in
which Belgium had become a different world from the Netherlands: the pairs
of military police that stood forbiddingly at the entrance to the mall, strolled
around the pedestrian cobbled streets, and kept watch in the squares. "This is
all since Paris," Anna observed. Since November's attacks in Paris, on the Stade
de France, the Bataclan theater, and several cafés and restaurants—and the mass
shooting in the *Charlie Hebdo* office just nine months before that—things in
Western Europe had become tense.

All around us surged a broad mix of people and cultures—groups of teenagers, young couples, businesspeople leaving work, shoppers—and I couldn't help
thinking of how charged this would feel in the US, with the ongoing surge in
visibility of police violence against communities of color.

In an open letter written after the shootings in Paris in November 2015, Butler notes: "The 'state of emergency,' however temporary, does set a tone for an
enhanced security state. People want to see the police, and want a militarized
police to protect them. A dangerous, if understandable, desire." She goes on to
ask, "are we grieving or are we submitting to increasingly militarized state power
and suspended democracy?" . . . and suggests that we "consider how the metrics
of grievability work, why the cafe-as-target pulls at my heart in ways that other
targets cannot. It seems that fear and rage may well turn into a fierce embrace of
a police state."

Several of the attackers in the Paris mass shootings were believed to have come from Molenbeek, a marginalized suburb of Brussels with poor schools and a nearly 27 percent unemployment rate for fifteen- to twenty-nine-year-olds. Peter Bouckaert of Human Rights Watch notes, "One of the gravest mistakes that Europe has made, several decades ago, is to put people into marginalized ghettos, basically, where extremism has built."

I recently reread Elif Shafak's *The Happiness of Blond People*, in which she writes:

> The one who leaves his or her homeland for good is often stalked by mixed emotions of guilt, longing, confusion, anticipation and insecurity, some or all of which can spring up from out of nowhere, for no reason at all. . . .

> The sharper the conflicts at work in the host society and the more negative the reception of outsiders, the greater the newcomer's inner divisions.

This has increasingly become an issue in Europe, especially in France and Belgium, which have large immigrant communities but are frequently accused of doing little to help them integrate and thrive. In ghettoizing entire communities, these countries have not only othered them but told them they are without value.

When we walked into the Liège train station to return home later that afternoon, we found the swooping, airy white station with its vaulted glass and steel canopy was also heavily patrolled by police in black uniforms, tall black boots, and large guns. On the train back to Maastricht that afternoon, watching the green of the countryside unfurl in front of us, I pondered how it affects all of us, having such a level of militarized surveillance and policing around us at all times; thought about the ways it makes me feel intimidated and scrutinized, and how much stronger that feeling must be for anyone not treated as part of the privileged norm.

After seeing the militaristic police standing or patrolling all over Liège, feeling a heightened awareness of the ways in which policing contributes to and enforces a sense of otherization, I did a little research to learn more about policing in the Netherlands.

"An Amnesty International Report published in October 2013"—writes political geography scholar Marijn Nieuwenhuis in one article I read—"demonstrates that what Dutch [police] officers categorise as 'suspicious behaviour' is strongly correlated to specific ethnic characteristics."

Nieuwenhuis also notes:[i]

> The national chief of police, Gerard Bouman, recently revealed that phrases such as "fucking Muslims" (*kutmoslims*) and calls for the "burning of mosques" are frequently overheard in police circles. . . . One of the former police officials revealed that many officers share the views of the extreme right-wing PVV [Partij voor de Vrijheid (Party for Freedom)] and [its] fanatical call for "fewer Moroccans."
>
> According to the former police official, "we used to say that we would go on 'Murk hunting' [i.e., a Dutch contraction of the words 'Turk' and 'Moroccan']. It is all good fun, everybody laughs, nobody protests . . ."
>
> [This forms] part of a much wider existing and (worryingly) growing societal trend of . . . racial Othering. A particularly damning report by the European Commission against Racism and Intolerance concluded that the "settlement of Eastern Europeans in the Netherlands—as well as of Islam and Muslims—has been portrayed by politicians and media as a threat to Dutch society."

Though as a recent *Christian Science Monitor* article points out, police shootings are still rare in many industrialized countries around the world, the Netherlands has not been entirely without unjustified police killings. There have been several widely protested incidents of police shooting and killing men of color, including Mitch Hernandez, an Aruban man visiting family in the Netherlands, and a seventeen-year-old, Rishi Chandrikasing, shot in a railway station in The Hague. Chandrikasing, unarmed, was shot in the neck as he was running away, and CPR on him was not started for a full minute and a half after police reached his body. The shot was fired while the officer was running, which goes against police policy: officers are supposed to take a braced stance and aim at the legs of a suspect. The officer who shot him was acquitted.

Although Hernandez's murder "has been largely ignored by the international press," writes Nieuwenhuis, "the event is important because it is symptomatic of a broader international trend towards an ever-increasing level of police violence against minorities in the western world."

And now, not only is Europe dealing with the ramifications of its treatment of immigrant communities from decades back, as well as the aftereffects of centuries of colonial policy in the Middle East and north Africa, but there are hundreds of thousands of newcomers arriving, cold and wet and nearly drowned, in boats on its shores.

Over the course of the winter of 2015–16, as the weather turned colder and rainier, thousands of people—families, children, elderly parents—were stuck, living in tents, all across Europe. And as winter weather settled in, conditions in these camps—in Calais, the Balkans, and all over Greece—dramatically worsened. As I walked or cycled the streets of Maastricht, heavily wrapped in a chunky, knitted gray scarf and wool jacket, people were camping all over Athens, in the public squares and near the ferry terminals. More than ten thousand waited at Greece's northern border.

"Absent a political solution, NGOs estimate that within the next two weeks, there could be up to 70,000 migrants trapped in Greece. Everyday more arrive on its shores," says a CNN correspondent in one news video.

As she speaks, we see a towering vehicle ferry arrive at a dock, its lower deck painted blue, the upper deck white. At the bottom, dwarfed by the size of the ferry, a line of children, teenagers, and a few adults stand with their hands grasping the safety lines, clad in sweatshirts and coats, trepidation on their faces. A few policemen step up, let down the lines, and the crowds of people slowly surge forward and emerge, some of them smiling, many looking tired, sad, or afraid.

In another video I watched, refugees blocked a road in Greece—desperate for some attention, some information, *something*. A Syrian woman whose face is half hidden by her headscarf says: "We have reached this point, and we are asking, What is going to happen to us? What is our fate? We who ran away from our country, not because we were hungry. We didn't leave because we were hungry. We left because there is a war. Is it our fate to die here also? No one is paying attention to us. Absolutely no one." She is weeping now.

I think about our need to be seen, to be regarded. To *matter*. To become invisible—truly invisible, unseen, or even ignored in your moment of greatest need—is a horror, an unimaginable trough of despair for any of us.

An older man with grizzled, salt-and-pepper stubble who is interviewed says: "We have a war. Imagine there is war in your country. What would you do?" He pauses for a long time, then shrugs, as if to say, *eh, what could you do?* "You would have to leave."

———

What struck me so profoundly, during those winter months of 2015–16, was seeing the political response to the refugees flowing into Europe: an almost shocking increase in the policing of geographical borders, in a post–UN treaty, "borderless" Europe.

Paul Mutsaers is a researcher focusing on policing in the Netherlands; some of his research has focused on the "Psy-Cops" program in Amsterdam, in which police have joined with military forces to gather intelligence on ethnic minority residents in the Netherlands. This, he points out, "boils down to nothing less than a thickening of borderlands. The border is no longer geographically fixed; it is all around us. But this does not mean that it imposes the same constraints on everyone. Borders mean different things to different groups."

If you look white enough and affluent enough, Europe at this moment is still essentially borderless to you. But look different from that privileged "norm," and things in Europe have been changing fast.

"It is striking to watch European societies investing so much in health at home and, at the same time, erecting ever more impermeable legal and material barriers to keep refugees at bay, actively contributing to human deaths," notes Stephane Baele, author of "Live and Let Die: Did Michel Foucault Predict Europe's Refugee Crisis?"

In 1976, Foucault introduced his ideas of biopower and biopolitics as "a new logic of government, specific to Western liberal democracies"—a logic through which power structures and procedures were aimed at either *disciplining* the human body to render it docile and extract its labor—or gaining influence and control over a population through *regulating* the biological processes of the human body: birth rates, mortality, life expectancy, and so on.

Thus, biopolitics aims to use disciplinary technologies for the purpose of control, while at the same time expending substantial resources and focus on the health of the population—so that the traditional "sovereign right to seize, repress, and destroy life is complemented by a new form of power that aims to develop, optimize, order, and secure life."

But this focus on health has a dark side. As Baele notes, Foucault "warn[ed] that paying so much attention to the health and wealth of one population necessitates the exclusion of those who are not entitled to—and are perceived to endanger—this health maximisation programme" and contended that "for people to find such extreme policies normal and even moral, they have to perceive those who die as different, not as members of their own group."

"Biopolitics," writes Baele, "is therefore the politics of live and let die. The more a state focuses on its own population, the more it creates the conditions of possibility for others to die."

The conflicts in the Middle East that people have been fleeing are both brutal and extremely deadly: "Extremist groups such as the Islamic State display unimaginable levels of violence. They have beheaded people with knives or explosives, burned people locked in cages, crucified people, thrown people from the tops of buildings, or more recently exploded people locked in a car."

And yet, as Western nations increasingly bulk up their border control, build impassable fences, and use sophisticated military technologies of control, those fleeing such violence are either left at the mercy of the war zone their home has become or forced to "undertake highly risky journeys towards a safe but fully sealed place."

———————

Almost five years later, when I look up Calais to see what has happened there in the years since—where people went after the main camp was shut down in 2016—I see that they've simply atomized, scattered into smaller and more dispersed camps.

And those camps are under constant harassment and attack by local police forces: according to the *Guardian*, there were 973 evictions from camps in Calais in 2020, nearly three per day.

"'It's been like this for months,' said Isabella Anderson, an HRO [Human Rights Observers] field coordinator. 'These constant evictions are part of a policy by the French government to wear down asylum seekers, to fatigue them and take away their hope. It's like torture.'"

The evictions, according to the *Guardian*, take place "on a rolling 48-hour schedule to prevent refugees acquiring limited rights and the police requiring a court order to clear the land" and "are seen by the French authorities as a key weapon in preventing" refugees from establishing another large camp like the Jungle. Violent acts committed by police as part of the evictions "have included minors being teargassed, a tent with a refugee inside being dragged by a tractor and an Eritrean [man being] shot in the face with a rubber bullet from 10 metres, hospitalizing him for two months."

> "They come at 5am, circle around your tent and cut it with knives," said Abdul [pseudonym], a 20-year-old from Sudan who has been in Calais for five months, camping in the bushes in the hope of one day crossing to the UK by boat or lorry. "It has happened to me so many times. They treat us like animals, not humans. In Sudan there is war, people are killed, women are raped. But in some ways, it is better than here."

As of January 2021, there were an estimated 1,200 refugees living under the condition of constant eviction in Calais and Dunkirk, including children and pregnant women. In another *Guardian* article, a Syrian man, seeking to reach his brothers in the UK, said, "It is like the authorities think we are animals and they are taking us from one farm to another."

In *Lande*, Hicks and Mallet cite several sources reporting that the police use "'tactics of exhaustion,' designed to weaken the chances of people successfully crossing the Channel at nighttime, [which] include the sustained use of sleep deprivation, the use of tear gas in the face or on sleeping people, or kicking them awake . . . combined with the destruction of mobile phones with batons or by stamping on them, baton strikes on the top of the legs to break items in trouser pockets."

Such "practices of assault, bodily harm, negligence, poisoning with gas, endangerment, despoliation, harassment and psychological violence have become 'an integral part of border management'" in a continual "cycle of 'cleansing' migrant camps."

One other practice that has become common is taking one or both shoes from migrants to hamper their movements, leaving them barefoot and vulnerable in the mud and broken glass of the camps.

This is a degree of precarity that is difficult to imaginatively comprehend. At its root, as Lauren Berlant writes, "precarity is a condition of dependency"—a dependency created or enhanced by the "destabilizing scenes" of capitalism, and by economic and political practices that "mobilize this instability in unprecedented ways." These movements and migrations of people are essentially the postcolonial realities of a neoliberal economic system resting on centuries of empire. They are provoked and amplified by not only ongoing geopolitical military conflicts but also, in the words of geography scholar Ruth Wilson Gilmore, the practices of "structural abandonment of vulnerable communities" and the increased policing that such practices necessitate.

The image of riot police—bulky and intimidating in black body armor and tall, heavy boots, standing on the corners and at the train station in Liège, patrolling the cobblestoned blocks of Brussels, forcibly evicting residents of the Jungle—plays over and over in my mind.

Frédéric Gros, another scholar of Foucault's ideas, sees biopolitics as an age of security in which structures of power are increasingly concerned with controlling mechanisms of human circulation and tracing human movement—*security* is thus perceived as directly rooted in the ability to control the flow of both human movements and human communications.

In *Lande*, the forensic archeologists' exploration of the camp at Calais, Dan Hicks and Sarah Mallet write, "Calais is just one location among many around the world at which a global process of wall construction by western governments against the movement of people from the Global South is underway."

And yet, borders—as noted by Paul Mutsaers in his research on the Dutch "Psy-Cops" program—are no longer geographically fixed, no longer just lines delineating the edges of a territory. I think of his phrase, "a thickening of borderlands," quite often. The identity-checking, control techniques, and wall-building originally associated with border checkpoints are now found "wherever the movement of information, people, and things takes place"—in cities, for example, or near camps of people seeking refuge or asylum.

Hicks and Mallet note:

> This includes . . . the biopolitics of the body at one remove, refracted through biometrical records and screens, photographs of the face, fingerprints, scans of bodies and eyes, alongside X-rays of lorries to look for human life. . . . The dispossession traced above in the form of statelessness, impermanence, timelessness are refractions of a broader status of being "without" that can begin with slippages of language around the lack of papers (*sans-papiers*) towards definitions of being without humanity.

Sans-papiers, sans-titre. Without papers, without title, without status. Without humanity.

In an introduction to a new nationalism-themed issue from the Racial Imaginary Institute, the curators observe that we are in what Trinh T. Minh-ha calls "an epoch of global fear," a moment in which "the idea of a globally interconnected future of interchange and national coexistence—widely shared after the end of the Cold War—has given way to talk of walling off people, rights, and resources to reinforce existing allocations of power and privilege."

As Hicks and Mallet point out, "It would be impossible now to mistake the 1990s debordering of the EU through Schengen and the building of the Channel Tunnel as indications of a post–Cold War world as a global borderless space."

I think about borders, about bodies and control, think back to Mark Quinn's series of frozen death-masks: "If you unplug it, it turns to a pool of blood. It can only exist in a culture where looking after art is a priority. It's unlikely to survive revolutions, wars and social upheaval."

We are in such a moment of social upheaval, though at this moment, the upheaval, the disruption, is only for some—the preponderance of walls, for now, ensures that. But I read in the news the other morning that one in thirty-three people on this planet currently needs humanitarian aid or protection—"more than at any time since the second world war," according to the coordinator of the UN's relief program.

My friend Poupeh Missaghi, who speaks Persian and was translating documents for people stuck in the flow of migrants, refugees, language, barriers, and fences, writes about her experience in a powerful essay called "The Death Card."

She describes watching drone footage from October 2015, which showed "a river of refugees . . . flowing through green patches of land," and realizes that it was only in the moment of watching those bodies move together en masse through the landscape that she truly understood the magnitude of the exodus. She writes, "devoid of the context of disaster and a background of calamity, devoid of any sound or voiceover, the drone footage becomes even more troubling."

> This is not a war zone in which the wounded and the surviving are running and struggling to find shelter. The image disrupts because it is a peaceful landscape of beauty and bounty, the earth being there for the human with the promise of growth, a future, and yet this river of suffering, of pain and loss, of forced exile, cannot stop and can only continue to run, to flow, to flee, moving through the green fields, wherever the humans in charge of the land allow them an opening to move through, to breathe and to be, disheartened and broken but still clinging to a hope arising from urgency

or lack of choice that somewhere someone or some government can accept their humanity.

In 2015, the Serbian artist Marko Risovic took photographs of the shoes of people who were migrating, fleeing, moving across the land. "All the shoes have a different story," Risovic said. "Shoes were torn apart by long walking or by the circumstances or conditions at the border crossing."

Focusing on people's shoes allowed him to represent an aspect of their experience without invading their privacy; in a world of biometrics and passports, shoes were safe to photograph because they didn't show people's faces, couldn't be used as inadvertent pieces of data in their asylum claims, didn't give them away in terms of where they'd entered the EU.

In one photo, an older woman in a long gray skirt is seated, her feet partly out of her shoes, the tip of a crutch planted in the gravel beneath her feet. Her shoes are of reddish leather, the backs crushed down, the rest bent and worn like an old shirt stretched out of shape.

Another shows a person clad in black pants, standing on a gray blanket atop a black tarp. One foot is wrapped in a swath of gold foil rescue blanket, knotted off just below the knee. The other foot is bare, red from the cold, and marked with traces of muddy sand.

A third image shows someone standing in fuzzy socks and black Keds with neon green laces. Their shoes are painted wetly with a coat of brown, claylike mud.

"In an era of resurgent and terrifying ethnic and racial nationalism around the world," write the curators of the Racial Imaginary Institute, "how can

contemporary writers, artists, and thinkers reimagine the concept of nation itself? What does it mean to belong?"

I think of those shoes I passed, sitting by the side of the path as I cycled to the
church on that blustery Maastricht morning. They were wet from the rain, sitting
at the edge of a muddy field, and yet they looked as if they'd been so carefully,
neatly placed there. To whom did they belong, and why were they abandoned by
the side of the field? Where were the feet that had once worn them, the human
who had walked around in them? The body and its disorderliness—so many
things beyond our control.

The wind tore across the fields that morning, blustering and bullying, in sporadic
gusts that could push you off the path into the bushes. The trees still just fingers,
their gold and green yet to return. Behind them, curtains of sky hung heavily,
bellies breaking open.

CHAPTER TEN

Seeking Refuge

In the art of Syrian American artist Diana Al-Hadid, figures and bodies twist and melt, and classical-looking structures with pillars collapse, the decay of a layered civilization. One piece, *Nolli's Orders*, reminds me of the photos of bombed-out buildings that were superimposed over Mokhalled Rasem's dance piece, or of the vacuum bomb in Darwish's *Memory for Forgetfulness*. The piece, a precarious set of tiers stacked atop each other, protruding out into space like Escher's platforms, rests on a small base, a replica of a pillared building with pointed arches like an ancient Islamic or Gothic ruin.

The layers drip and melt and liquesce into each other, quiescent and ruined. Beneath them, but still atop the small, pillared building at the base, a landscape of papery hills angles downward, the stark white cubes of art-gallery boxes protruding from them anachronistically, as though to declare a violent collision of past and present.

Melded into the skeletal, dripping strata, at an entirely larger scale, are five semi-reclining human figures, spread out around the wreckage, cast in white plaster, and truncated: like any classical Greek sculpture, their rendering stops at the neck. Though their postures echo the repose of classical sculpture, they seem somehow slumped and sprawling, casualties in the aftermath of disaster or war. They, too, are covered in the streaks and drips of a world that is ending.

Some years ago, in 2012 or 2013, a Syrian student at my school gave a talk. She was an intelligent, beautiful, joyful young woman, beloved by almost everyone, students and teachers alike. She had traveled home to Damascus for the summer, and she was furious and full of grief at what she'd seen there: the warping of what had begun as a set of democratic protests and grown into armed conflict, into a ballooning proxy war funded by the US and Iran and other parties. Her country was being torn to pieces before her eyes, she'd told us.

———

It is the early spring of 2016 now, and each morning in my round apartment on the outskirts of Maastricht—as the still wintry sunrise begins to turn the sky a deep indigo blue, and the pastures begin to emerge from the inky dark, and the horse barn across the road glows with its row of lights—I sit and read the news, try to understand the events of this world.

I read that in Deir-al-Zour, Syria, the price of milk has gone up 20,000 percent from prewar prices. The cost of bread, up 6,500 percent. Imagine if you went to the supermarket and found that a loaf of bread now cost $260, a gallon of milk $600.

I watch a BBC video of two Turkish coast guardsmen hitting a boat full of refugees with sticks. We can hear a woman's voice screaming. The boat is crowded, small, and low in the water. It holds perhaps twelve people, with several children in the middle. As the sticks hit it, we see the people at the edges flinch, duck down. There is a chaos of frightened, urgent voices, speaking in Farsi and Arabic. The two boats veer apart: "They've gone, gone." Then, "Oh god! They are coming back!" a man's voice narrates. "Hopefully we'll be OK, please God," says another. Finally the small coast guard boat turns away and the video cuts off.

I have been reading these narratives daily, obsessively. So many of them repeat. *I bought the boat tickets for myself and my children with our last money.* The tickets were expensive, even a thousand dollars per person. *When we came down to the boat that night, the sea was huge and I was very afraid. I tried to back out, to say we would go the next day, but the smuggler had a gun and he forced us to get on board. I thought we were all going to die.* Most of the boats are steered by one of the refugees, whichever one the smuggler picks and tells to drive. Many times the engine cuts out at some point during the crossing. Many nights the seas are huge, many nights there are boats overturned.

"I have watched the devastation in the faces of volunteers here as the bodies of children they worked with in the days before are brought in from the sea," an old classmate of mine writes from the coast of Turkey, where so many people are departing. "Many of the bodies are already missing limbs."

I don't know how to process, describe, or voice my furygrief at the bewildering violence of the world that so many people are up against. "The feeling that something is happening beyond our control—a mouth of blood dragged through each dark day," writes Bhanu Kapil in *Ban en Banlieue*.

I have been considering traveling to Greece, to the isle of Lesvos where the boats full of those fleeing Syria and elsewhere—arriving wet and hypothermic and often injured—are mostly landing. I have medical skills that could be of use.

But already I am skeptical of my impulse, skeptical of my desire to help. Writing of her translation work in "The Death Card," Poupeh says: "I am aware that this is to try to help to alleviate the pain of the victims, but I know too well that it is also to soothe my own feeling of shame and guilt caused by being seemingly safe and secure amidst the attacks and the exodus, to alleviate the sense of passivity and helplessness in the face of the horrific events."

Eventually, I decided to try to go. By then borders had closed, tens of thousands of people were backed up in camps along the northern border of Greece, masses of frustrated, frightened, desperate people piling up in the ports, bused out to camps, amassed at the border and rioting. People there were angry. They were afraid. They had heart conditions, pregnancy complications, diabetes, bomb blast injuries that were poorly healed.

The sky that day was energized, the still bare branches gesticulating wildly in the wind, the clouds skimming by as though driven by some mighty hand. A white coat of blossoms moved frenetically in the wind; even the birds swerved and veered through the sky.

On the day of my travel, as I scrolled through the Facebook feeds of all the various volunteer groups and camps, I saw that police had begun clearing people out of Piraeus, the main port of Athens where so many refugees had been camping. People were resisting, fearful of where they were being taken and what would happen to them there. Things were moving fast, conditions on the ground shifting, available information changing almost by the hour.

Among all the other news shared by volunteers on the ground were rumors that hate groups were planning a protest at Piraeus, and there were mentions of a possible Golden Dawn presence near Malakasa camp, where I was headed. My plane floated over the Greek fields, lit reddish by the setting sun, and I thought of Golden Dawn—such a beautiful name for something so ugly, these groups of angry, hate-filled men. Men ready to do violence to those most vulnerable, those come from one terror into another.

As we descended into Athens, the hillsides were patchworked with various shades of green. The city, an undulating blanket of red tile roofs, spread between the hillsides like the sea between islands. Next to the twilit runway stood an IKEA, garish in its bright yellow and blue.

An hour north of Athens, Malakasa camp had about 1,100 people living in it, almost exclusively from Afghanistan. Many had walked for months to reach Europe, some for years. Some were pregnant; some carried infants in their arms. One young man told me some of them had even walked in the cold and snows of winter through the high mountains of Iran, Iraq, and then Turkey to get to Greece from Afghanistan.

What I didn't know while I was there but learned much later was that cousins of my friend and former student Farid could easily have been among the people in Malakasa camp. Around that same time, Farid, on break from university in the US, had traveled home to Afghanistan and found that his cousins had been slipping away, slowly disappearing from the town they grew up in, without a word, without anyone knowing where they had gone.

While Syria had been a war zone for four or five years at that point, Afghanistan had been in a state of war for almost forty years. The Taliban particularly targets the Hazara minority, and many of the people I met in Malakasa were Hazara. There were also Afghans fleeing Iran, whose government had been forcibly recruiting among the millions of Afghans who live there, forcing them to go join the fight in Syria or risk being deported back to the war zone of Afghanistan.

There were rows and rows and rows of white tents in Malakasa, each of which housed two families. Between them red dirt and dust; between them endless sunshine, soon to become scorching heat. There were a few trees on the edges of this camp, but not enough to shade a thousand people. There were twelve showers and twelve toilets, which were divided, half for women and half for men. According to the Greek volunteers in the camp, there were at least 350 children in Malakasa, at least thirty pregnant women, and a couple of newborns. There were estimated to be at least thirty-five or forty unaccompanied minors, though it was difficult to get any sort of accurate count as they often blended in with families and went uncounted.

Malakasa camp was on military ground and controlled by the Greek army, which turned most other organizations away at the front gate, so unlike some of the other camps, there weren't many NGOs working there. A group of Greek people from local towns—an informal "solidarity network," in their words—were doing much of the support work inside the camp. Almost all the translation and communication between the residents of Malakasa and the volunteers, doctors, and army was done in English by Afghan people in the camp, in varying degrees of fluency.

When people first arrived at Malakasa, which opened in late winter, a retired Greek schoolteacher named Nikos recounted, it was cold, still the rainy season. The babies had no shoes and no foot coverings; many people had no socks. He showed me a photo of the flooded mud around the latrines; water ran out from the structures for the first several weeks people were there, he said, and they had to hop from stone to stone to avoid walking through puddles of mud and sewage.

There was still no internet at the camp, no Wi-Fi, which meant anyone living there was totally cut off from the news, cut off from any real access to information. Camp residents were free to come and go, but Malakasa is a small village many kilometers from anywhere, so unless they had the money for the train to Athens, there wasn't much of anywhere to go.

So many of the things we take for granted in our lives are not accessible to people who are living in camps like these. Information. Internet. Pediatricians. Birth control, prenatal visits. Lights—the camp at Malakasa was pitch-dark at night. Unsafe dark, with no lights in the tents, no flashlights.

The reality of camp life is steeped in the lethargy of a sluggish governmental system, the stagnation of lives lived with little sense of agency and even less sense of daily purpose. I had imagined the waiting, fear, and uncertainty that people living in camps might feel—but the degree of boredom I had not anticipated. Stagnation is deeply damaging, I realized during my time at Malakasa: being stripped of purpose for such long periods of time, dependent on and subject to the whims of fate and those in the camp around you—it heightens the tensions between people over petty things; wastes people's potential and education; encourages a sort of black market in things, if not bodies; and increases domestic violence.

Families disappeared daily with smugglers who promised to get them to Germany. The unaccompanied minors in the camps, so hard to keep track of in the first place, also sometimes vanished. Stories abounded of their disappearing, particularly from Piraeus, kidnapped into the organ or sex trades.

And those who came to help sometimes ended up adding to the chaos, the hardship. A former student of mine, volunteering in a camp near Malakasa, told me that some well-meaning outsiders had shown up one afternoon, given out hundreds of packs of Hot Hands—those little chemical hand warmers—and then left. Most of the people living in the camp had no idea what the little white packets were, and volunteers found people all over the camp, including children, pouring them into their tea.

Besides adding to the chaos at times, short-term volunteer work offers little continuity, little service to anyone. And as soon as you get there, you realize, I can be here or not be here, it makes not one iota of difference, the systems people are up against are so massive and intractable. Europe does not want to help them, to accept them, so for now, these giant camps full of people are functioning as a sort of human stop sign, a message to those refugees stuck in Turkey and Lebanon and Jordan who might have hoped to follow: DON'T COME. Europe does not want you.

———

For so many of the people I met in Malakasa, their whole lives, all the belongings left to them, were on their phones. Their legal documents (often the only copy

remaining); photos of family and loved ones; videos and photos that document
the persecution, threats, and violence they were subject to at home, the direct
danger to their lives. One young Afghan woman, who had worked for the US
Army, showed me the photos of her brother's dead body, shot by the Taliban as
retaliation because of her work.

Cell phones and language skills: both struck me, unexpectedly, for the degree to
which they become essentials when people's lives are upended.

My friend Poupeh writes of her work with Translators without Borders: "I have
been reminded of how a lack of language can lead to irrevocable consequences
for people who are already in life-and-death situations; of how language is, before
anything else, a means of survival. In the process of transferring seemingly simple
words from one language to another, I have felt the urgency and necessity of
translation, of it not being a choice but a need as basic as food and medical care."

I had similar epiphanies during my time in Greece. About how something as
conceptual and intangible as a national border can profoundly change the course
of someone's life. About how something as simple as what language is spoken in
a country can determine whether people seeking refuge feel able to settle there
or strive—even risk their lives—to travel farther, to arrive somewhere they know
the language better. About how the physical landscape, the placement of a river
or a mountain range, can drastically impact the ability of a family to walk to
help, to safer terrain; about how a small stretch of sea can become a treacherous
obstacle, an impasse, a life threat.

Language matters. There is simultaneously a fetishization of refugees, a patholo-
gizing of them, and a sort of errant, groundless sympathy—which is not the same
as empathy, infused with pity as it is. Rather, it is evidence of what Susan Sontag
called "the imaginary proximity to suffering" on the part of those of us watching news coverage from afar—and out of such an imaginary proximity grows a

sympathy that can cloak our complicity in the structures causing the suffering in the first place.

In an interview, Saidiya Hartman and Frank Wilderson discuss the structural divisions that prevent genuine empathy for the Other. So often, to arrive at empathy rooted in our common humanity, we require that the Other must be assimilated—stripped of their identity—so that we can easily see ourselves in them. There is a "'species' division between what it means to be a subject and what it means to be an object," Wilderson writes.

We—those of us who are white, those of us who live in wealthy nations—are so deeply trained to see people of color or people from other parts of the world as *object* rather than *subject* that it leaks out all over the place in our language.

One problem I have struggled with in this writing is echoing news reporting that so often reinscribes and reinforces this object-ism: even when people are given some expression, granted direct quotations, they aren't really given the power of voice or of autobiography or of self-definition because they're already defined by the labels (refugee, migrant, helpless, war, poverty, fleeing) that have been applied to them as a group at large.

In another of Diana Al-Hadid's pieces, *Actor*, a netlike steel structure of rods, bent and slanted, stands upright like a pier that has withstood a hurricane. At its base is something like tangled seine nets, full of white plaster in slumping curves like drowned bodies. Looking at this piece from every angle, I cannot stop seeing bodies, and I think perhaps Al-Hadid's pieces become a kind of Rorschach ink blot for their viewers.

Christina Sharpe writes, "my experience of photographs of disasters that happen in Black spaces and to Black people is that they usually feature groups of Black people . . . in 'pain for public consumption.'" This is not limited to disasters in

Black spaces, though it is centrally characteristic of them—we see it again in the public attention to the photo of Alain Kurdi or the photo of Óscar Alberto Martínez Ramírez and his infant daughter, Valeria, who drowned in the Rio Grande.

I come back to Sontag's words again, to the ways in which our "imaginary proximity to suffering" allows us to avoid self-interrogation, avoid thinking about the power structures that benefit us, and allows us to evade blame by indulging in the public consumption of sentimentality.

At a recent writing conference, on a panel called "Beyond the Event," Vanessa Angélica Villarreal says: "I don't want to create trauma porn. . . . I don't want to hold suffering up as spectacle." I write her words down in my little notebook and hold on to them.

———————

I have tried for several years after this trip to make sense of it to myself. And I have avoided writing this chapter of the book because I didn't want it to be the climax, the culminating white-savior journey that gives meaning to all the rest.

Shortly after I returned from Greece, I wrote an essay about my experience there, which I published and which got lots of attention and interest. But when I look back at that essay, I feel deeply uncomfortable with it.

When I was a college student studying in East and South Asia and in Central America, we spoke with many local activists and learned about significant issues impacting peoples' lives. And yet, whenever any of us asked what we could do to help this issue, to change it, we were met with an extremely consistent answer: go home. Use your voice in your own country, which wields such immense power over our countries. You have a kind of power and access, by accident of birth, of nationality, that we—also by chance of birth and nationality—will likely never have.

I went to Greece because I wanted to feel as if I could give back some of the support and hospitality that had been given to me during years of living abroad, which of course, in the context of camps and the hundreds of thousands of people in them, I couldn't.

Perhaps it is simply I who was seeking refuge against my own feelings of impotence, complicity, and inaction. I was the innocent interloper, arriving with my little backpack of medical supplies, representing a country that has in many ways *created* this flow of people seeking refuge—through military intervention in the proxy war in Syria, through our Cold War machinations and CIA support for the mujahadeens in Afghanistan, through our invasions of Iraq—and yet, despite my awareness of those things, still buying into the narrative of crisis, of disaster, still thinking I could in some way *help*. My experience in Greece was not of heroism but that of the antihero.

The EU has reacted to the refugee situation (to quote Poupeh again, "I am not sure if *refugee* and *situation* are the best words I can use, but I will concede to them for now") much as the US has in Central America: by making another country its proxy, forcing Turkey to turn people back or let them stay. That way we all—the US, Germany, Netherlands, all the EU—get to keep our self-image, safely untouched, of ourselves as compassionate humanitarians. And, at the same time, our cocoon is protected.

I think we—we as a country, we as Americans—need to look at what makes a *disaster*, what makes a *crisis*. And where the benefits are flowing from the underlying conditions preexisting those catastrophes.

We need to learn, in the words of Teju Cole, "to think constellationally" and "see the patterns of power behind the isolated 'disasters.'" We need to push against the focus on an immediate event and see the "larger disasters behind [the humanitarian disaster], larger disasters in which, as Cole points out, we often bear a great deal of responsibility: through militarization, resource extraction, food scarcity, our backing of brutal and corrupt governments, and climate change.

As my "Beyond the Event" panel notes observe about responses to an immediate crisis, "Too often these violences are cast as disastrous events that eschew the intersection of geography, race, class, and infrastructure"—and our ahistoricism, as Americans, contributes to our ignorance of our own responsibility, our nation's responsibility, for these disasters.

Too often, to paraphrase Cole, we are driven by our sentimental urge to "make a difference," which can come to function not only as disguise but even as a release valve for the guilt and discomfort of living in a society built on exploitation of people and natural resources.

In Athens's Venizelos airport, sitting at a table by a glass wall overlooking the runway and waiting to board my flight back to Amsterdam, I thought of how difficult, how agonizing, every moment of uncertainty, of unclear decision-making, has felt in my life—and then tried to imagine how it would feel to be living in Malakasa, having committed all your resources to get there and cut all ties at home, sometimes having escaped near death—how it would feel to be living with such absolute, utter uncertainty and lack of control. The future of every person in that camp is opaque—as all our futures are, to some extent, but this opacity is of a vastly different texture and dimension, so intensely bounded by forces outside each individual's control.

———

The morning after I returned from Greece, I woke up to find the world around me spinning. Every time I moved my head or my body, the world moved, too fast, and in dizzying, blinding circles. If I lay flat and still, everything seemed normal.

So I lay in bed, unable to leave it, trying not to notice the longing looks and eventual agitation of the dog, and used my phone to research positional vertigo, which I eventually concluded was the source of this spinningness. I thought about hunger and thirst and needing to pee, and I thought about helplessness. I thought about what it would have been like if this had happened while I was in Greece, or if it had ever happened to someone who was—like almost everyone I'd met in Malakasa—walking the immense distance and rugged mountainous terrain from Kabul or Kunduz or Feyzabad, through the massive length of Iran, through Turkey, and then crossing the sea to Greece.

In Diana Al-Hadid's *Antonym*, a figure is a shell, hollowed out, like what might be left if a body were encased in ash and then dissolved, or turned to dust, inside that casing. The figure—leaning to the side, slightly slumped—is seated on a white pedestal, but melting in, as if flash heat had softened the world, and I think again of Darwish's vacuum bomb. One leg dangles over the edge of the pedestal, and the foot that hangs below is blown out on the bottom, only a partial crust of its instep and heel leading up to the hollowed-out leg, mottled with missing patches like skin from a burn patient.

In *Suspended after Image*, a figure melts through stairs, white plaster contours of the body emerging only into the empty space between the perfectly geometric sharp edges of the stairs. It is unsettling, alarming, like watching someone being devoured by another object, and it reminds me of N. K. Jemisin's stone eaters. At its base, the figure's leg melts into the floor. Driplines of paint run down the entire project, stair after stair, though none taint the alabaster of the body itself. One arm ends below the shoulder, in classical sculpture form. The other reclines, gracefully, along the stairs to the figure's left.

In Maastricht, the spring warmth comes slowly back into the world. The days stretch long and longer, a skin of thin blue light.

A while later, I will hear from other volunteers in Malakasa that a government inspector has come now, and she is getting in everyone's way, making their work more difficult. I hear that the young woman from Afghanistan whom I'd hoped would be able to get a special immigrant visa, is just two months short of the required period of work for the US—her brother's having been killed in retaliation for that work, irrelevant to whomever made the decision.

So many people are waiting, but the late spring does not swell ripe or pregnant with it. No golden haze to the afternoon light; instead there is a bluish tinge to the air as it stretches toward dusk. The waiting feels restless, edgy, lined at its endpoint with the sandpapery rub of what is next.

CHAPTER ELEVEN

American Innocence

"The first word I learned in English was a Greek swear word," Anna said to me one day, apropos of nothing.

"I didn't know for the longest time that it wasn't even English. That's what happens when you send your immigrant kid to an immigrant school." She laughed.

The US pioneered some of our most insidious empire-building strategies in Greece during the early Cold War era, before going on to use them globally in its trumped-up fight against communism, so it seems somehow apropos that one of the first words my Soviet-Russian wife learned after moving to the US was a Greek swear word.

The word was *malaka*, which immediately took my mind to Malakasa: how everyone whom I met there was faring, whether claims for asylum had been answered, whether conditions in the camp had improved at all. It made me think again about the ways in which the precarious passage of so many people from Syria, Afghanistan, and Iraq to the shores of Greece has been described as a "crisis," of the ways in which the stretch of time from 2015 to 2016 has felt like a continual upheaval of violence and chaos.

"The term 'crisis' derives from the Greek 'krisis,' meaning decision or judgment. From this, we also get terms such as critic (someone who judges) and critical condition (a medical state that could go either way)," writes William Davies. "A crisis can conclude well or badly, but the point is that its outcome is fundamentally uncertain. To experience a crisis is to inhabit a world that is temporarily up for grabs."

But when is the world not up for grabs, despite all our wishing and pretending otherwise?

In an interview with Chris Kraus, Olivia Laing describes trying to write a nonfiction book "about the body and violence and protest" during the same time period that I was living in Maastricht. She says: "I was finding it impossible . . . because the world was changing too rapidly. . . . To write from a stable point of view meant losing the feeling of chaos and perpetual disruption that was the signature of [that moment]."

In a photo, eight figures walk through a small street in a European city, sidewalk cafés on either side. The silent figures all wear white painting suits, the words "Save Iraqi People" written in thick black marker on the back of each suit. They are a Vienna-based performance-artist group called Iraqi Autumn; their members, young Iraqis who have sought asylum in Europe after fleeing Iraq because it was so dangerous for them to stay, to continue to be activists.

They are protesting the silence of the international community about state violence in Iraq; trying to call attention to the many young Iraqis protesting nonviolently, despite the tear gas, live ammo, and other immense violence being directed at them in return.

The article accompanying the photo speaks of silence and of cutting hair:

> One of the group's members gathers his long hair, covers it in mud, then begins cutting it off. In Iraq, the wives of soldiers have traditionally cut their hair as an act of erasing their femininity, viewing hair as both sexy and holy. Cutting it allows its owner to perform their grief. Much of Iraqi Autumn's work points to the notion of autonomy and how, particularly in spaces of political oppression, this liberty is muzzled.

The metaphoric quality of the group's performances is one mode of opening the space between what is stable and known and what may be possible to imagine. In the words of Aristotle, "ordinary words convey only what we know already; it is from metaphor that we can best get hold of something fresh."

In art lies this same possibility: for metaphor, for expanding beyond what can be comprehended totally, for seeing outside preconceived possibilities, beyond even our own imagination.

While the "objective" conceptual system often fears or looks down on metaphor—believing that "to use words metaphorically is to use them in an improper sense, to stir the imagination and thereby the emotions and thus to lead us away from the truth and toward illusion," write Lakoff and Johnson in *Metaphors We Live By*, "metaphor is one of our most important tools for trying to comprehend partially what cannot be comprehended totally." In the sense of making meaning, too, we live in a world that is always up for grabs.

Most of us tend to think of both language and self as stable, and yet, as Henry Giroux and Peter McLaren point out, by recognizing the manifold ways we are produced through language, we can begin to develop a "critical language" that will help us to become conscious of our own self-formation and of "the subject positions which we assume uncritically."

It is a different kind of a move toward disruption, this time in our self-perceptions: away from a stable, undisrupted point of view; away from a stable sense of self.

By holding the idea of ourselves as solid, unchanging, we are better able to cope with the constant external flux of this world we live in. And yet, as anyone participating in cultural exchange quickly begins to learn, sense of self and identity are not at all independent of context.

When I lived in Hangzhou, China, as the country was just beginning to open to foreigners, I discovered that all the external markers of identity I'd learned to read growing up in the US meant nothing in a late nineties Chinese context: clothing, haircut, personal style, or dress. It was a strange disorientation that told me how much I relied on those markers to indicate with whom I might be "compatible"—socially or personally—as well as who *I* was.

"The term 'identity'. . . implies that there is a fixed essence that exists independently . . . allegedly constituted outside of language, history, or power," write Giroux and McLaren. "The term 'subjectivity' permits us to acknowledge and address the ways in which individuals make sense of their experiences, including their conscious and unconscious understandings . . . [and] underscores the contingency of identity." We human beings are, they argue, essentially "a decentered flux of subject positions."

This "decentered flux" is what intercultural learners begin to become aware of through the unsettling of their identities; it is, essentially, what Buddhism describes as *no-self.*

Not long after my return from Malakasa to Maastricht, my friend Sandhya came from South Africa to visit me, eighteen years after we'd been schoolmates together, eighteen years of writing letters and long emails back and forth.

The weather in Maastricht had dropped from lovely April sunshine that felt truly like a storybook spring back to wintry cold and incessant rain. The day she arrived, it snowed for a while, comically large clumps of white falling heavily from the sky into the bone-cold day.

The cold cut straight through Sandhya's Durban sensibilities. We decided to go to see the caves as a way to stay out of the rain and wind, so one morning we climbed the street to the Sint Pieter fortress and sat in the chalet to have a cocoa while we waited for our tour to start.

The caves under Maastricht spread under the entire ridgeline of Sint Pieter's and continue down into nearby Belgium in a connected system. They are not truly caves, actually, but tunnels dug to extract yellowish blocks of limestone called marl. People from the area have sheltered in these caves on multiple occasions— to hide from the French in 1794 and again during World Wars I and II, when the caves served as a refuge for many Jewish people. There is also a vault built deep in the passages that protected a number of precious artworks, including Rembrandt's *Nightwatch*, during the bombings of the world wars. As Sandhya and I followed the tour guide through, I couldn't stop imagining the profound disruption that would have required whole families to relocate into these caves, to spend years harboring down here without daylight, to even build chapels and shops in this labyrinth.

The only way I can try to understand other people's experience of turbulence is through my own experience of disruption, which has come primarily through the isolation and inner turmoil of upheaving my sense of self. Seeing Sandhya in person, after not seeing her since I was a teenager, it was disconcerting both to slip into my old self, as she had known me—or at least to be reminded of that self through her eyes and memories—but also to see clearly the self I am now and the self that she is now, so different from who we were as young people. When I look back at things I wrote—from the years Sandhya and I were schoolmates in a community of students from all different cultures, or from the time I lived in China and felt lonelier and more culturally isolated than I'd ever experienced—I see a mind trying to make sense of *self*, of the world, of cultural difference, and of vast differences in the ways people around me experienced the world.

To see outside or step outside—though oftentimes not an action made by choice—can be both uncomfortable and instructive. Naomi Goldenberg writes that "an outsider is someone who, because she feels outside the social structure, can see some of the ways 'outsides' and 'insides' are constructed." This is valuable, she goes on to say, because "anyone who is aware of their own experience of confusion about identity has some important things to teach us about what we call the sense of self."

Reading Goldenberg's words helped me see a pattern in my life where I hadn't seen one before: all the disparate travels and moves to different places, all the wanderings, were actually part of this attempt to place myself outside, to try to step outside so as to better see in. So as to learn. It wasn't always a choice—there were also unavoidable experiences of *being* outside: growing up furious at the patriarchal structure in my family and alienated by the social strictures of what was expected of me as a "girl" made me a feminist, and something in me led me to a nondiscriminatory kind of queerness.

Not only does being on the outside teach us about the self, continues Goldenberg, but through positioning themselves on the "outside," intercultural learners may also begin to become aware of power imbalances and how they are constructed between cultures. Or, to put it in the words of Gayatri Spivak: "What we are asking for is that . . . the holders of hegemonic discourse, should de-hegemonize their position and themselves learn how to occupy the subject position of the other."

———

As a part of my identity, my sense of self, I grew up learning—and believing—in American benevolence and goodness, that the US was a benign world leader, a proponent of enlightened democracy and human rights around the world. I grew up believing, in short, in the beneficence of US hegemony.

I did not have what James Baldwin describes Black Americans as possessing, that "great advantage of having never believed that collection of myths to which white Americans cling, believing that their ancestors were all freedom-loving heroes, that they were born in the greatest country the world has ever seen, or that Americans are invincible in battle and wise in peace."

In my four years abroad in college, however, I lived in Latin America twice—in Mexico and later in Costa Rica—and ever since, I've believed that if you want to see the role of the US in the world with a clear gaze, a short study of our foreign policy and actions in Latin America will suffice as a succinct introduction, a thumbnail sketch of the whole. In it, it is brutally clear the ways in which Monroe Doctrine–era land grabs and business interests morphed over time into US-backed coups to overthrow democratically elected leaders and install brutal dictators; to provide military funding, training (including in torture techniques), and weapons; to support paramilitary death squads, structural adjustment policies, and externally enforced transnational corporate ownership of resources. As Suzy Hansen lays out so neatly in *Notes on a Foreign Country*, for example, from 1954 to 1973 the US "would stage or support" seven military coups in Latin America: first, Guatemala in 1954, then "Argentina in 1962, Guatemala again in 1963, Brazil in 1964, Bolivia in 1964, Uruguay and Chile in 1973."

While studying in Costa Rica with a small group of students and our professors, we at one point traveled for two weeks in Nicaragua and Honduras. We met with former gang members and came to understand the ways in which gang violence there was essentially of US creation: the economic devastation, the exported weapons, and the weaponry left over from US-armed groups such as the Contras or belonging to undocumented gang members who had been deported from the US. We spoke to young men growing up in barrios in Managua in which unemployment rates were exceptionally high and for whom the opportunity to work—to have some sense of purpose, of possibility, of hope—was bitterly distant. One young man said to me directly, "There's nothing to do here, no way to better your life, nothing to work for—only, on all sides, drugs drugs drugs and violence." We spoke to Sandinistas who had fought to provide land and opportunity to the impoverished majority in the country and had been crushed by US opposition, both militarized and economic. We spoke with young women, younger than us—fifteen, sixteen—who had little access to birth control or medical care, who were mothers before emerging from their teens, who had so little access to any kind of health care for very serious medical issues.

Most stunning to me was the discomfort of our own bodies traveling through those spaces: in a vehicle with tinted windows, we were constantly approached by people asking for money, and I saw the differences in reaction: the discomfort and refusal of most of the white students; the way several students of color refused to *stop* giving. The ways all of us struggled when confronted with our Americanness and our different relationships to what that meant.

I remember driving through the streets of Managua one evening, and several girls on our small bus slamming closed the bus windows at a stoplight, shrieking, "What are you looking at?" "Go the fuck away!" "Ewww, stop *looking* at me!!!" at the street vendors who came up to the side of our bus and stared in at us, laughing and talking, one of them pantomiming kicking the tire. *What do they think they're looking at?* I wrote in my journal at the time. *A bunch of white American girls, their bodies and sexuality sold by Hollywood; all our shiny jewelry, watches, clothes; the packaged junk food we're all munching on.*

On our last night, as we were sitting in the stopped bus waiting for a few group members, a woman approached the vehicle with three ragged, disheveled little children in tow. It was dark out, and there was Spanish reggae music blasting on the bus radio—everyone was dancing in their seats, and few noticed the woman or her children standing beside the bus, looking in at us. "Levanten los manos," went the song, and the woman and her children stood outside the windows, their raised hands outstretched toward us. Inside, students shrieked and laughed as they danced. It felt like the sentiment was, "phew, we've done our time 'confronting poverty,' now we can return home to our comfortable lives and not have to think about it." Outside the windows the woman and children stood looking in, their gazes all but unnoticed.

When I first read Suzy Hansen's "Unlearning the Myth of American Innocence," every single sentence in it resonated powerfully with me—it felt like so many echoes of my own learning process abroad. Beginning with an emerging awareness of her own whiteness and how it shaped her upbringing, Hansen then widens her lens to living abroad, seeing the ways whiteness and Americanness are intertwined in their power dynamics in the world.

Reflecting on her childhood, she writes:

> We were all patriotic, but I can't even conceive of what else we could have
> been, because our entire experience was domestic, interior, American.... I
> don't remember a strong sense of civic engagement. Instead I had the feel-
> ing that people could take things from you if you didn't stay vigilant. . . .
> The world was white, Christian; the world was us. . . . There was no sense
> of the US being one country on a planet of many countries. . . .
>
> I knew I was white, and I knew I was American, but it was not what I
> understood to be my identity. For me, self-definition was about gender,
> personality, religion, education, dreams. I only thought about finding my-
> self, becoming myself, discovering myself – and this, I hadn't known, was
> the most white American thing of all.

When I think back on the years I spent living abroad in my late teens and early
twenties and to the many people who opened their homes to me—many of them
the parents or families of friends I'd made abroad—I feel immense discomfort
at how much I was given, how casually I sailed in and out. I was grateful for their
hospitality, even touched by the extent of it. But even so, I think now, on some
level I expected nothing less. It felt, at that time, as if the world just opened to
me, and in many ways I took that for granted, as if it were a natural part of what
I'd learned growing up: I could do or become anything I wanted, if I just worked
a little to achieve it. It's not that I didn't believe I would have to work for things,
but that I had no real understanding of the massive foundation of privilege and
access underlying the small amounts of work I actually had to do to make these
opportunities happen for myself, when for others in the world, no amount of
hard work could ever lead to such opportunity.

Later in her essay, Hansen acknowledges:

> Young white Americans of course go through pain, insecurity and heart-
> ache. But it is very, very rare that young white Americans come across
> someone who tells them in harsh, unforgiving terms that they might be

merely the easy winners of an ugly game, and indeed that because of their ignorance and misused power, they might be the losers within a greater moral universe.

Living abroad, I experienced both deference—which I was uncomfortably aware was based solely on my nationality, skin color, and perceived wealth—and hostility; I remember being confronted, asked, "Why can you come to our country, and yet I can't get a visa to go to yours?" During those years of living abroad as a late teen and early twenty-something, I slowly became a great deal more aware of that "greater moral universe" Hansen speaks of, and when I at some point read Ivan Illich's famous 1968 speech, "To Hell with Good Intentions," I recognized at once the truth in his criticism of young American volunteers abroad who were, at best, "alleviating the damage done by [US] money and weapons, or 'seducing' the 'underdeveloped' to the benefits of the world of affluence and achievement, . . . [to US] ideals of acquisitive and achievement-oriented 'Democracy.'" At worst, we were doing a kind of damage we couldn't even see, bumbling around with "sentimental concern for newly-discovered poverty south of the border combined with total blindness to much worse poverty at home."

Illich was for me that voice that Hansen refers to: the rare speaker willing to tell young white Americans in "harsh, unforgiving terms" that they are the "easy winners of an ugly game."

He was a voice that burst the bubble of self-congratulatory "goodness" we aspired to: "I am here to challenge you to recognize your inability, your powerlessness and your incapacity to do the 'good' which you intended to do." And he echoes Baldwin in saying, "it is profoundly damaging to yourselves when you define something that you want to do as 'good,' a 'sacrifice,' and 'help.'"

In Illich's words, the experience of living abroad could lead to a damning new awareness: "the awareness that even North Americans can receive the gift of hospitality without the slightest ability to pay for it, that for some gifts one cannot even say 'thank you.'"

I realized some little bit of this at the time, as a twenty-one-year-old—even wrote in a journal:

> *This is how my own culture runs flat out over so many other cultures—they are still giving, out of tradition and generosity, and we are only taking and taking and taking—and have been for centuries and centuries. And how do I ever return that immense kindness and generosity, that giving? It is not something repayable.*

But I have grappled with how to *live* with this understanding, for decades more.

And I have found, in returning to the US, that those awarenesses are difficult to hold on to, so alluring is the siren call of capitalism, the beckoning to settle into a comfortable house, a regular job, the evening escapism of TV entertainment, the bar with friends, keeping up with email and social media and all the demands of adulthood. The cognitive dissonance of holding on to the awarenesses so easily developed when living outside the US is a strain, one comfortably relinquished in what Hansen refers to as the "palliative effects of [one's] own ignorance."

———

Years later, during graduate school in Arizona, I had the incredible opportunity to moonlight in the visual arts grad program, taking some classes on theory and practice, working in the metal shop, putting up an installation at a gallery off campus. The installation, *This the Body: An Historical Perspective*, was a faux museum exhibit designed to interrogate the authority of the museum and the Western history of displaying and scrutinizing the bodies and selves of those designated as Other.

That history includes, as Coco Fusco has neatly laid out in "The Other History of Intercultural Performance," a long list of performances and exhibits resting on colonial notions of primitivism, savagery, and exoticism from 1493 to 1992.

Inspired by a study of the history of the World's Fair and by the performance art of Fusco and Guillermo Gómez-Peña in *The Couple in the Cage: A Guatinaui Odyssey*, I wanted to find a way to take the othering gaze and turn it back on the gazer.

In my own performance piece, the multimedia installation featured various metalwork sculptures of bones—a pelvis, sections of spine, a shoulder blade.

> Display. Look at this body. Here is a
> body for you to look. Here, for your
> eyes. Your delection. & your
> entertainment. This body. These bodies.
> Here, skin eyes legs. Here: look.
>
> Look here. This the primitive. This the
> tattooed, this the freak, this the other.
> Look here. Look here. Look harder.
>
> Here are the labels you may affix:

On the wall were museum labeling plaques that were lyrical and interrogatory of eugenics and other discriminatory body practices.

> These bodies. Can be found. These
> bodies, brought from afar for your
> discerning gaze. These bodies:
> see how they are different, see here
> & here how they are not like you.
>
> Abu Ghraib. Abner Louima. Trans
> bodies on display. St. Louis World's
> Fair. Bronx World's Fair. Ota Benga.
> The Bronx zoo is not a home. This is
> nothing new. Why do we think Other.
> Why do.

A low, soothing voice-over spouted museum-speak nonsense about fields of inquiry, representation, and authenticity.

The central feature of the exhibit was a tall, wooden, 1950s museum display case, inside which I and two others stood naked and on display. A mirrored panel ran across the section where our faces were, so that viewers saw themselves reflected when they came to gaze at our bared bodies. Unbeknownst to them, a video camera filmed them, catching them as they looked. In time-lapse projection on a wall outside the exit, when they left the room they saw their own faces staring in at us.

In *The Couple in the Cage*, Fusco and Gómez-Peña pose as two previously "undiscovered" Amerindians who have agreed to travel to various cities to be displayed—for their own safety and that of onlookers—in a caged enclosure. They travel with faux handlers who feed them bananas and water.

"What distinguishes *The Couple in the Cage* is . . . the impossibility of an appropriate reaction," writes Barbara Kirshenblatt-Gimblett. "There is no tenable audience position."

"To buy into this performance at face value, when one should know better, is to fail dramatically." But to "play along"—knowing it is performance art—"tests the moral limits of theatrical representation."

The Couple in the Cage is a work of performance art that "rehearses . . . a mode of encounter" and "shifts the locus of repudiation and admonishment from the 'other' to the practices of othering," in the words of Kirshenblatt-Gimblett.

And the practice of othering is so deeply dangerous exactly because it is such a small step from "other" to "less than human." Sudhir Kakar, in his psychological analysis of Hindu-Muslim riots in India, writes, "empathy with members of the other group, even when considered the enemy, defends the Other from the untrammeled aggression which can so easily be let loose against all those considered subhuman."

And author and nonviolent resistance theologian Walter Wink argues: "Once children have been indoctrinated into the expectations of a dominator society, they may never outgrow the need to locate all evil outside themselves. Even as adults they tend to scapegoat others for all that is wrong in the world. They continue to depend on group identification and the upholding of social norms for a sense of well-being."

Wink's ideas tie directly to what Anna keeps pointing out to me in American culture: we do not see all humans, ourselves included, as complex mixtures with flaws and fallibility; rather, our dualistic notions of people being good or bad and of ourselves as "good people" are not only at the root of our inability to see ourselves clearly but also a fundamental factor in our need to project onto an Other.

On that same Central American college trip, we spoke with a Honduran scholar, Darío Euraque, who told us that when he was younger, it was "as if history was dead—there was very little sense of the relevance it has to the contemporary situation." Later on, however, he realized that "if you really grasp the extent to which history matters, it can create a kind of existential crisis—it's frightening."

Americans, conveniently, tend to have little memory for history, a kind of expedient erasure that protects our sense of goodness and innocence, and are shocked when any other people seem to hold our history of interventions and strongarming against us because, in Hansen's words, "we don't acknowledge that America is an empire; it is impossible to understand a relationship if you are not aware you are in one."

Euraque talked to us about Honduran history: the military regimes that governed almost without exception from 1900 to 1982, with their authoritarian culture and military police; the immense debt taken on by Honduras and other Central American countries in their bids to industrialize—debt that had to be repaid with US dollars, which later drove the desperate prioritization of whatever part of the economy could produce US dollars over the needs of the citizens of the country. Those military regimes were US-supported and often US-created: from the era of the American fruit companies' domineering grip to the Cold War, the Contras and the death squads, and more recently, the 2009 coup to overthrow Manuel Zelaya, the country's democratically elected president, and ongoing military and police training and support. I remember my despair and anger at learning about this history: how was it possible I had learned nothing, known *nothing* about any of this, growing up?

As we'd neared Tegucigalpa in the middle of the afternoon, the city had looked so colorful as it sprawled up the surrounding steep hillsides. Above it all, tall white letters perched on one of the highest hills, overlooking all the rambling slums and half-dirt streets: COCA COLA.

In Comayagüela—the sister city of Tegucigalpa, just across the river—we drove through long, narrow streets, packed with vending stalls on both sides: underwear and bras stretched on hangers, plastic objects of every type, vegetable stalls, mud puddles. A woman in a "Feminist Majority" T-shirt smiled and gave us a big wave as we drove by. The public buses were all old, retired, donated yellow school buses from the US.

Leaving Comayagüela, with its high rates of crime, gangs, drug use, and prostitution, we crossed the river and drove up toward the richer, sleeker Barrio Buenos Aires, where cell phone stores and convenience marts could once again be found, even in this sprawling, poverty-racked city. Historically, to cross the bridge over the Choluteca River from Comayagüela into the barrio, you had to show a certifying card allowing you to enter that wealthier area.

We passed by the mall district, with a PriceSmart in front, all shiny and new and big, and the houses were new and big too. The mall was covered with gleaming glass panels. We could have been just about anywhere in the world—it was an entirely different city from the one we had been in at the bottom of the hills.

I remember realizing with shame that, even with all that I had learned—about the voraciousness and exploitative manipulations of capitalism, about the debt crisis in Latin America underpinned by the World Bank and the IMF, about the underlying history of the Monroe Doctrine and American fruit companies and other business interests—a part of me felt relieved to be going back into a part of a city that was shinier, newer, more recognizable with its many things to buy.

Elsewhere in her essay, Suzy Hansen describes her experience living in Turkey, not only learning about cultural difference, but also developing an increased awareness of America's global role, and a greater understanding of her own cultural and psychological character. Within that learning, she says, she became aware of her own prejudices and assumptions:

> No matter how well I knew the predatory aspects of capitalism, I still perceived Turkey's and Greece's economic advances as progress, a kind of maturation.... I would never have admitted it, or thought to say it, but looking back, I know that deep in my consciousness I thought that America was at the end of some evolutionary spectrum of civilization, and everyone else was trying to catch up.

"Even when I disagreed with America's policies, I always believed in our inherent goodness, in my own," Hansen writes. She describes realizing that "American exceptionalism did not only define the US as a special nation among lesser nations; it also demanded that all Americans believe they, too, were somehow superior to others, a concept of goodness that requires the existence of evil for its own sustenance"—and that those beliefs are so profoundly bound up with capitalist development as a sign of enlightenment. This was a kind of nationalism, she writes, that was "so insidious that I had not known to call it nationalism . . . a limitation that was beyond racism, beyond prejudice and beyond ignorance."

Living and traveling in a variety of countries around the world, I, too, had become aware of this "limitation," this internalized idea of American superiority in myself, and had become deeply uncomfortable with it. And after three years abroad, returning to the US to live in New York City just before 9/11, I felt deeply aware of the ways this played out in the rhetoric and actions of 9/11's aftermath. In that moment, many Americans were expressing a deep bewilderment at how anyone else in the world could be so angry at us as a country, betraying such a deep ignorance of US foreign policy and global influence over the span of centuries, that I—after several years of meeting and speaking with people whose lives were directly and negatively impacted by both of those things—was both shocked and depressed by the lack of awareness of our country's historical actions and impact in the world.

I felt, in fact, much like Wendy S. Walters describes feeling in her book *Multiply/ Divide*, where she writes of returning to the Northeast after trying to help family recover after Hurricane Katrina:

> I returned from New Orleans more miserable than when I left. As much as I had wanted to come back from that trip with a sense of conviction, inspired to action that would distract me from my loneliness, I could not find a singular source of outrage on which to fixate. . . . I was faced with too much that was obvious about the way class and race work in America. . . .
>
> This is when I realized my loneliness had deeper roots than I had initially suspected, and that . . . it came from having a profound sense of disconnection from what I thought America was, and who, in that context, I knew myself to be.

There is a loneliness to being an outsider, to seeing the constructed world from a different angle. When I returned to the US, I felt that loneliness acutely, as if I were seeing a completely different version of reality than the people around me saw: all the advertising, the patriotic gestures, seemed so garish and hollow. I returned to the US only to experience the tumult of 9/11 in New York. Sent home from work in midtown Manhattan after the planes crashed into the towers, I walked down Sixth Avenue, pausing numbly with a group of others to watch the event replayed on multiple screens in the display window of a TV store; walked home across the Brooklyn Bridge amid the thousands of other people also streaming across that bridge as ash and paper fell down out of the sky onto us. And I returned to witness the violence that followed, threats and attacks against anyone seen as other—Sikhs, Muslims, anyone else perceived in a moment as *different*, as *unamerican*—the ongoing violence, as our country tumbled headfirst into what would become an endlessly expanding war.

In a recent interview, scholar Ruth Wilson Gilmore describes her research, asking "what are the conditions under which it is more likely that people will resort to using violence and harm to solve problems?" She states emphatically, "what we found is that where life is precious, life is precious." In other words, where the systems and structures and very culture of a society treat all lives as precious, then individual people also respond by treating life as precious. And where they don't, individuals respond with nihilism, selfishness, and violence.

"Violence, as it says in the Zohar, causes actual disturbance in the heavens as it does in the upper spheres of the human imagination," writes Fanny Howe in *The Winter Sun*. "It is the same as the subtle social nihilism that is manifested as pragmatism."

The subtle social nihilism that is manifested as pragmatism. As I read Howe's words, I think that this is in fact the dominant US paradigm. An individualistic social nihilism that is in service to capitalism, the market, and to profit and a mindless belief in eternal growth.

And as our world feels both increasingly finite and increasingly up for grabs, we are seeing an increase in violent, aggressive means—at least at this moment in the

US—to cope with the sense that *language* and *self* are not stable concepts, that the world is neither stable nor secure.

Of course, the sense of a world "increasingly up for grabs" is very American—and probably specifically very white, middle-class American—because for much of the world, it has always been grimly evident exactly to what extent life is up for grabs. The "chaos and perpetual disruption" that Olivia Laing describes as emblematic of recent times , are an ongoing fact of life for a great many people on this shared globe, for whom economic stability and justice are elusive.

In thinking of violent, aggressive means, of instability and injustice—and in thinking of our future as a planetary species, in thinking of our humanity—I keep returning to the case of Israel and Palestine, and the extensive US funding of Israel's military-security establishment. To the idea that this tiny country, effectively functioning as a well-funded apartheid regime, has—by its displacement and caging in of Palestinian populations, using settler colonialism, surveillance, militarized crowd-control techniques, one-sided warfare, and psychological warfare to squeeze Palestinians into tinier and tinier spaces—caged *itself* into a hawkish, hyperright, warlike state.

In Israel and Palestine, I see the possible future of the world if wealthy nations—who have emitted the overwhelming majority of the carbon causing the climate emergency—refuse to start planning now for open, humanitarian ways of integrating mass migrations of people displaced by famine and fatal heat waves and other climate change disasters. If, instead, these wealthier nations—of which I am a part—build more walls, increase their militarization of borders and strategies for population suppression, refuse to educate their own citizenry about the displacements to come, then we lose all possibility of a humanitarian model, rooted in justice, of responding to the changes beginning to amplify in our world.

Mohsin Hamid, whose novel *Exit West* I teach with my students—a novel that begins in the Syrian conflict and then beautifully, humanely chronicles the unfolding of a world in which millions of people have been displaced and moved around the globe—says in one interview:

> I think there's been a failure of imagination. Everywhere around the world, people are having difficulty imagining a future. People are going to move. Things are going to change. And yet all of our leaders seem to be telling us to go back to a previous time when things were better. You know, in Britain, it's go back before the EU. In America, it's make America great again. In much of Iraq, Iran, Pakistan, it's go back to the caliphate of 1,000 years ago. The danger is that we're not imagining futures, not imagining something we can go to that's different and progressive.

So much of the reaction now is rooted in fear and resource guarding—or on business as usual, plausible deniability, and protecting the status quo—instead of in creativity and vision. It's the job of writers and artists, as Hamid argues, "to start imagining those futures, . . . to make people comfortable with . . . the inevitable reality of a world where billions of people are going to move in the next couple of hundred years. . . . Climate will change, sea levels will rise, people will move."

"And if we can't find a way to be hopeful and optimistic and find beauty in that, we're in real trouble."

As he speaks, I picture miles and miles of stretching walls, coils of razor wire and jutting metal and guards with guns and surveillance drones. The shadows of all those walls, stretching long across the land.

Gómez-Peña, who together with Fusco performed in *The Couple in the Cage*, has had a long and prolific art career in the US, and many of his pieces grapple with migration, dislocation, and cultural alienation.

In 1979, he performed a solo piece called *The Loneliness of the Immigrant* in which he "transformed his body into a mysterious package," wrapped in batik fabric, with cord tied around his waist, legs, and ankles. His body—the mysterious package—was positioned lying on the floor of a public elevator.

His poetic communique, on the wall of the elevator, read:

> Moving to another country hurts more than moving to another house, another face, another lover. . . . In one way or another we all are or will be immigrants. Surely one day we will be able to crack this shell open, this unbearable loneliness, and develop a transcontinental identity.

Over the twenty-four hours that Gómez-Peña performed this piece, "many passersby interacted with the cocooned person/object: talking, kicking, poking, confessing, and verbally threatening," and finally security guards picked up his body and dropped him into an industrial trash bin.

Gómez-Peña described *The Loneliness of the Immigrant* as "a metaphor of painful birth into a new country, a new identity . . . and a new language." Metaphor is one mode of opening the space between what is stable and known and what may be possible to imagine.

His piece is deeply rooted in an activist consciousness, but also a poetic-spiritual one—one that calls for expanding beyond what can be totally comprehended, for seeing outside the preconceived possibilities, outside even of our own imagination.

This is what I desperately hope for, that we humans can imagine beyond our current concepts of *self.* That we can find, in ourselves, the capacity to feel how we are akin to not just our immediate family, not just the community of people like us, not just the people in our nation, but to every being on this shared piece of rock and water that supports all our lives. That in a moment of disruption, when everything feels up for grabs, we can somehow come to define ourselves as *more than*, that our identities can expand enough to hold a transformative notion of self.

CHAPTER TWELVE

Black Squares and Summer Storms

June now in the Netherlands, and green has exploded. Foliage looms over sidewalks, paths, and walkways, thick and dark, its fecundity almost menacing. Where there used to be space, air, light, now there is a heavy blanket of green. I have just returned from Iceland, and compared to its barren, wide open spaces and midnight sun, the dark and thick of the vegetation here is overwhelming.

Slugs are everywhere, and a pine marten or hedgehog has chewed the red-and-white gemeente trash bags left outside for today's pickup.

I've been away for weeks of teaching in Naples and Reykjavik, and come home to several days of rain: the deep, geometrically angular ridges of the ploughed fields are filled with water, the bike paths and neighborhood streets flooded with the fine silt of ploughed fields.

Today, though the sky is heavy and gray with it still, we've been granted a respite from the rain that yesterday was incessant, soaking me multiple times: walking the dog, taking out the recycling, going to the store.

I hold J'Lyn Chapman's new little book, *Beastlife*, in my hands, and already the words lining the pages feel electric to me. Living in Europe, I rarely get the physical weight and page of new English-language, small press books in my hands. And Chapman's book, as it unfurls its pages and the words trip and tilt in the dust mote haze of afternoon sun, proves the perfect complement to the heavy summer fields as they drape this Dutch landscape: golden where the wheat has already matured, green where the small shoots of corn are only just beginning. The muscularity of the ruddy horses as they sprint, nuzzle, wrestle in the fields across from me. The clouds of blackbirds that swirl up at twilight, swell, and narrow and tunnel across the sky. But this book, I find as I begin reading, is also the decaying worms, driven by flood to concrete, now feasted on by clustering dark slugs. The humid stench of things dying, rotting, and growing all at once. The swarms of small biting flies hovering at head height, glinting in the sun.

Beastlife is a beautifully designed little book, full of pages with fading traces of graph paper around their edges. On some, the ghost of an image, a spirit, so faint you think you might have imagined it by suggestion of the words above.

It is a sumptuous feast and a rotting: grotesque and greenly lavish all at once, an "oracle of entrails." Full of light, fur, palms, dusk, filament, pond, "the auspices of bones and chalk." Birds everywhere, minnows that are "early moons . . . flashing by my thighs," and a wood floor "soft with moss." This is a world of grasses, green water, ticks and deer and bear and fish and blood. Bones and sky constellations. Dying, seduction, rapacity.

How are we beings in time, mortal bodies in time? this book asks. How do we interact with language and imagination, with the sentence and the word. How do we see the world through light, bended and refracted and distorting. What is story, what is history. How do we find meaning in remembering and attention, in silence and agony, brutality and beauty and desire. In fecund nature, grotesquerie, and wild death.

In one section, "The Good Beast: Five Essays," Chapman turns to the recurrent motifs of wings and flight, the distortions and bending of light and time. She writes of the 1969 Soviet Union film by Andrei Tarkovsky, *Andrei Rublev*, which one film reviewer describes as "at once humble and . . . supremely tactile—the four elements appear as mist, mud, guttering candles, and snow."

The review continues:

> Undirectable creatures animate Tarkovsky's compositions—a cat bounds
> across a corpse-strewn church, wild geese flutter over a savaged city. The
> birch woods are alive with water snakes and crawling ants, the forest
> floor yields a decomposing swan. The soundtrack is filled with bird calls
> and wordless singing; there's always a fire's crackle or a tolling bell in the
> background.

Later, Chapman freezes us in Tarkovsky's slowed moments, a horse that is shot
and falls down a flight of stairs, forcing us to endure the view of a "contorted
beast / pain in the prolongation of a single moment."

"All of this life is the reflective index of a shimmering surface," she writes, and
light bends, refracts, scatters.

Chapman's writing of Tarkovsky makes me think of a moment from earlier in
the spring: in Vienna for a layover, Anna and I went to the Albertina to see an
exhibit of Russian avant-garde painters of the early 1900s.

The exhibit included paintings by Wassily Kandinsky, Kasimir Malevich, and
Marc Chagall, their work done almost entirely between 1910 and 1920, in the
decade before the revolution. They painted not so much in a progression of styles
and schools, as elsewhere in Europe, but messily all at once, tangentially, glancing
off of each other like light on the facets of a stone.

As we walk among the paintings, Anna points at one and says, "He was my great-
grandfather's student." The painting, by Boris Grigoriev, depicts a surreal, circus-
esque scene with a performer in a tux; behind him stands another in red silks,
holding a bow and arrow aloft. Called *Portrait of Vsevolod Meyerhold*, it depicts
a preeminent actor and director in experimental theater who was later executed

in a Stalinist purge. For a moment I am confused, thinking she is speaking of the painter, but she means Meyerhold himself, and I try to imagine that world, so long disappeared: a turn-of-the-century Russian school, a young theater prodigy-to-be, and her great-grandfather as school director.

In this Maastricht June, everything is a shattering of light, a kaleidoscopic green refraction. For days it has continued to rain—pounded, flooded—but finally today the skies are holding in their water. It floats silently above us, congealed into bellied clouds sitting near our heads, staring down, moving slowly. Water is everywhere on the ground. The red-silt mud holds it, the grasses hold it, the fields hold it in stripes. The Jeker, normally a placid little river, is rushing and brown with it.

The tree outside my writing window has long brown strings of pods, fingers drifting in the light wind.

A letter arrives from a friend in the camp in Greece, another volunteer: it was so hard to leave, so much still undone, and how do you decide *I must go now*. When you leave, you rejoin your life as though nothing has changed, but in this other world so many other lives continue along a trajectory you have just been witness to. Witness to the dust and heat and tents and saturating sunlight; the worries and the small children and the many closely held hopes and shreds of weathered cloth.

Today in the UK, there is a wave of pale-faced people claiming nostalgia and return; holding to dreams and imaginations of an older, better time; wishing for a history that is dubious in its purity. These pale voices are gaining strength, and it makes me feel sad, we who should if anything be moving toward a vision of self that includes the man on the other side of this round globe, bicycling with a mattress on the cart behind him; that includes the small silvery fox darting through a narrow field.

Out running on the paths, I saw a small hedgehog dead by the side of the trail, curled in, its tiny eyes shut against the world. Small paws curved across its chest. On its belly, several large flies with green heads strolled an exploratory amble.

Things in Europe are coming apart. On the day I'd initially planned to book my flight from Brussels to Athens, bombs exploded in Zaventem, the Belgian national airport, and in the Maelbeek metro station close to the EU buildings in Brussels. In the photos of the terminal where one of the bombs exploded, all the ceiling panels were on the ground, a layer of dust coating the suitcases left behind when people fled.

Greece is now on lockdown. Médecins sans Frontières is pulling out of the Moria camp in Lesvos, saying it has become more of an internment facility than a voluntary camp. Turkey has traded its way toward European favor by agreeing to a return of refugees. Supposedly, other nations are sending officials to help with the overload of asylum claims in Greece, though they have yet to materialize. In the meantime, boats are still arriving. There are at least seventy thousand migrants frozen in Greece, living in tents in Lesvos, Idomene, Athens, and elsewhere. Some of them are Kurds, who face serious danger if sent back to Turkey without their asylum claims being heard. So many of them are Syrians, who have nowhere to return to.

I read in the news that there is a movement toward better European coordination of cyber intelligence, which has been made difficult by the use of encryption in messaging platforms. As I read this, I think about how those who desperately want to will continue avoiding surveillance through increased technological evasion, leaving only the rest of us to have our data widely harvested. All our privacies, caught up in this undefined, ongoing war.

Bellicose is such a beautiful, rounded word, soft and tripping over the tongue, full against the roof of the mouth. Its sound, such a lie against the meaning it holds.

Second to the intrigue of Anna's familial declaration, the work of Chagall and Malevich captured me most in the exhibit of the Russian avant-garde. Chagall's paintings are all whimsical and colorful romantic surrealism, while Malevich's Cubo-Futurism is stern and shiny. After the revolution, he would proclaim his transition to an absolute nonobjectivity he called Suprematism: a "spiritual process of exposing the essence of the universe." I found it striking that his *essence of the universe* was so very geometric and angular: essentially modern, masculine, and antinature.

In a power struggle with Chagall, Malevich would take all of Chagall's students, sending them fleeing to Moscow. (Kandinsky experienced much the same, deposed from another art institute for his "spiritual outlook" on art.) In 1930, Malevich himself would be jailed under Stalin, the formalism of his work—initially declared the "official art" of revolutionary Russia—now "despised as an expression of degeneration."

But I found that his *Black Circle* and *Black Square*—from his "basic vocabulary of Suprematism," which sought the "zero of form"—reminded me of Rothko, and felt weighty and profound.

In a 1915 exhibition, Malevich hung his *Black Square* in the upper corner of the room, where religion icons are normally hung; according to one article: "The sacred spot where Malevich chose to hang his *Black Square* is known in Russia as 'the beautiful corner' or 'the red corner.' It is the point where the wall meets the ceiling, usually reserved for religious icons."

Like Tarkovsky, whose *Andrei Rublev* is described as "charged with resurgent Slav mysticism," Malevich has often been suspected of mysticism, at least in his later career, and is said to have drawn inspiration from the Orthodox church, which was sidelined and stigmatized after the revolution.

His relationship to the black squares shifted from anarchic—and arguably nihilistic—when he created the first one for the futurist opera *Victory over the Sun*, which ends with the world "in total darkness, symbolizing a destruction of Russian tradition and making way for the future," to a much more spiritual belief that the black square signified the essence of God's image "in the relationship between man and the universe."

And this, after all, is the essence of mysticism itself: the quest for "direct communion with ultimate reality," the belief that "ultimate reality can be attained through subjective experience (such as intuition or insight)."

I have often been drawn to those identified as mystics—from Simone Weil, Teresa de Avila, and Saint Francis of Assisi to Meister Eckhart and Kahlil Gibran and Pierre Teilhard de Chardin to Baal Shem Tov and Rumi and Shams of Tabriz—drawn to their strangeness and their excesses, the purity and clarity of their beliefs.

I am drawn, too, to their idea that the profoundly spiritual can be found steeped into the substance of the world around us, that it is in us, all the time.

The days are rolling into scorching, or at least the northern European version of it. Sun bakes down on us as we walk through the fields, shoulder-high corn offering no shade. Heat prickles on my shoulder blades, trickles down the insides of my elbows.

My dog and I go for a walk in the now lushly vegetated hills, beyond the fields and the windmill that sit beside our home. We pass oats, with their little braided heads, and then corn: still baby plants only shin high, soon they will become towering hedges along the bike path.

Reaching our trail, we turn off into the mud, sliding and slipping as we try to keep our footing. The path up the hill has become a dense tunnel, what was only a ravine in winter. Lush, fecund greenery spills and burrows and braids around us. Fetid air hangs heavy over the trail. The stench of things dying, rotting, and growing all at once. Cobwebs and tiny insects tickle my skin; every lungful of air is so humid and thick it clogs my throat, chokes me. Snails press their small meaty bodies to soil and stone, their shells standing upright above them. It is like walking through a verdant sauna, tangled with foliage and damp with decay. Brambles and nettles overhang the path. The mud is dark and oozing under our feet, with patches of dun-yellow clay.

Climbing upward, we shift suddenly from a hot sauna to a chill one, the air just as moist, but now clammy and cool. The dog pants, and a sheen condenses on my upper lip, my neck, my inner arms. Birdsong sparkles out over us like a net, little clusters everywhere, the sound full and constant.

We traverse and then descend the small ridgeline, emerging into a different field, the sunlight blinding, disorienting, and too hot. We walk through potatoes this time, just beginning to bud into bloom. The dog finds a mud puddle and leaps into it gloriously, joyfully, before I can protest. Biting flies attack any time I stop, so I continue walking, and he runs up behind, shaking muddy water over us both.

In Iceland the birds were white-and-black, some with bright orange beaks, blood orange almost, long and vivid and pointed. They moved against a barren landscape: the green of mud and tides and early spring, or iron-brown cracked expanses that had run in liquid lava and then solidified, where the land had bubbled up in rounds, cracked through as air escaped. Atop it, the yellow-green glow of tundra formed strange lumps, as though the entire barren field were covered with sunning harbor seals, their fur ashimmer in the light.

We ventured one evening into the dark of a lava tube, taller than us in a few places, mostly shorter, in some places belly-crawling small. The ceiling had strange formations, marbled black like raku pottery, in points and cones, or in a huge mawlike chandelier. The air was damp and cool, thick; in one cavern, breath condensed and dust rose to make an impenetrable fog. Everywhere, water trickled, oozed into the sandy floor. In some parts, a fungus grew in ceiling patches that reflected bright silver. In a few places the rocks of the ceiling had shattered, collapsed in piles. When we finally reemerged into the hours-long dusky light, the wind whipped across the lava field and its seal-like lumps of tundra and tried to push us back in, push us over, push us to the rock.

While I was away in Iceland teaching, someone broke into the pharmacy down below our apartment. Anna woke up to the crash of breaking glass, cabinets toppling, and the alarm screaming. Ours was the only residence in a little commercial plaza and shared an adjoining inside door with the pharmacy. She lay still, in bed, wondering whether the intruders would try to come through that door. Then, things went silent, and shortly after, the cops arrived. Our elderly dog slept through the entire thing.

The next day at the gym, Anna finished her workout and popped into the bathroom adjoining the changing room. Upon trying to exit, she found the door would not unlock. The next workout had started and her banging and shouting could not be heard over the loud music and weightlifting plates crashing to the ground. The only window was small, well above her head, and she'd just done an hour of pull-ups and other weight training. Nonetheless, she jumped and pulled and finally saw a pair of high-heeled legs walking nearby. "Hey! You, in high heels!" she shouted. (You can't believe it's actually you saying these things, she told me later. It's so cliché. But there I was.) "Can you go into the gym and tell them someone is locked in the bathroom?" Thankfully, the woman did go in, and a few minutes later Anna was rescued with pliers.

The day after that, Anna and our friend Dasha took the train three hours north to Amsterdam. Dasha, who is from Belarus, had an appointment at the US embassy to request a visa for a summer trip to Minnesota. Anna sat at a nearby café to wait while Dasha went in. The security was like security in US airports: long, stringent, intimidating, and not overly informative. Reaching the head of the line, Dasha was told she could not have a cell phone with her, so she sprinted two blocks to the café where Anna sat, depositing her cell phone into Anna's hands. Returning to the embassy, she had to wait in the long line all over again. About halfway through, Dasha, an avid geocacher, realized she also had her GPS in her bag. Despairing, she raced back out of the embassy. Other people in line had told her they'd been forced to make another appointment and come back again because they'd initially come with phones or other gadgets. They told her, *just stash it somewhere outside*. So Dasha ran down the block, beyond the embassy building, and tossed the GPS into the grass behind a bike rack. When she returned, security all but assaulted her. They'd seen her on the cameras, they told her. They took her passport, her papers. They interrogated her for more than an hour. What was she plotting? Who was she working with? "I have never been so terrified in my whole life," Dasha said later. "I really thought I was never going to leave that building again." Finally, they let her go through to the offices inside, where she collapsed in tears before going to her appointment. Her application, after all that, was approved with two quick stamps, and she was back outside again in minutes. Her GPS was still tucked there in the bushes.

All of our privacies, caught up in the formalities of borders and intelligence. A bellicosity of bureaucracy, an onslaught.

In contrast to Iceland, in Maastricht the birds are almost all blackbirds, little eyes rimmed in yellow, beaks sharp and yellow against the sky. They move in tornadoes over the fields, wheeling and swerving and dipping in one body, like ink when it is poured into water.

We have entered into July, and everywhere ticks, beetles, slugs proliferate. Clouds of gnats, swarms of flies hang in the air, illuminated golden by the setting sun. The tips of the corn stalks are turning crimson. The potatoes are flowering. The wheat, even more golden.

The burros down the street are as clumpy and sideburned as ever, but munch happily on the green rather than standing miserably in cold rain. Snails haul their bodies along the sidewalk. The air itself is tinged with green, pregnant with moisture, building up into big bodies of cloud, looming sky high. Finally, it has not rained in days and the mud on the paths is almost dry. Nettles overhang all the paths, stinging any unwarily bared skin. The green is neon, it is electric, it is surging. It waves, vibrates, sways in the breeze. It pulsates and hums.

It is a physical world full of—pregnant with, humming with—possibility, potential, life. And at the same time, with rotting, excess, and death. A paradox of the sacred and the profane, of multiplicity and constant change.

What does it mean, really, to be so many different people in a lifetime? How do we know who we are, where we stand? *My actions are my only true belonging*s. I feel defined by questions these days, where once there were certainties. Nothing frenetic, broken, and yet neither is anything certain.

I want to bury myself in the voices that acknowledge this uncertainty, this complexity, this shifting.

This morning, I passed the body of a bird dead in the grasses, crawling with worms, swelling and alive with motion. The thick, gray quills of its feathers stood up askew, like the many picas stuck into the side of a fighting bull, or like the shifting quills of a porcupine as it climbs. One feather moved back and forth, waving at the sky, as something burrowed at its base.

I thought of the Buddhist training I did the previous fall, which included contemplating the decomposition of a corpse, those many stages of heat and life and swell and bloat. I thought about my dog, whose aging pains me so much right now, and imagined his body, also lying in the grasses, patches of blond fur matted and interspersed with feasting worms. I thought about my father, who has reached that age where I frequently hear of celebrity deaths on the news and realize they were the same age or younger than he is; I thought that his body, too, will one day be vacated, returned to earth and its processes of decomposition. This itself does not bother me; it is the loss that we are—I am—terrified of. The grief of losing, of that permanent absence. Can I, I thought, pour all the energy of that would-be grief into loving them now?

The children are out of school for the summer and travel in rowdy, indifferent packs on the bike paths, yelling and laughing as they ride. Swerving is a necessary adaptation.

Everywhere, people walking small dogs and small children. Garden parties and sidewalk cafés.

Europe is on holiday, and no one wants to think about the thousands of refugees sweltering in primitive camps across the continent. The situation has shifted again, this time to invisibility. If you put people away into camps and stop showing images of boats crashing on rocky shores, it is easy to forget about all those lives stagnating, unseen, in the summer heat.

Europe's deal with Turkey—to return refugees to that country—carries on, despite Turkey's own spiral downward into repression. The current of boats has shifted paths, but still they come, despite increasing border checks, despite the agreement with Turkey, despite everything. They come to the shores of Italy now, and Spain, longer and more dangerous routes, but still the boats come.

A young man from Afghanistan has taken an ax and drawn blood on a train in Germany. Two weeks ago, a man in France ploughed a large truck through a holiday crowd in Nice, killing many people. In the US, a man shot up a nightclub full of revelers, more Black men have been killed by police, and several police have been killed in retaliation. The escalation in this moment, on both continents, feels spiraling, violent, out of control. The language of hatred builds like the massive wall of a summer storm, gray and dark and terrifying.

In the meantime, political parties riding an anti-immigrant wave tap into people's fear and gain momentum all over Europe, from Marine Le Pen to Geert Wilders to Norbert Hofer to Nigel Farage—and elsewhere, with Rodrigo Duterte, Jair Bolsonaro, Narendra Modi. In the US, our own candidate for hate spews anti-immigrant rhetoric along the campaign trail.

For a few days, as the news circles around the actions of this Afghan teen—a refugee, an unaccompanied minor—and his bloody rampage on a train, the sorrow of hearing it sits heavy in my chest. I think of all the Afghan people in Malakasa, their hope worn thin and tattered. Each time one angry, violent person commits an action like this, a tally is added to the accounts of every person in that camp, in all the camps across Greece, and all the camps that stretch out in a fractured network through Turkey, Lebanon, Jordan, and onward.

Tonight, a long column of crows floated across the sky, a loosely sketched line of birds riding some evening current, their wings still as they glided, piecemeal, against that faded blue. Below them, the fields glowed in the evening light, as gold as any Van Gogh. The spiny arms of the windmill reached up toward night that was sinking down the hill, and at the windmill's foot the corn brushed its tasseled heads in a slight stir of breeze.

The blackbirds rode a long, dispersed column across the sky, a flock stretched out and gliding over miles. They rode an invisible river of air toward the setting sun, as though streaming west in some ancient ritual of the sun god: dark birds floating against a paling sky.

Our days in Maastricht are drawing to a close. We've packed boxes and boxes and boxes in the July heat, temperatures reaching ninety-five degrees in our little apartment with no air conditioning and lots of sunlight. The boxes are gone now, our home stripped down to a skeleton of furniture and clothing. The fields are so green and the air so heavy with summer. Everywhere, the nettles, ants, flies, grasses of summer.

CHAPTER THIRTEEN

Radical Hope

Hope locates itself in the premises that
we don't know what will happen and that in the
spaciousness of uncertainty is room to act.
—Rebecca Solnit

Two years after we left the Netherlands, I found myself leading a trip to Yellowstone in November. I'd never been to the park at that time of year. Unlike the summer months when it is crammed with people, the park was nearly empty, and the early winter cold drives wildlife down to lower terrain where they can more easily be spotted.

At Yellowstone I learned many things. That, for instance, while the earth's crust is in most places around forty miles thick—forty miles down until you get to the plasticky, warmed earth we call the mantle—in Yellowstone there are spots where it is only three to five miles thick.

That you can trace the boundaries of the basalt flow from Yellowstone's giant volcano, which erupted 640,000 years ago , by tracing the waterfalls around the park; where the hard basalt cap ends, the water has eroded the sedimentary rock, creating huge waterfalls.

That when Yellowstone's volcano last erupted, eight feet of ash fell across all the American west, from Arizona and California up to the border with Canada.

I learned that pronghorn antelope are not true antelope, but most closely related to giraffes. That they are not adapted to snow and migrate from Yellowstone to lower lands near Livingston in the winter or down to Green River, Utah.

That elks' seasonal movement is called surfing the green wave; they follow their summer grazing upward as new green growth emerges, because that first month of growth is when the plants offer the most nutrients.

I learned that grizzlies are picky about their hibernation dens; they pick north-facing, forty-degree slopes at about 7,000–8,000 feet of elevation and then dig in fifteen feet, lining the den with moss and detritus. That mama bears give birth in their dens and don't even fully wake up while the young are being born.

I learned that osprey from Yellowstone travel as far as Cuba and Guatemala in their winter migration. That magpies have been observed having "social" funerals, mourning the death of one of their own. That some of the Rocky Mountain junipers in the park are more than a thousand years old.

And that the very existence of wolves and their impact on the ecosystem changes the course of rivers, making them less erosive and richer habitats for trout and beavers and myriad other species.

I learned, too, that Yellowstone has outcroppings of "basement rock," the foundation of the continent itself and some of the oldest rock on the planet.

In *Trace*, Lauret Savoy writes:

> Sand and stone are Earth's memory. . . . Stanley Kunitz wrote in his poem "The Testing-Tree" that "the heart breaks and breaks and lives by breaking." At a young age I began to hope that despite wounds a sense

of wholeness could endure. That each of us possesses a *hardness*—not harshness, not severity, but the quality of stone or sand to retain some core though broken again and again.

The starkness and purity of the Yellowstone landscape—no power lines or human habitations in sight, just us and this stretching land and the musky scent of bison nearby—possesses that same kind of *hardness*, in which I find my own sense of wholeness.

It makes me think of a book a friend described to me, about the romanticization of austere northern landscapes and the European-colonialist fear of the southern, the fecund and the humid, the tropical, the dark and wet of the rainforest (and the female), the global South, the polytheist, the nonwhite, nonlinear, many-godded, many-tongued South.

I love this northern landscape, though, love it deeply and bracingly and starkly, and whenever I am here I feel a longing for something I cannot name, for life itself perhaps, or for a life lived outdoors in constant contact with the air and the ground and the skies, in motion instead of seated.

Each news story and observation of this landscape's destruction evokes Savoy's words: the heart breaks and breaks and breaks again, a devastation that is almost unspeakable. Despite wounds, this place offers a sense of wholeness, a sense of enduring.

I remember a John Rybicki passage I read once, in which he says: "I tell all my writing students that 'You're holy-men and women in the making. Sing for the broke-down rest of us who feel profoundly but can't express it.' The best writing is summoned out of those two extremes of wonder and wound."

And Dan Beachy-Quick writes that "we read the poem to keep our wounds open, to refuse to let the damage diminish, to betray our own need of order with a continually renewed capacity for disorder. To let the world in."

Walking through the yellow grasses and light snow of Yellowstone, the wind bit into my legs, and thinking about words like *orogeny* and *geothermal* called to mind N. K. Jemisin's Broken Earth trilogy, made me think of geologic time, of the multiple mass extinctions that have come before, of the earth covered with sea and then covered with ice and then covered with sea again. In some perhaps twisted way, that relieves my deep grief just a little, to think of that kind of scale of time, to think that change is constant, to think that the complex web, this paradise of earth that we've destroyed, corrupted, consumed, and killed wouldn't have gone on forever unchanged, even without the locust plague of humans devouring it.

The time span of geologic change makes it easier to bear the thought of climate devastation now. The morning we left for this trip, I read of a report finding that we've lost 30 percent of all of Earth's wildlife, mostly in recent decades, and it had me so heavy with grief that it felt hard to keep moving. But in geologic terms, all is constant change: this landscape was sea once, then all ice—Yellowstone was covered by a 2,000–4,000-foot-thick glacier at one point. From dust we come and to dust we shall return—and apparently, if you think in geological time, that applies not only to our individual lives but to all life, or at least all life as we know it now.

It doesn't have to be this way, at least in our lifespans: we can still change it, I believe; if enough collective action manifests quickly and powerfully enough, we can still keep this lush verdancy, this paradise we know as today's Earth. But still, there is some consolation in knowing a kind of duration exists, even outside of the existence of humans and polar bears and blue whales and glaciers.

At COP 21, the UN Climate Change Conference held in Paris in 2015, twelve large chunks of ice, "harvested from free-floating icebergs in a fjord [in] Greenland, were arranged in clock formation to melt symbolically on the Place du Panthéon. . . . [They were] eerie, beautiful, terrifying. A visceral and powerful reminder of why [this work] is so desperately important," wrote one attendee.

My friend Kimi, a writer and dancer, was there for the conference, which took place during an unusually warm December in Paris. In a video she shared of the Place du Panthéon at night, Kimi dances with one of the pieces of ice, still taller than she is, but visibly smoothed by the melt of day. It is a spectral, otherworldly white against the cobbled dark of the cityscape. She bends toward it, and then away, her black clothing in sharp contrast to the ghostly ice as she spins, glides, and stretches around it. Behind them, the stone plaza shines with water, lit by quaint streetlamps against the tall façade of old buildings.

In an interview from around that time, professor of glaciology Jason Box describes being stunned, on a visit to the ice in Greenland, to see the ice sheet's darkening, caused by microbial blooms and the soot from wildfires burning more and more frequently in Greenland. Darkened glaciers absorb more solar heat and thus melt faster. "The glacier is decanting," he says.

Box speaks of his crowdfunded study, the Dark Snow Project, which has found a continued increase in melt related to the darkening glaciers.

The photos I find after hearing this are staggering: the glacier is a flat, cracked expanse, like a giant mud field that has dried in baking sun. It looks like a drought-stricken desert landscape.

Each morning I sit and practice a kind of meditation that is focused on compassion, an articulation of intention. This is the kind of meditation, researchers have found, that grows the muscles of the brain, the kind that increases our capacity to care for one another. It is a profound act of hope to say these words each morning, knowing they are impossible, knowing they can never be true. And yet wanting them to be, more than I want anything else in my entire life.

May all beings, everywhere, be happy.
May all beings be safe from harm.

This is, of course, an immense exercise in paradox. Even as I sit and offer these wishes, I am deeply, profoundly aware of the vast gap between what I am wishing for the planet and the reality of bloody warfare, child abuse, domestic violence, abuse and cruelty toward animals, destruction of natural spaces, and myriad other meannesses taking place around the world, even in the moment I am wishing them away.

But, like setting good intentions and promising to hold to them despite knowing that one will certainly break them in various ways, this practice of offering compassion to all beings is one of immense softening, toward oneself and toward others. It grows kindness, despite its seeming like the equivalent of trying to move all the grains of sand one by one, as the fairy tales go.

It must be acknowledged, though, that *kindness* on its own is not enough. Contrary to the yard signs that have become so popular in the US, kindness is not everything, just as heartbreak without action is mostly sentimentality.

In her 2003 book, *Regarding the Pain of Others*, Susan Sontag describes compassion as an unstable emotion. "It needs to be translated into action," she writes, "or it withers."

Political and structural change is bigger and more important than individual acts of kindness in terms of actually offering any sort of concrete, tangible kindness to the other beings of this world. If we want change, want to work toward this sort of *systemic kindness*, it involves not just interpersonal work but also systems change—to prevent cataclysmic climate change, but also to create societies that are in any way more just. Even if that change is not going to last forever, even if this struggle to create more just societies is always tentative, always an act of *balancing* rather than ever finding a solid, static place of *balance*.

"You can't avoid the struggle," says my handwriting on one scrap of paper I find tucked among my notes, "but to be engaged in a meaningful struggle, versus a meaningless one—there's no comparison." I have no idea whose words they are, or where they came from, but I am grateful to find them there.

They make me think of a recent article I read about the artist Cannupa Hanska Luger's work at Standing Rock, in North Dakota. I'd known his work already, been enamored with an exhibit I'd seen at the Museum of Contemporary Native Arts in Santa Fe when I lived in New Mexico, and the article had caught my eye.

"The media's general interest is in 'struggle porn,' so people have missed what is beautiful" about the communal gathering to protest, says Luger.

"When you first arrive [at Standing Rock]," he recounts, "your first interaction is being included, which is not something that people are used to in this country. . . . [For] everyone who has interacted with the space, there is something transformative that has happened." Those who came were "hoping to experience something new, something profound. But when they got there, they realized they're not a part of something new, they've just been absorbed into something that is much older than the entire country. That's incredibly humbling."

Luger explains: "Our original bible . . . is the land. . . . Where everyone else sees a pipeline and 'progress,' what we see is someone going through our bible and editing things without any care, ripping a line straight through that story."

Luger made a set of mirrored shields for those protesting at Standing Rock to use in self-defense. "I was inspired by these activists in the Ukraine," he says. "These women—old women and children—came out and carried mirrors from their bathrooms and into the street to show these riot policemen what they looked like. From the photos I saw, it seemed profoundly effective."

But at Standing Rock, hired guards and police were already hitting people with hoses. "I didn't want people to bring mirrors to the front line and get hit with batons and cause more damage than good." So he came up with a design for simple, inexpensive mirrored shields, of which six hundred were eventually made by him and others.

The photograph accompanying the article is beautiful: stretching hills, yellow with wintry grasses, that look just like Yellowstone in November. A thin dusting of scattered snow in the grasses, heavier against the base of the hill. Stretched across the foreground of the photo, in the gold-crimson of late day sun, sixty or more tall, mirrored shields are being held up, reflecting the landscape before them, the long orange skirts or tan boots of the people holding them showing beneath. In the background, the winter sky goes from turquoise to purple. A few trees, their arms bare, are just visible in the background.

Asked about the role of artists in protest, Luger reflects:

> Artists, we live on the periphery. But we are the mirrors. We are the reflective points that break through a barrier. You don't have to be in the same economic place that I am to relate to the work that I make. That is the power of art.

> We are not rich people. But we are incredibly wealthy. We have ideas.

Another image accompanying the article shows a single mirrored shield held aloft. It reflects a blurred, dreamlike image of what lies before it: sandwiched in between yellow grasses and the stretching gray-white sky is a row of black-clad riot cops, faces obscured by helmets, indistinct weapons held aloft.

In days spent hiking through a wintry Yellowstone, I am reminded that there is a different kind of violence—the violence of necessity that also is a part of nature, the interconnected web of survival that forms a chain of dependency, one species dependent on and hunting another, wolves on elk and deer, coyote and fox on mice and voles, grizzlies on fish and elk. And the brutality and harshness of winter, the desperation that can come late into it, that is simply a part of living in the natural world. There is a kind of everyday violence many of us are inured to, protected from in this modern consumer society, and this is one aspect of that violence: the beauty but also the harshness of the natural world, the simple violence of survival in an interconnected net. So there is a way in which violence is simply part of the fabric—a part we struggle to comprehend, to reconcile with, often—the elk calf taken down by a grizzly, the lone moose starving to death, the wolf attacked and killed by members of another pack.

We held the cured pelt of a young wolf who had died years earlier of unknown causes, with a partly healed injury to his front leg. His fur was so long and so soft, a mixture of gray and black, his long front claws indicating he hadn't been moving well for several months.

We looked at the skull of another wolf, a male who had left his pack, who even with a fully cracked lower jaw took down a bull elk and fought off an entire other pack to defend a carcass, his much-needed winter food.

I heard an episode of *On Being* recently that featured Kate Braestrup, who serves as chaplain for the game warden service in the state of Maine, where I grew up.

At one point, Braestrup comments: "One thing the Buddhists say, or the Tibetan Buddhists, anyway, is that you prepare your whole life for your death. . . . We are all practicing all the time for the test, and we don't know what the test is going to be. And I encounter people at those moments when all of a sudden here it is. . . . You don't choose. You just be whatever it is you've been."

Later in the interview Braestrup muses:

> A continuous argument I have with Christianity . . . is I always felt that it
> was answering a question I wasn't asking. . . . If you decide that the most
> important thing, . . . the highest possible value is life, that it's breath in the
> body and walking around and eating sandwiches and whatever, then you're
> lost. Then you've lost . . . because we're all going to die. . . .
>
> If I posit instead that the most important thing is love, then . . . yes, I have
> a world that's full of suffering and evil and pain, and I have something to
> do. I have something to look for. . . . You and I are willing to risk our lives
> just, you know, to get to the grocery store two minutes faster. So . . . don't
> tell me that human beings value life that highly. We really don't. . . . But
> we definitely value our connection to each other. And that, I think, we are
> less likely to risk.

Braestrup also talks about the devastating loss of her husband, Drew, a state
trooper killed in a car accident:

> A big part of that first day, [of what I understood from Drew's death,] was
> not just I've lost Drew, but I've lost Drew and here come all these people
> who are going to hold me. And that was . . . just astonishing to me and—
> and beautiful. . . .
>
> The most traumatic thing is not suffering; it's suffering alone.

One of the naturalists we spent time with at Yellowstone, a man named Owen,
told us the story of a bison calf that had died near a research station, where rangers had been able to observe what occurred after its death. Its mother, he told us,
remained by its body for two days. The rest of the herd stayed nearby, moving up
the hillside across the valley. When, on the second day, a grizzly bear came and
started sniffing around the calf's body, the mother moved away—but then, as
rangers watched, she brought the entire bison herd charging down the hillside to
drive the grizzly bear away from the little calf's body.

After that, every single member of the herd walked by the calf, one by one, and nudged it with their noses.

Being asked to live with the unthinkable, it seems, is just the basic core of what it means to be human (and perhaps that also extends beyond the human realm more than we know, as we might intuit from the story of the bison). It is both unremarkable and unthinkable at once; it is the central paradox, at once mundane and profound, of our existence.

How do you live with the unthinkable, the unbearable, and still keep *living*? Still keep feeling, still keep moving with intention and energy into the circumstances of your life?

This is the paradox Barry Lopez describes in *Arctic Dreams*, this challenge of living not only with questions that are unanswerable but with realities that are excruciatingly unjust, unbearable:

> No culture has yet solved the dilemma each has faced with the growth of a conscious mind: how to live a moral and compassionate existence when one is fully aware of the blood, the horror inherent in all life, when one finds darkness not only in one's own culture but within oneself. If there is a stage at which an individual life becomes truly adult, it must be when one grasps the irony in its unfolding and accepts responsibility for a life lived in the midst of such paradox. . . . There are simply no answers to some of the great pressing questions. You continue to live them out, making your life a worthy expression of leaning into the light.

This writing project has, in the end, been a kind of quest, a grappling with the things I myself am grappling with, spiritually and ontologically, with exactly what Barry Lopez describes—the question of how to come to terms with the darkness in both my society and myself.

How to come to terms with my own fears, but also my laziness, my desire to lead a comfortable, creative life without the despair and exhaustion and frustration of activism and activist losses, of the grief of loss. How to come to terms with my ongoing impulse to put the discomfort of cognitive dissonance to the side, to hold on to my own amnesia and innocence about the role of my country in the world. To think about my whiteness, but not all the time, not when it's most uncomfortable.

And, again and again, how to grapple with my own growing sense of aging, of mortality, of the complexity and paradoxes and bafflement of human existence, of life itself—its grotesqueries and brutalities as well as its exhilarations; its longings, sometimes overpowering.

At a recent training for educators, a woman who is also a minister said that all her teaching about world religions and spirituality revolves around asking these three questions: Who am I? What do I believe? How will I live?

I set out wanting to explore human violence, trying to understand its hows, its whys. But I found that I couldn't understand it, even after researching for years, that it is baffling and bewildering and brutal and filled with agony.

And what I came to in the end was not here's what we understand about violence and how to end it but rather here's what we can focus on doing instead. Here's what we can train our brains to do instead, through repeated acts of contemplation and compassion. Here is what some people, faced with immense violence and brutality, and against all odds, chose instead. Here is some light, breaking across the darkened sky.

None of that offers any reassurance that there won't be massive human outbreaks of violence in the present, in the future, or that any one of us—or all of us—won't be subject to them. Thinking of the threat of such violence, what I ultimately found gave me some measure of peace was looking to the natural world, to the way the Yellowstone landscape and ecosystem have been carved, shaped, changed over the millennia. And also to the dynamics in the packs of wolves that have been reintroduced there, a reminder that life is very often hard and brutal and violent, for all creatures, that it's not just humans that evidence this type of behavior. I don't know why that makes it more bearable for me, but it does.

And so, ultimately, maybe this whole quest is about needing to find that measure of hope. To refind, rebuild it, which is an active process requiring certain breakthroughs. And, I think now, to find, cultivate, and keep hope is an ongoing, lifelong process, probably involving many losses and rekindlings.

Carmen Maria Machado writes in her recent book, *In the Dream House*: "That there's a real ending to anything is, I'm pretty sure, the lie of all autobiographical writing. You have to choose to stop somewhere. You have to let the reader go."

Part of me fears to end the book in Yellowstone, with its wild, harsh, enduring landscape as a source of hope and consolation for this profound grief; worries that to end with the scale of geologic time too easily lends itself to a sense of nihilism in the present moment, which is not at all what I am advocating.

In "Kabbalah and the Inner Life of God," Lawrence Kushner defines a mystic thus: "A mystic is anyone who has the gnawing suspicion that the apparent discord, brokenness, contradictions, and discontinuities that assault us every day might conceal a hidden unity."

Pierre Teilhard de Chardin, whom the Catholic church prohibited from publishing his philosophical writings while he was still alive, believed in this singularity, this unity. He believed that our knowledge wrapped the earth, an innervated layer almost: a skin.

And in the documentary film *Cage on Cage*, John Cage speaks of his belief that for our survival we will need to become a *we* instead of billions and billions of *I*'s.

Across the screen of the film, an entire flock of birds, thousands of small black birds, swirling and turning back on themselves, swelling and curving like a crescent of ink dropped into water, expanding and curling in on themselves. Taking up the whole sky. A *we* instead of thousands separate. Voices like a throat full of joy, and deep.

Cage is speaking in the shadow of the Cold War. Today we stand beneath a different shadow but still in the shade.

In "The Empathic Civilization," social theorist Jeremy Rifkin talks about the extension of human empathy over time. "If we have gone from empathy in blood ties to empathy in religious associational ties to empathy based on national identification, is it really a big stretch to imagine the new technologies allowing us to connect our empathy to the human race writ large in a single biosphere?" he asks. "And what reason would we stop here at the nation-state identity and only have ideological empathy?" After so many years of living and spending time abroad, of meeting people and building friendships and trying to truly understand deeper aspects of cultural difference, I find the idea of patriotism—some kind of claiming that the people of one nation-state are better, more deserving of care or loyalty than the people of another nation-state—bewildering.

I think back to Suzy Hansen's book, which begins with her early exposure to James Baldwin's statement that "Americans have no sense of 'tragedy,'" and her incomprehension of his assertion that it was only the power of love that could overcome "white people's absence of tragedy and fear of death and irredeemable 'innocence.'"

And yet, she finally concludes:

It is not until one contemplates loving someone, caring about that person's physical and emotional well-being, wanting that person to thrive, wanting to protect that person, and most of all wanting to understand that person, that we can imagine what it would feel like if that person was hurt. . . . Only if that person's suffering becomes your suffering—which in a sense is what love is—and only when white Americans begin to look upon another people's destruction as they would their own, will they finally feel the levels of rational and irrational rage terrifying enough to vanquish a century of their own indifference.

The need is pressing for us to extend our neurologically wired empathy to include the whole world. If we are going to survive, we have to actually expand. Become more than we are, more than we have ever been. Birds flowing through the sky in one body.

Is it possible? I don't know. I only know that it's imperative. And it feels hopeful to even say that there's a way forward.

Of the idea of *radical hope*, the philosopher Jonathan Lear writes, "What makes this hope *radical* is that it is directed toward a future goodness that transcends the current ability to understand what it is."

Radical hope is a paradoxical hope, and in the words of John Paul Lederach, "A paradox suggests that truth lies in but also beyond what is initially perceived." A paradox is a gift, one that "holds together seemingly contradictory truths in order to locate a greater truth."

Paradoxical hope is rooted in our ability to act at the same time as it grows out of a clear-eyed gaze about what is. It is, to borrow from Lederach's description of the moral imagination, "the fundamental belief in and pursuit of the creative act . . . [even] in the lands of violence."

It is the role of the artist, Lederach argues, to continually imagine the many possible futures, outside and beyond the single narrative that power structures suggest is the inevitable one. This requires, according to him, a profound belief that the creative imagination is always accessible to us, "even in settings where violence dominates and . . . creates its greatest lie: that the lands it inhabits are barren. Artists shatter this lie, for they live in barrenness as if new life, birth, is always possible."

Artists and mystics—the visionaries of our society, of a unity which, it would seem, we must find our way into before we destroy ourselves—these are where I put my hope, for it is their visions that keep hope alive. And the natural world— the stark, wintry plains of Yellowstone meadows, herds of bison grazing placidly, each one larger than a small car—is where I find my consolation.

The rabbi Jonathan Sacks says: "I think God is setting us a big challenge. A really big challenge. We are living so close to difference with such powers of destruction that he's really giving us very little choice. To quote that great line from W. H. Auden, 'We must love one another or die.'"

It is a risk, to hold on to hope—for any of us, on the journey of human existence— and the risk feels especially salient and pressing in this moment, though perhaps that is a human delusion, to always believe our time is the most precarious.

"To risk is to step into the unknown without any guarantee of success or even safety," Lederach tells us, and Braestrup adds: "The question isn't whether we're going to have to do hard, awful things, because we are. We all are. The question is whether we have to do them alone."

As I write these words on our return from the journey to Yellowstone, we are surrounded by the paintbrushed white and red sandstone of Paria Canyon in

Utah. It is dark. Across the wash, the students laugh as they make dinner, and someone plays the guitar. Beside me stands an uneven red stone pillar, no taller than me, with a perfect round hole in the top of it, a tiny window. Far down the canyon, there are a few yips by coyotes, barely discernible over the other noise. A sharp, white quarter moon hangs in the inky sky above and beside it, the seven sparks of the Pleiades.

NOTES

Prologue

xiii | "growing up in a dominator culture . . . educated toward a complete innocence of that empire's excesses and indifferences and violences": Suzy Hansen's *Notes on a Foreign Country: An American Abroad in a Post-American World* (New York: Farrar, Straus and Giroux, 2018) offers compelling examples of this phenomenon.

xiv | *The personal voice has persisted*: Ann Cvetkovich, introduction to *Depression: A Public Feeling* (Durham: Duke University Press, 2012), 9.

xv | *How connected we are with everyone*: Juliana Spahr, *This Connection of Everyone with Lungs: Poems* (Berkeley: University of California Press, 2005), 8–9.

Chapter One

1 | "the story of Joseph Schmidt—a world-famous Jewish tenor": Geoffrey Shisler, "Joseph Schmidt," Music and the Holocaust, http://holocaustmusic.ort.org/places/camps/josef-schmidt/.

2 | "Some of the arguments used in Germany at that time against people with AIDS": Raimund Hoghe and Bonnie Marranca, "Dancing the Sublime," *PAJ: A Journal of Performance and Art* 32, no. 2 (2010): 24–37, 25.

2 | *We could hear the awful thump*: Angelique Chrisafis, Sofia Fischer, and Mark Rice-Oxley, "France Stunned after Truck Attacker Kills 84 on Bastille Day in Nice," *Guardian*, July 15, 2016.

5 | "Linyekula arranges two lines of small, round stones": Deborah Jowitt, "Raimund Hoghe, Faustin Linyekula, and the New York City Ballet Help Open the Season," *Village Voice,* September 22, 2010.

5 | "Hoghe tells the story of coming to the US": "Raimund Hoghe interview, Dance Umbrella 2010," Vimeo.com.

7 | *When I display my own hunchbacked body*: Program notes for *Sans-Titre—A Piece for Faustin Linyekula*, Kaaitheater, January 2011.

7 | *With me, you have this break*: Hoghe in "Dancing the Sublime," 37.

8 | *Pier Paolo Pasolini wrote*: "Raimund Hoghe" (English), raimundhoghe.com.

Chapter Two

16 | *We are sitting motionless at either end of a rectangular table*: Marina Abramović, quoted in Klaus Biesenbach, *Marina Abramović: The Artist Is Present* (New York: Museum of Modern Art, 2010), 138.

16 | *Then we had an almost physical fight*: Ibid., 14.

17 | *I am the object*: Ibid., 74.

18 | *Human beings are always afraid of very simple things*: "Marina Abramović: An Art Made of Trust, Vulnerability, and Connection," TED.com, March 2015.

18 | "the last divided capital": See, for instance, Helena Smith, "In Nicosia, The World's Last Divided Capital, A Spirit of Reconciliation Is Stirring across the Fence," *Guardian*, January 14, 2017.

19 | "the Turkish Cypriot minority and Greek Cypriot majority": When the Ottoman empire had control of Cyprus centuries before, Muslims were taxed less than Christians, which compelled a number of Cypriots, largely those who were poorest in the country, to convert—but in many ways, they were of the same people, much like the former Yugoslavia, where ethnic differences between Serbs and Bosnians were amplified and often invented by those provoking the conflict.

27 | *No . . . not yet, and probably not for a long time*: Susan Sontag, quoted in Edward Hirsch, "Susan Sontag, The Art of Fiction No. 143," *Paris Review*, no. 137 (Winter 1995).

28 | *imagining ourselves in a web of relationships*: John Paul Lederach, *The Moral Imagination: The Art and Soul of Building Peace* (Oxford: Oxford University Press, 2005), 5.

28 | *each meeting with each different armed group required careful preparation*: Ibid., 16.

29 | *rooted in the challenges of the real world*: Ibid., 29.

Chapter Three

33 | "the Stasi even kept 'data' of people's scents": Hubertus Knabe, "The Dark Secrets of a Surveillance State," TED.com, June 2014.

33 | "One psychologist outlines four conditions": Sudhir Kakar, *The Colors of Violence* (Chicago: University of Chicago Press, 1996), 35.

33 | *One of my teachers at Columbia was Joseph Brodsky*: "Marie Howe, "The Power of Words to Save Us," *On Being*, May 4, 2017; original air date, April 25, 2013.

34 | *The war began with words, but none of us paid any attention*: Chris Hedges, *War Is a Force That Gives Us Meaning* (New York: Public Affairs/Hachette, 2014), 110.

34 | "the current atmosphere in Hungary": Shaun Walker, "Hungary: Pithy Insults Fly as Anti-Orban Protesters Resort to Ridicule," *Guardian*, January 20, 2019.

34 | "'filthy rats' and 'inevitable bloodshed,'": Walker, "Hungary."

34–35 | *Since there was, in essence, one shared language . . . The nationalist myths stand*: Chris Hedges, *War Is a Force That Gives Us Meaning* (New York: Public Affairs / Hachette, 2014), 33.

35 | *Bosniak human rights activists, led by Ms Bakira Hasečić*: "Bosniak Women Use Human Shield to Stop Serb Nationalists from Destroying Memorial," Bosnia Genocide blog, December 25, 2013, www.bosniagenocide.wordpress.com. The website is no longer available.

36 | *One of the identifiable factors of a massacre*: Fanny Howe, *The Winter Sun: Notes on a Vocation* (Saint Paul, MN: Graywolf, 2009), 100.

37 | *To one who teaches about civil rights*: Jeanne Theoharis, "My Student, the 'Terrorist,'" *Chronicle of Higher Education*, April 3, 2011.

37 | "Reinhold Niebuhr cautioned": Chris Hedges, "Moral Man and Immoral Society: Rediscovering Reinhold Niebuhr," *On Being*, October 25, 2007; original air date, February 10, 2005.

38 | *When dying regimes collapse, they do so with dizzying speed:* Chris Hedges, *Wages of Rebellion* (New York: Nation Books, 2015), 8.

39 | *That mass killings and genocides recur*: Annie Dillard, *For the Time Being* (New York: Vintage Books, 1999), 58.

39 | *Only the dead have seen the end of war*: George Santayana, "Tipperary," *Soliloquies in England and Later Soliloquies* (New York: Scribner's, 1922), chap. 25.

40 | *Tyrants don't care if you believe them*: Peter Maass, "What Slobodan Milosevic Taught Me about Donald Trump," Intercept, February 7, 2017.

40 | *modern strongmen seek merely to discredit journalism*: David Frum, "How to Build an Autocracy," *Atlantic* (March 2017).

40 | *It was as though I pointed to a black wall*: Maass, "What Slobodan Milosevic Taught Me."

42 | *at least 14,000 people were tortured to death*: Seth Mydans, "Out from behind a Camera at a Khmer Torture House," *New York Times*, October 26, 2007.

42 | *I'm just a photographer; I don't know anything*: Nhem En, quoted in ibid.

42–43 | *Before killing the prisoners, the Khmer Rouge photographed*: "Tuol Sleng: Photographs from Pol Pot's Secret Prison," www.tuolsleng.com.

43 | *What it showed was how context and circumstance*: "The Magic Shop of the Brain," unedited version, *On Being*, February 11, 2016.

44 | "The science shows that when we see another person": Ibid., paraphrasing Doty.

44 | *Or . . . you can do a form of exercise . . . whether our species survives or not*: "The Magic Shop of the Brain."

45 | *Peace is visible already*: Marguerite Duras, *The War*, trans. Barbara Bray (New York: Pantheon, 1986), 47; quoted in Hedges, *War Is a Force*, 60.

45 | *Each generation again responds to war as innocents*: Hedges, *War Is a Force*, 173.

45 | "the American antiwar protest movement": Thich Nhat Hanh, quoted in Christopher S. Queen, *Engaged Buddhism in the West* (Summerville, MA: Wisdom, 2012).

45 | *be engaged, not live for yourself alone*: Jacques Lusseyran, *And There Was Light: The Extraordinary Memoir of a Blind Hero of the French Resistance in World War II*, trans. Elizabeth R. Cameron (Boston: Little, Brown, 1963), 312.

46 | *Never mind how*: Ibid.

46 | *The first of these is that joy does not come from outside*: Ibid.

46 | *If you can form close human attachments to those around you*: Fanny Howe, *The Winter Sun*, 93, commenting on Lusseyran's work.

46 | *Yeah, the time is so bad*: Maria Ohileb, quoted in Joanna Kakissis, "Settled Migrants in Greece Reach Out to Help Newcomers," *Morning Edition*, NPR, August 31, 2015.

46–47 | *Every time we try to identify God*: Martin Sheen, "Spirituality of Imagination," *On Being*, December 16, 2015.

Chapter Four

51 | *What I have been thinking about, lately*: Fanny Howe, "Bewilderment," in *The Wedding Dress* (Berkeley: University of California Press, 2003), 5.

51 | *"That, to echo Marie Howe"*: Marie Howe, "The Gate," in *What the Living Do* (New York: Norton, 1997), 58. Howe writes: "This is what you have been waiting for, he used to say to me. / And I'd say, What? // And he'd say, This—holding up my cheese and mustard sandwich. / And I'd say, What? // And he'd say, This, sort of looking around."

53 | *meticulously re-created the aftermath of a rape*: Maggie Nelson, *The Art of Cruelty* (New York: Norton, 2011), 78.

53 | *a large amount of what appeared to be chunky blood* (and following quotations): Nelson, ibid., 79–80.

53 | *There is a Muslim prayer that says*: Howe, "Bewilderment," in *The Wedding Dress*, 6.

54 | *In order to be bewildered*: Kaveh Akbar in an interview with Thora Siemsen, "Bewilderment Is at the Core of Every Great Poem," Literary Hub, November 3, 2017.

55 | *One definition of the lyric*: Fanny Howe, "Bewilderment," 21.

55 |*The creator meant his light to emanate*: Dillard, *For the Time Being*, 50.

57 | *had the vessel under surveillance*: Christina Sharpe, *In the Wake: On Blackness and Being* (Durham, NC: Duke University Press, 2016), 55.

57 | *Already determined by blood*: Josué Guébo, *Think of Lampedusa* (Lincoln: University of Nebraska Press, 2017), 24.

58 | "I imagine the voices of the dead speaking to": I owe this line in part to Dionne Brand, who writes in *A Map to the Door of No Return* (Toronto: Vintage Canada, 2001), "Black experience in any modern city or town in the Americas is a haunting" (25); in part to Christina Sharpe, who in *In The Wake* describes the way "visual and literary culture evoke and invoke the Middle Passage with such deliberate and reflexive dysgraphic unseeing" and writes, "The haunt of the ship envelops and persists in the contemporary" (60); and also to M. NourbeSe Philip, who on her website describes her book *Zong!* (Toronto: Mercury, 2008) as "hauntological; it is a work of haunting, a wake of sorts, where the spectres of the undead make themselves present. . . . What is the word for bringing bodies back from water? From a 'liquid grave'?"

58 | "There was another ship": "The Left-to-Die Boat," Forensic Architecture, November 29, 2012; see also Sharpe, *In the Wake*, 58.

58 | *the ghosting of transatlantic slavery*: Sharpe, *In the Wake*, 55.

58 | *Who explains this total loss*: Guébo, *Think of Lampedusa*, 4.

59 | *In cataclysmic moments*: Avivah Zornberg, "The Transformation of Pharaoh, Moses, and God," *On Being*, April 21, 2005.

59 | *Do we believe the individual is precious . . . Nothing to it*": Dillard, *For the Time Being*, 59.

60 | *As if each corpse in this Mediterranean*: Guébo, *Think of Lampedusa*, 46.

60 | *cannot be mourned*: Judith Butler, "Precariousness and Grievability—When Is Life Grievable?," blog, Versobooks.com, November 16, 2015.

61 | *The differential distribution . . . publicly display and avow the loss*: Ibid.

61 | *Precariousness . . . implies living socially*: Ibid.

62 | *For us, there is only the trying . . . The rest is not our business*: T. S. Eliot, "East Coker," *The Four Quartets* (New York: Harcourt, Brace, 1943), 31.

Chapter Five

64 | *The people are being reduced to blood and dust*: Mohammad Ehsan Osmani, quoted in Emma Graham Harrison, "Inside the Kunduz Hospital Attack: 'It Was a Scene of Night-marish Horror,'" *Guardian,* April 10, 2016.

65 | "news emerged of erroneous military intelligence": Ken Dilanian, "AP NewsBreak: US Analysts Knew Afghan Site Was Hospital," AP News, October 15, 2015.

65 | *Our main question is*: Jason Cone, quoted in "Rejecting U.S. Claims, MSF Details Horrific Bombing of Afghan Hospital and Demands War Crimes Probe," *Democracy Now*, November 9, 2015.

65 | *among the most brightly lit buildings in Kunduz*: Joseph Goldstein, "Doctors without Borders Says Clues Point to 'Illegal' U.S. Strike on Afghan Hospital," *New York Times*, November 5, 2015.

65 | "drone strikes in Afghanistan—despite their supposed precision": Spencer Ackerman, "US Drone Strikes More Deadly to Afghan Civilians than Manned Aircraft—Adviser," *Guardian*, July 2, 2013.

65 | "caused ten times more civilian casualties than strikes from manned aircraft": Ibid.

66 | "Wim Wenders's documentary": *Pina*, directed by Wim Wenders, Germany, 2011.

66 | *There are situations, of course*: Pina Bausch in ibid.

66–67 | *Drones hover twenty-four hours a day . . . trauma among civilian communities*: James Cavallaro, Sarah Knuckey, and Stephan Sonnenberg, "Living under Drones: Death, Injury, and Trauma to Civilians from US Drone Practices in Pakistan," International Human Rights and Conflict Resolution Clinic, Stanford Law School; NYU School of Law, Global Justice Clinic, September 25, 2012, vii.

67 | *Proper burial ceremonies and grieving rituals*: Ibid., 33; brackets in source.

67 | *Will this be the longest day in history*: Mahmoud Darwish, *Memory for Forgetfulness* (Berkeley: University of California Press, 1995), 36.

68 | "Uncontrollability . . . is a key element": Cavallaro, Knuckey, and Sonnenberg, "Living under Drones," 82.

68 | *Before the drone attacks, it was as if everyone was young*: Ahmed Jan, quoted in ibid.

68 | *Do you remember 9/11 . . . wake up with a start to every noise*: Peter Brenner (pseud.), quoted in ibid.

68 | *the shadow of September 11 and its ongoing consequences*: Cvetkovich, *Depression*, 1.

68 | *If you bang a door, they'll scream*: Noor Behram, quoted in Cavallaro, Knuckey, and Sonnenberg, "Living under Drones," 87.

69 | *a city of broken teeth*: Solmaz Sharif, "Drone, in *Look* (Minneapolis: Graywolf, 2016), 93.

69 | "The language used to talk about the ethics of drone use": The terms *dronespace* and *distant intimacy*, as well as *radically asymmetrical relationship*, come from John Williams, "Distant Intimacy: Space, Drones, and Just War," *Ethics and International Affairs* 29, no. 1 (March 2015): 93–110.

70 | *Though the [Razzo family] hadn't known it*: article, Azmat Khan and Anand Gopal, "The Uncounted," *New York Times*, November 16, 2017.

70 | *While the drone operator knows a great deal*: Williams, "Distant Intimacy," 104.

70 | *You cannot surrender to a Reaper*: Ibid., 103.

70 | *loosened or simply shredded*: David Axe, "While No One Is Looking, Trump Is Escalating America's Drone War," *Vice*, June 22, 2018.

71 | *When you hear the drones . . . they decide our fates from their position in the sky*: Jonathan Cook, "Gaza: Life and Death under Israel's Drones," *Al Jazeera*, November 28, 2013.

71 | *apprehensive silence carrying the weight of metal*: Darwish, *Memory for Forgetfulness*, 75.

71 | "During Operation Cast Lead in 2008. . . ten-minute warning for inhabitants to escape": Cook, "Gaza."

71 | "A United Nations commission found that the tactic was not effective": Idrees Ali and Yeganeh Torbati, "U.S. Military Used 'Roof Knock' Tactic in Iraq to Try to Warn Civilians before Bombing," Insider, April 27, 2016.

72 | "A potent crowd-control technology": Anna Feigenbaum, "100 Years of Tear Gas," *Atlantic,* August 16, 2014.

73 | *widespread, frequent, and indiscriminate . . . I can't see or work or think all day*: Rohini Haar and Jess Ghannam, "No Safe Space: Health Consequences of Tear Gas Exposure among Palestine Refugees," Human Rights Center, UC Berkeley School of Law, January 2018, 24, 14–16.

73 | *People of Aida refugee camp, we are the occupation forces*: "Border Cop Suspended for Threatening to 'Gas' Palestinians," *Times of Israel,* October 2015.

74 | *dramatically more potent, longer lasting, and dangerous . . . it is poison*: Ibrahim Husseini and Liam O'Hare, "'Devastating': Israeli Tear Gas' Effect on Palestinians," *Al Jazeera,* December 28, 2017.

74 | "According to Major Assaf Shaish": Yoav Stoler, "The Israeli Military Has Big Plans for Small Drones: The IDF Continuously Increases Use of Off-the-Shelf Machines Manufactured by the Likes of DJI and Israeli Aeronautics," *CTech,* www.calcalistech.com, June 29, 2018.

74 | "from white phosphorus": Peter Beaumont, "Israel Admits Troops May Have Used Phosphorus Shells in Gaza," *Guardian,* January 21, 2009.

74–75 | "'butterfly bullets' and DIME bombs": Conn Hallinan, "Israel Treated Gaza Like Its Own Private Death Laboratory," AlterNet, February 13, 2009; "Medics in Gaza Report Israel Forces Using Devasting 'Butterfly Bullet," Middle East Monitor, May 3, 2018. (DIME is an acronym for Dense Inert Metal Explosive.)

75 | *showcase its weaponry with the intention of selling it on*": Daniel Hilton, "Drones over Gaza: How Israel Tested Its Latest Technology on Protesters," Middle East Eye, May 16, 2018.

75 | "Israeli weapons companies are actively partnering": Todd Miller and Gabriel Schivone, "Gaza in Arizona: How Israeli High-Tech Firms Will Up-Armor the US-Mexico Border," *Mother Jones*, January 26, 2015.

75 | "When Jarrar was invited to the US": Khaled Jarrar, "Crossing Borders, Looking over Walls," Creative Time Reports, March 14, 2016.

76 | "The 'break the bone strategy'": "Colonel Says Rabin Ordered Breaking of Palestinians' Bones," *Los Angeles Times*, June 22, 1990; Amira Hass, "Broken Bones and Broken Hopes," Haaretz, November 4, 2005.

76 | "A recent US State Department map shows": Adam Entous, "The Maps of Israeli Settlements That Shocked Barack Obama," *New Yorker*, July 9, 2018.

76 | *As Palestinians, we cannot know our landscape*: Khaled Jarrar, "Visual Occupation/s: The Image and Palestine," Thinking Its Presence conference, October 19, 2017, University of Arizona Poetry Center.

77 | *No one has pointed out yet*: James Baldwin, "From 'Nationalism, Colonialism, and the United States: One Minute to Twelve—A Forum,'" in *The Cross of Redemption: Uncollected Writings* (New York: Pantheon, 2010), 14.

77–78 | *For me, this was a material evidence . . . our struggle for that liberation is intertwined*: Michael Rakowitz, "Michael Rakowitz Discusses Withdrawing from the 2019 Whitney Biennial, and His Leonard Cohen Problem," *Art Movements* (podcast), *Hyperallergic*, May 17, 2019.

79 | *"Body Revolution" is about violence*: Irina Angerer, "Mokhallad Rasem: 'Through Art We Can Fix a Broken World' @ TransArt 16," Franzmagazine, September 15, 2016.

79 | *It creates an immense emptiness*: Darwish, *Memory for Forgetfulness*, 76.

80 | *In this show the body screams*: Mokhalled Rasem, "Dancing on the Edge Festival 2015 presents Mokhallad Rasem—Body Revolution," YouTube, November 4, 2015.

Chapter Six

83 | "on the top floor of AZM": AZM is the abbreviation for Academisch Ziekenhuis Maastricht.

83 | "boats are carrying groups of people from Turkey to Greece": Migrants attempted the sea crossing into Greece in part because there is an imposing barbed-wire fence along the Turkey-Bulgaria border; and in part to avoid both Bulgaria, whose police force has been accused of innumerable acts of violence against migrants trying to cross through that country, and Albania, whose strong mafia presence threatened violence that deterred crossing.

85 | *As the recent events in Paris so tragically demonstrate*: "Active Shooter and Complex Attack Resources," Office of Health Affairs, Department of Homeland Security, November 17, 2015, https://www.acep.org/globalassets/uploads/uploaded-files/acep/clinical-and -practice-management/ems-and-disaster-preparedness/active-shooter-and-complex-attack -resources2.pdf.

85 | *It is no longer acceptable . . . to stage and wait for casualties to be brought out to the perimeter*: Joint Committee to Create a National Policy to Enhance Survivability from Intentional Mass Casualty Shooting Events, "Active Shooter and Intentional Mass-Casualty Events: The Hartford Consensus II," *Bulletin of the American College of Surgeons* 98, no. 8 (September 2013): 18–22.

86 | *surround and contain*: Ibid.

86 | "titles such as 'See Something, Do Something' . . . and 'Active Shooter Study'": see "Active Shooter and Complex Attack Resources" for links.

86 | "THREAT": Lenworth M. Jacobs and Joint Committee to Create a National Policy, "Active Shooter and Intentional Mass-Casualty Event." The Harvard Consensus III: Implementation of Bleeding Control," *Bulletin of the American College of Surgeons* (July 2015).

86–87 | *The most significant preventable cause of death . . . Immediate responders must now "see something, do something."*: Ibid.

87 | *Unfortunately, the time has come*: Lenworth M. Jacobs Jr., Karyl J. Burns, Norman McSwain, and Wayne Carver, "Initial Management of Mass-Casualty Incidents due to Firearms: Improving Survival," *Bulletin of the American College of Surgeons* (June 2013).

89 | *facing aggression and hatred*: Dave Grossman, *On Killing: The Psychological Cost of Learning to Kill in War and Society* (Boston: Little, Brown, 1995).

89 | *may be especially severe or long lasting . . . our mental and physical health*: Ibid., citing *Diagnostic and Statistical Manual of Mental Disorders*, 4th edition, 309.81: "Posttraumatic Stress Disorder."

89 | *We want desperately to be liked, loved, and in control*: Grossman, *On Killing*.

90 | *highlight the violence and racism of US culture after 9/11*: Wafaa Bilal, "Domestic Tension," in *Net Art Anthology: Retelling the History of Net Art from the 1980s to the 2010s*, Rhizome, October 27, 2016.

90 | *fire on repeat . . . describe it as a war zone*: Ibid.

90–91 | *defined by the horrific rule of Saddam Hussein . . . the air is not circulating*:: Bilal, "Shoot an Iraqi," wafaabilal.com/shoot-an-iraqi/.

91 | "In early video blogs from the piece": Bilal, "Domestic Tension."

91 | "By later days of the video blog": Ibid.

91 | *the difficulties and joys of the American immigrant experience*: Bilal, "Shoot an Iraqi."

91 | *We may think we are surviving*: Ibid.

92 | *A mode of collective paralysis*: Ronak K. Kapadia, "Death by Double-Tap: (Undoing) Racial Logics in the Age of Drone Warfare," in *With Stones in Our Hands: Reflections on Racism, Muslims, and US Empire*, eds. Sohail Daulatzai and Junaid Rana (Minneapolis: University of Minnesota Press, 2018), 201–18, 208.

94 | *collective outcomes can seem paradoxical . . . These are the* instigators: Mark Granovetter, "Threshold Models of Collective Behavior," *American Journal of Sociology* 83, no. 6 (May 1978), 1420–43, 1422.

95–96 | *There is now empirical evidence to suggest . . . the way a scaffolding can support a crumbling building*: Kakar, *The Colors of Violence*, 149.

96 | *Lurking beneath the surface*: Hedges, *War Is a Force That Gives Us Meaning*, 45.

96 | *self-sameness and continuity in time and space*: Kakar, *The Colors of Violence*, 143.

96–97 | *What happens in the period of tension . . . evoke stronger hostility and hate than do wide disparities*: Ibid., 42.

97 | *the incontestable fundamentals of a person*: Teju Cole, "Black Body: Rereading James Baldwin's 'Stranger in the Village,'" *New Yorker*, August 19, 2014.

97 | *proposes that the perceived precariousness of an Other*: Nelson, *The Art of Cruelty*, 91.

97 | *All of us*: Grossman, *On Killing*.

98 | *advances in ethics and politics are erratic . . . regularly succumbs to barbarism*: John Gray, "Steven Pinker Is Wrong about Violence and War," *Guardian*, March 13, 2015.

98 | *the radical precariousness in which we all share*: Nelson, *The Art of Cruelty*, 92.

100 | *Auschwitz Survivors*: Tzvetan Todorov, *Facing the Extreme: Moral Life in the Concentration Camps* (New York: Holt, 1997), 141.

100 | "D. W. Winnicott, describes such fragmentation": Maggie Nelson, *The Argonauts* (Minneapolis: Graywolf, 2015), 33.

100 | "Kakar writes of the need of egoically fragile strongmen": Kakar, *The Colors of Violence*, 149.

101 | *Compassion and brutality can coexist in the same individual*: Primo Levi, *The Drowned and the Saved*, trans. Raymond Rosenthal (1988; New York: Simon and Schuster, 2017), 44.

101 | *the moral imagination that rises beyond violence has but two*: Lederach, *The Moral Imagination*, 35.

Chapter Seven

103 | *as if we're not all in this together*: Kara Walker in Carolina Miranda, "Q&A: Kara Walker on the Bit of Sugar Sphinx She Saved, Video She's Making," *Los Angeles Times*, October 13, 2014.

103–104 | *The Chinese empire grew from the loess soil*: Dillard, *For the Time Being*, 46.

106 | *While some say that their darkness comes from climbing through chimneys*: Markha Valenta, "Saint Nicholas: The Hard Politics of Soft Myths," December 20, 2010.

108 | *hands out sweets and gifts from his big bag*: Lutz Krebs, "Sinterklaas, Zwarte Piet, and Everything in Between," Maastricht University School for Public Policy and Human Development blog, Oct 30, 2014.

108–109 | *Midway through Candide . . . but all over the world*: Edwidge Danticat, "The Price of Sugar," Creative Time Reports, May 5, 2014.

109 | "In Central America, one report found that laborers worked": "New Reports on Labor Conditions in Sugar Industry in Central America," Global Labor Justice-International Labor Rights Forum, July 18, 2009.

110 | *I wanted to make a piece*: Kara Walker, "Creative Time Presents Kara Walker's 'A Subtlety,'" YouTube, March 20, 2017.

110 | *Europe's black possessions remained*: James Baldwin, "Stranger in the Village," *Notes of a Native Son* (Boston: Beacon, 1955, 1984), 159–75, 170.

111 | *There's this insane amount of pressure*: Kara Walker in interview with Kara L. Rooney, "A Sonorous Subtlety: Kara Walker with Kara Rooney," *Brooklyn Rail*, May 6, 2014.

111 | *It takes bones to get sugar white*: Shailja Patel, "Shailja Patel: Unpour," Creative Time Reports, May 8, 2014.

111 | *Basically, it was blood sugar*: Kara Walker, in interview with Audie Cornish, "Artist Kara Walker Draws Us into Bitter History with Something Sweet," *NPR*, May 16, 2014.

112 | "In the background, a woman's voice keens in song": The recording is of a young woman singing during Memre Waka, a street event held at every opening of the Commemoration Month (for Keti Koti) in Amsterdam. According to Getty Images, "1 July 1863 marked freedom for the Surinamese from slavery. Nowhere is that more celebrated than in Amsterdam, home to a thriving Surinamese community. . . . Keti Koti, meaning 'Broken Chains' in Surinamese, is a free celebration of liberty, equality, and solidarity. . . . It opens with a memorial procession called Memre Waka, around the canal houses of Amsterdam which have a slavery history." "Koti Festival Was Opened in Amsterdam: 10 Pictures," Getty Images, June 1, 2017.

112 | *These sugar loaves were baked in Amsterdam . . . still reminds us of these sugar bakers*: Patricia Kaersenhout, in *Amsterdam, Traces of Sugar / Amsterdam, Sporen van Suikker*, directed by Ida Does, Ida Does Productions, 2017.

113 | *The Dutch sold an estimated 600,000 African people*: Ibid.

113 | *Revenue from the goods produced with slave labor funded much of The Netherlands' Golden Age*: Mia Mitchell, Marie-Ann Ricardo, and Belma Sarajlic, "Whitewashed Slavery Past? The (Lost) Struggle against Ignorance about the Dutch Slavery History," *Humanity in Action* (blog), February 2014.

114 | *white Dutch people are often ignorant*: Ibid.

115 | *This is not the case . . . as structurally racist as the United States*: Gloria Wekker, "Never Be Indifferent: 400 Years of Dutch Colonialism," TEDx Talks, YouTube, November 15, 2016.

115 | *anti-Black to anti-Muslim . . . maintain or gain a sense of place*: Nancy Jouwe, "Reflections on the Netherlands Now," *Etnofoor* 26, no. 1 (2014): 173–78, 176. At the beginning of her essay, Jouwe points to "explicitly racist comments in the mainstream media and on social media (often referring to the Black Piet discussion)."

116 | *I cut out parts from the book . . . is bound to have consequences*: Kaersenhout, in *Amsterdam, Traces of Sugar*.

117 | *You cannot say "it's time to move on"*: Ibid.

118 | *that we have been an empire*: Gloria Wekker, "Toward a Decolonized University, Part 1/3," Nieuwe Universiteit, YouTube, March 17, 2015.

118 | *Much like other former colonial powers*: Markus Balkenhol, "The Changing Aesthetics of Savagery: Slavery, Belonging, and Colonial Melancholia in the Netherlands," *Etnofoor* 22, no. 2 (2010): 80–82, 82.

119 | *If slavery persists as an issue*: Saidiya Hartman, *Lose Your Mother: A Journey along the Atlantic Slave Route* (New York: Farrar, Strauss, and Giroux, 2007), 6.

120 | *White supremacy is usually less a matter*: Paul Lipsitz, *The Possessive Investment in Whiteness*, rev. ed. (Philadelphia: Temple University Press, 2006), viii.

121 | *I wish I could explain how my entire life . . . you must have been wearing strange clothing*: "Sylvana Simons: Zwarte Piet Hoeft Niet Meer Terug Te Komen," online video clip, Joop, December 5, 2015.

123 | *Healing trauma involves recognizing*: Resmaa Menakem, *My Grandmother's Hands: Racialized Trauma and the Pathway to Mending Our Hearts and Bodies* (Las Vegas: Central Recovery, 2017), 165–66.

124 | *It doesn't matter any longer what you do to me*: James Baldwin in Kenneth Bancroft Clark, "A Conversation with James Baldwin," WGBH Boston, June 24, 1963.

124 | "tolerant, worldly Dutch": paraphrasing Balkenhol, "The Changing Aesthetics of Savagery," 80.

124 | *A black man was entombed. . . . We shared this moment of stillness*: Kaersenhout, *Traces of Sugar.*

Chapter Eight

130–31 | *From all available evidence . . . no suggestion that I was human*: Baldwin, "Stranger in the Village," 159–75.

132 | *As a first-generation Greek Bahamian woman who is also queer*: Helen Klonaris, "If I Tell These Stories: Notes on Racism and the White Imaginary," in *The Racial Imaginary: Writers on Race in the Life of the Mind,* ed. Claudia Rankine, Beth Loffreda, and Cap Max King (Albany: Fence, 2015), 83–90, 88.

133 | *I think that a great deal of the psychic pain*: Jess Rowe, "To Whom It May Concern," in *The Racial Imaginary*, 62–63.

133–34 | *anxiety . . . over maintaining my status . . . and through therapy*: Ibid., 61.

135 | *The story of the Negro in America . . . embrace the stranger they have maligned so long*: James Baldwin in *I Am Not Your Negro,* directed by Raoul Peck, footage of James Baldwin and narration by Samuel L. Jackson, Velvet Film, 2016.

136 | "In the Dutch town of Enschede": "12 Pigs' Heads Dumped next to Dutch Refugee Centre Site," DutchNews.nl, November 25, 2015; "Origin of Pig Heads at Asylum Site Still Unknown," NL Times, November 27, 2015.

136 | "a civil servant with the Enschede city council": "Enschede Civil Servant Stabbed Close to Refugee Centre Site," DutchNews.nl, November 2, 2015.

137 | *What white people have to do is try to find out*: James Baldwin, from the WGBH-TV broadcast, May 24, 1963; transcript in "A Conversation with James Baldwin: Kenneth B. Clark, *Freedomways* 3 (Summer 1963): 361–68; reprinted in *Conversations with James Baldwin*, ed. Fred L. Standley and Louis H Pratt (University of Mississippi Press, 1989), 45.

137 | *We feel alienated from other people*: Casey Llewellyn, "What We Could Do with Writing," in *The Racial Imaginary*, 43–48, 47.

138 | *is that race can really keep us from each other*: Ibid., 46.

141 | *I learn that silence is a way of refusing to see*: Klonaris, "If I Tell These Stories," 85.

144 | *Nouns are magical to an immigrant*: Bhanu Kapil, *Ban en Banlieue* (Brooklyn: Nightboat, 2015).

145 | *What can we do?*: Baldwin in *I Am Not Your Negro*.

145 | *I do not believe the twentieth-century myth*: Baldwin, "From 'Nationalism, Colonialism, and the United States,'" 11.

Chapter Nine

149 | *In a funny way I think "Self," the frozen head series*: Mark Quinn, interviewed by Priscilla Frank, "Mark Quinn Discusses Self-Portraits Made of His Own Blood," HuffPost, June 8, 2012; updated December 6, 2017.

150 | "which he preserved in medical refrigerators": Andrew Roth, "Russian Artists Invite Visitors to Donate Blood to Exhibition," *Guardian*, February 8, 2019.

150 | "a power structure that would rather crack down": "Young Blood," from *Dossier Pedagogique: Black Horizon*, BPS22, Musée d'art de la Province de Hainaut, for exhibition opening February 9, 2019.

150 | *intended to encourage visitors to reject propaganda and censorship*: Roth, "Russian Artists Invite Visitors to Donate Blood to Exhibition."

150 | *open world . . . without censorship*: Andrei Molodkin, quoted in ibid.

151 | "A remarkable photo series in the *Guardian*": Mary Turner and Getty Images, "Inside the Homes of the Calais Jungle Camp—in Pictures," *Guardian*, February 27, 2016.

151 | "One striking photo of the operation to clear the camp": Jess McHugh, "EU Refugee Crisis in France: Calais 'Jungle' Camp on Fire, Woman Slits Wrists in Protest," *International Business Times*, March 1, 2016.

152 | *use of the environment as a kind of weapon against the weak . . . slowly embarked on acquiring an empire*: Dan Hicks, quoted in Charlotte Higgins, "Lore of the Jungle: Unearthing Treasures from the Calais Camp," *Guardian*, May 16, 2019.

152 | "In *Frames of War*, Judith Butler": The following two paragraphs paraphrase and quote from Holly Brown, "Judith Butler in Belgium: Reflections on Public Grief and Precarity in the Wake of the Paris Attacks," *DiGeSt.: Journal of Diversity and Gender Studies* 3, no. 1 (2016): 7–16.

152 | *to emphasize our mutual dependency*: Birgit Schippers, *The Political Philosophy of Judith Butler* (New York: Routledge, 2014), 3, quoted in Brown, "Judith Butler in Belgium," 10.

153 | *European governments to conduct airstrikes . . . minimizing precariousness for others*: Ibid., 10–11.

153 | *We are not terrorists so please don't destroy our homes*: Natasha Rees-Bloor, "Calais 'Jungle' Camp Clearance—In Pictures," *Guardian*, February 29, 2016.

154 | *The "state of emergency," however temporary*: Judith Butler, "Mourning Becomes the Law: Judith Butler from Paris," Sexual Policy Watch, November 18, 2015.

155 | *One of the gravest mistakes that Europe has made*: "Peter Bouckaert of HRW: Shutting the Door on Refugees Would Be Propaganda Victory for Islamic State," *Democracy Now!*, November 18, 2015.

155 | *The one who leaves his or her homeland*: Elif Shafak, *The Happiness of Blond People: A Personal Meditation on the Dangers of Identity* (London, Penguin UK, 2011), ebook.

156 | *An Amnesty International Report published in October 2013 . . . a threat to Dutch society*: Marijn Nieuwenhuis, "The Netherlands' Disgrace: Racism and Police Brutality," Open Democracy, July 23, 2015.

157 | "*Though as a recent Christian Science Monitor article points out*": Sara Miller Llana, "Why Police Don't Pull Guns in Many Countries," *Christian Science Monitor*, June 28, 2015.

157 | *has been largely ignored by the international press*: Nieuwenhuis, "The Netherlands' Disgrace."

158 | *Absent a political solution, NGOs estimate*: "EU Council President to Migrants: Do Not Come to Europe," CNN video, March 3, 2016.

158 | *We have reached this point*: "Refugees Block Road in Greece over Closed EU Borders—Video," *Guardian*, April 3, 2016.

159 | *boils down to nothing less than a thickening of borderlands*: Paul Mutsaers, "From the Field: Psychological Operations and the Policing of Migrants in the Netherlands," Oxford Law Faculty, *Border Criminologies* (blog), October 15, 2014.

159 | *It is striking to watch European societies*: Stephane Baele, "Live and Let Die: Did Michel Foucault Predict Europe's Refugee Crisis?," Conversation, February 25, 2016.

159 | *a new logic of government, specific to Western liberal democracies*: Ibid., quoting Foucault.

159 | *sovereign right to seize, repress, and destroy life*: Michael Laurence, "Biopolitics and State Regulation of Human Life," Oxford Bibliographies, April 28, 2016.

159–60 | *paying so much attention to the health and wealth . . . journeys towards a safe but fully sealed place*: Baele, "Live and Let Die."

160 | *"It's been like this for months"*: Peter Yeung, "'Like Torture': Calais Police Accused of Continued Migrant Rights Abuses," *Guardian*, January 13, 2021.

161 | *on a rolling 48-hour schedule*: Ibid.

161 | *"They come at 5am, circle around your tent"*: Ibid.

161 | *It is like the authorities think we are animals and they are taking us from one farm to another*: Diane Taylor, "French Police Clear Migrant Camp at Launch Point for Britain," *Guardian*, September 29, 2020.

161 | *"tactics of exhaustion," designed to weaken . . . cycle of "cleansing" migrant camps*: Dan Hicks and Sarah Mallet, *Lande: The Calais "Jungle" and Beyond* (Bristol, UK: Bristol University Press, 2019), 34, 32–33.

162 | *precarity is a condition of dependency*: Lauren Berlant, *Cruel Optimism* (Durham, NC: Duke University Press, 2011), 192; quoted in "Precarity and Performance: An Introduction," by Nicholas Ridout and Rebecca Schneider, *TDR: The Drama Review* 56, no. 4 (2012): 5–9.

162 | *structural abandonment of vulnerable communities*: Ruth Wilson Gilmore, "Intercepted Podcast: Ruth Wilson Gilmore Makes the Case for Abolition," podcast, Intercept, June 10, 2020.

162 | *Calais is just one location among many*: Hicks and Mallet, *Lande*, 24.

162 | "Frédéric Gros, another scholar of Foucault's ideas, sees biopolitics as an age of security": Nicolae Morar, discussing Gros's chapter, "The Fourth Age of Security," in her review of *The Government of Life: Foucault, Biopolitics, and Neoliberalism*," by Miguel and Vanessa Lem Vatter, *Notre Dame Philosophical Reviews* (May 2015).

163 | *a thickening of borderlands*: Mutsaers, "From the Field."

163 | *"wherever the movement of information, people, and things takes place"*: Hicks and Mallet, *Lande*, 27.

163 | *This includes . . . the biopolitics of the body*: Ibid., 73–74.

163 | *an epoch of global fear*: "On Nationalism: Borders and Belonging," The Racial Imaginary Institute, January 2021.

163 | *It would be impossible now to mistake*: Hicks and Mallet, *Lande*, 25.

164 | *If you unplug it*: Mark Quinn, quoted in Frank, "Self-Portraits Made of Frozen Blood."

164 | *more than at any time since the second world war*: Patrick Wintour, "Humanitarian System Not Listening to People in Crises, Says UN Aid Chief," *Guardian*, April 21, 2021.

164–65 | *a river of refugees . . . somewhere someone or some government can accept their humanity*: Poupeh Missaghi, "The Death Card," Entropy, August 16, 2016.

165 | *All the shoes have a different story*: Marko Risovic, quoted in Rachel Lubitz, "These Powerful Photos of Shoes Show a Different Side of the Refugee Crisis in Serbia," Mic, October 23, 2015. See also "Refugee Crisis: Every Shoe Has a Story," CNN, October 23, 2015, https://edition.cnn.com/2015/10/22/europe/refugees-serbia-shoes/index.html.

165 | *In an era of resurgent and terrifying ethnic and racial nationalism*: "On Nationalism."

Chapter Ten

168 | "I watch a BBC video of Turkish coast guardsmen": Migrant Crisis: Turkish Guards Hit Migrant Boat with Sticks, March 12, 2016, BBC.

169 | *The feeling that something is happening*: Kapil, *Ban en Banlieue.*

169 | *I am aware that this is to try to help*: Missaghi, "The Death Card."

174 | *I have been reminded of how a lack of language*: Ibid.

174 | *the imaginary proximity to suffering*: Susan Sontag, *Regarding the Pain of Others* (New York: Farrar, Straus and Giroux, 2003), 102.

175 | *"species" division between what it means to be a subject and what it means to be an object*: Saidiya V. Hartman and Frank B. Wilderson, "The Position of the Unthought," *Qui Parle* 13, no. 2 (2003): 183–201, 190.

175 | *my experience of photographs of disasters that happen in Black spaces*: Sharpe, *In the Wake*, 53.

176 | *I don't want to create trauma porn*: Vanessa Angélica Villarreal, speaking at "Beyond the Event" panel, facilitated by Kathleen Blackburn, Nonfiction Now 2018.

176 | "I wrote an essay about my experience": Arianne Zwartjes, "These Dark Skies: Seeking Refuge on Europe's Shores," *Catapult*, February 27, 2017; originally appeared in *Southern Review* 53, no. 1 (Winter 2017): 37–47.

177 | *to think constellationally*: Teju Cole, "The White-Savior Industrial Complex," *Atlantic,* March 21, 2012.

178 | *Too often these violences are cast as disastrous events*: "Beyond the Event" panel.

Chapter Eleven

181 | "The US pioneered some of our most insidious empire-building strategies in Greece during the early Cold War era": For a discussion of the subject, see Suzy Hansen, "Benevolent Interventions: Greece and Turkey," *Notes on a Foreign Country: An American Abroad in a Post-American World* (New York: Farrar, Strauss and Giroux, 2017), 142–50.

181 | *The term "crisis" derives from the Greek "krisis"*: William Davies, "The Last Global Crisis Didn't Change the World. But This One Could," *Guardian,* March 24, 2020.

182 | *about the body and violence and protest*: Olivia Laing, in interview with Chris Kraus, "Becoming Kathy Acker: An Interview with Olivia Laing," *Paris Review*, September 11, 2018.

182 | *One of the group's members gathers his long hair*: Cleo Abramian, "Iraqi Performance Artists Use Silence as a Gesture of Dissent," *Hyperallergic*, November 22, 2019.

183 | *ordinary words convey only what we know already*: Aristotle, *Rhetorica* 1411b, quoted in George Lakoff and Mark Johnson, *Metaphors We Live By* (Chicago: University of Chicago Press, 1980), 190.

183 | *to use words metaphorically*, Lakoff and Johnson, *Metaphors We Live By*, 191, 193.

183 | *critical language . . . the subject positions which we assume uncritically*: Henry Giroux and Peter McLaren, "Writing from the Margins: Geographies of Identity, Pedagogy, and Power," *Journal of Education* 174, no. 1 (1992): 7–30, 26.

184 | *The term "identity" . . . implies that there is a fixed essence . . . decentered flux of subject positions*: Ibid., 14.

185 | *an outsider is someone who*: Naomi Goldenberg, "Stepping Out of the Circle: Overcoming Tribal Identities," quoted in Arianne Zwartjes, "A Critical Look at Cross-Cultural Education and Service Learning," thesis submitted to the Friends World Program of Long Island University, June 2001.

186 | *What we are asking for*: Gayatri Spivak, *The Postcolonial Critic* (London: Routledge, 1990), 121.

186 | *great advantage of having never believed*: James Baldwin, "Down at the Cross: Letter from a Region in My Mind," *The Fire Next Time* (New York: Delta, 1964), 115.

187 | *would stage or support . . . Argentina in 1962, Guatemala again in 1963*: Hansen, "Benevolent Interventions," 149.

189 | *We were all patriotic*: Suzy Hansen, "Unlearning the Myth of American Innocence," *Guardian*, August 8, 2017.

189 | *Young white Americans*: Ibid.

190 | *alleviating the damage done . . . with total blindness to much worse poverty at home*: Ivan Illich, "To Hell with Good Intentions," address to the Conference on InterAmerican Student Projects (CIASP), Cuernavaca, Mexico, April 20, 1968; reprinted in *Combining Service and Learning: A Resource Book for Community and Public Service*, ed. Jane C. Kendall, vol. 1 (Raleigh, NC: National Society for Internships and Experiential Education, 1990, 314–20, 316, 317, 315.

190 | *I am here to challenge you to . . . one cannot even say "thank you"*: Ibid., in *Combining Service and Learning*, 320, 316.

191 | *palliative effects of [one's] own ignorance*: Hansen, *Notes on a Foreign Country*, 156.

191 | *"as Coco Fusco has neatly laid out"*: Coco Fusco, "The Other History of Intercultural Performance," *TDR: The Drama Review* 38, no. 1 (Spring 1994): 143–67, 146–47.

192 | *"the performance art of Fusco and Guillermo"*: Gómez-Peña *The Couple in the Cage: A Guatinaui Odyssey*, directed by Guillermo Gómez-Peña and Paula Heredia, Third World Newsreel, 1993.

193 | *What distinguishes* The Couple in the Cage *. . . tests the moral limits of theatrical representation*: Barbara Kirshenblatt-Gimblett. "The Ethnographic Burlesque," *TDR: The Drama Review* 42, no. 2 (Summer 1998), 175–80, 178.

193 | *rehearses . . . a mode of encounter . . . the practices of othering*: Ibid., 176, 177.

193–94 | *empathy with members of the other group*: Kakar, *The Colors of Violence*, 140–41.

194 | *Once children have been indoctrinated*: Walter Wink, "The Myth of Redemptive Violence," in *The Powers That Be* (New York: Doubleday, 1999), 53.

194 | *we don't acknowledge that America is an empire*: Hansen, "Introduction," 11.

196–97 | *No matter how well I knew the predatory aspects . . . beyond prejudice and beyond ignorance*: Hansen, "Unlearning the Myth of American Innocence."

197 | *I returned from New Orleans*: Wendy S. Walters, *Multiply/Divide* (Louisville, KY: Sarabande, 2015), 9.

198 | *what are the conditions*: "Intercepted Podcast: Ruth Wilson Gilmore Makes the Case for Abolition," Intercept, June 10, 2020.

198 | *Violence, as it says in the Zohar . . . subtle social nihilism that is manifested as pragmatism*: Fanny Howe, *The Winter Sun*, 50.

199 | *chaos and perpetual disruption*: Laing, quoted in Kraus, "Becoming Kathy Acker."

200 | *I think there's been a failure of imagination . . . we're in real trouble*: Mohsin Hamid, "Magical Novel 'Exit West' Explores What Makes Refugees Leave Home," *PBS NewsHour*, March 16, 2017.

200 | *transformed his body into a mysterious package . . . and a new language*: Guillermo Gómez-Peña, "Essential Works," guillermogomezpena.com/works/.

Chapter Twelve

204 | *oracle of entrails . . . soft with moss*: J'Lyn Chapman, *Beastlife* (Rome: Calamari, 2015), 7–10.

204 | *at once humble and cosmic*: J. Hoberman, "*Andrei Rublev*: An Icon Emerges," Criterion Collection, January 11, 1999, https://www.criterion.com/current/posts/43-andrei-rublev-an-icon-emerges.

205 | *contorted beast . . . index of a shimmering surface*: Chapman, *Beastlife*, 30–31.

208 | *spiritual process of exposing the essence of the universe*: wall text from "Chagall to Malevich" exhibition, *Albertina Museum*, Vienna, 2016.

208 | "for his 'spiritual outlook' on art": Natalie Hegert, "From Chagall to Malevich: The Competitive Drama of the Russian Avant-Garde," Mutual Art, March 9, 2016.

208 | *despised as an expression of degeneration*: wall text from "Chagall to Malevich" exhibition.

208 | *basic vocabulary of Suprematism . . . zero of form*: Ibid.

208 | *The sacred spot where Malevich chose to hang his Black Square*: Shira Wolfe, "Stories of Iconic Artworks: Kazimir Malevich's *Black Square*," *Artland*, March 27, 2020.

208 | *charged with resurgent Slav mysticism*: Hoberman, "*Andrei Rublev*: An Icon Emerges."

209 | *in total darkness, symbolizing a destruction of Russian tradition*: Wolfe, "Stories of Iconic Artworks."

209 | *in the relationship between man and the universe*: Evgenia Petrova, "Malevich's Suprematism and Religion," in *Kazimir Malevich: Suprematism*, ed. Matthew Drutt, exhibition catalogue (New York: Guggenheim Museum, 2003), 89–95, 91, https://archive.org/details/kazimiroomale.

209 | *direct communion with ultimate reality*: *Merriam-Webster*, s.v. "mysticism."

Chapter Thirteen

217 | *Hope locates itself in the premises that we don't know what will happen*: Rebecca Solnit, *Hope in the Dark*, 3rd ed. (Chicago: Haymarket, 2016), xiv.

218 | *Sand and stone are Earth's memory*: Lauret Savoy, *Trace: Memory, History, Race, and the American Landscape* (Berkeley: Counterpoint, 2015), 16.

219 | *I tell all my writing students*: John Rybicki, author's notes, source unknown.

219 | *we read the poem to keep our wounds open*: Dan Beachy-Quick, "A January Notebook," *Evening Will Come: A Monthly Journal of Poetics*, no. 4 (April 2011), https://thevolta.org/ewc4-dbeachy-quick-p1.html.

220–21 | *harvested from free-floating icebergs in a fjord . . . so desperately important*: Claire Bonham-Carter, "Notes from COP 21: #icewatchparis," AECOM (blog), December 16, 2015.

221 | *The glacier is decanting*: Jason Box, quoted in "Voluntary Pledges Aren't Enough: Glaciologist Says Nonbinding Emission Reductions Won't Cut It," *Democracy Now!*, December 11, 2015.

222 | *It needs to be translated into action*: Sontag, *Regarding the Pain of Others*, 101.

223 | *The media's general interest is in "struggle porn"*: Cannupa Hanska Luger, quoted in Miranda, "Q&A: The Artist Who Made Protesters' Mirrored Shields," *Los Angeles Times*, January 12, 2017.

223–24 | *I was inspired by these activists in the Ukraine . . . more damage than good*, Luger, in ibid.

224 | *Artists, we live on the periphery*: Ibid.

225–26 | *One thing the Buddhists say . . . it's suffering alone*: Kate Braestrup, "A Presence in the Wild," *On Being*, June 26, 2008.

227 | *No culture has yet solved the dilemma*: Barry Lopez, *Arctic Dreams* (New York: Scribner, 1986), 173.

229 | *That there's a real ending to anything*: Carmen Maria Machado, *In the Dream House* (Minneapolis: Graywolf, 2019), 239.

229 | *A mystic is anyone who has the gnawing suspicion*: Lawrence Kushner, "Kabbalah and Everyday Mysticism," *On Being,* March 21, 2019; original air date, May 15, 2014.

230 | "And in the documentary film *Cage on Cage*": *Cage on Cage: An Interview,* directed by Barry Harris, 1982, https://sitesantafe.org/event/cage-on-cage-an-interview/.

230 | *is it really a big stretch to imagine*: Jeremy Rifkin, "RSA Animate: The Empathic Civilization," YouTube, May 6, 2010.

230 | *white people's absence of tragedy and fear of death*: Hansen, *Notes on a Foreign Country*, 21, quoting James Baldwin, "Nobody Knows My Name."

231 | *It is not until one contemplates loving someone*: Hansen, *Notes on a Foreign Country*, 246.

231 | *What makes this hope* radical: Jonathan Lear, *Radical Hope: Ethics in the Face of Cultural Devastation* (Cambridge, MA: Harvard University Press, 2009), 103; quoted in

Junot Diaz, "Under President Trump, Radical Hope Is Our Best Weapon," *New Yorker,* November 21, 2016.

231–32 | *A paradox suggests that truth . . . new life, birth, is always possible*: Lederach, *The Moral Imagination*, 36, 5, 38.

232 | *I think God is setting us a big challenge*: Jonathan Sacks, "Enriched by Difference," *On Being*, April 25, 2016.

232 | *To risk is to step into the unknown*: Lederach, *The Moral Imagination*, 39.

232 | *The question isn't whether we're going to have to do hard, awful things*: Kate Braestrup, "The Paradox of Suffering and Love," *On Being*, May 2, 2016.

ACKNOWLEDGMENTS

To play on Dana Ward's "many gendered-mothers of my heart" in the poem "A Kentucky of Mothers," I would like to express thanks to the "many-*genred* mothers of my heart" for this and all my writing: to all the authors, from Wendy S. Walters to Anne Carson and Bhanu Kapil and Fanny Howe, Jenny Boully and Rae Parris and Noam Dorr and onward, who have written projects that were "mixed"—variable and hybrid and multilayered, and at times uneven in all the best ways possible.

I love this part of every book and read them eagerly because they are a kind of acknowledgment that, even though it often feels solitary and so very alone, writing is actually a deeply communal act. The acknowledgments page is a way of claiming community, of saying "these are the people I owe a debt to, these are the people who stand around me, who offer support and inspiration." To that end: I am more indebted than I can ever acknowledge to my dear friends, support network, and incredibly talented writers Aisha Sabatini Sloan, Beth Alvarado, and Debbie Weingarten. They have read and reread drafts and essays from this manuscript and offered insightful comments and suggestions for revision over and over with grace, generosity, and brutal honesty.

Thanks especially to Aisha, for so many conversations over the years that have helped prompt ideas and parts of this book, but more importantly have helped me stay sane and find my way through the world. I would be lost without our friendship.

Thanks, too, to Boyer Rickel, Riley Beck Iosca, and Hannah Ensor for your generous readings and comments, and to Amy Frykholm for the walks and writing-talk and encouragement through the entire snowy winter of 2016–17 and onward. And to the Maastricht Writers Workshop: Martine, Becky, Colette, Steve, Ariane, Katya, Bob.

To my parents, William and Georgia. Thank you so much for all of your love and support—despite the not insignificant discomfort of having a nonfiction writer in the family.

A huge thanks to Angeliki & Stratis, Nikos, Hilde, Kylie, Christos, and everyone else living in and volunteering in Malakasa. Thanks to Kimi Eisele, Poupeh Missaghi, and Ida

Does; John Hovey for suggesting I check out Grossman's book and for the conversations in Reykjavik; Jeremy for suggesting *War Is a Force That Gives Us Meaning*; Dasha and Rebecca for your ongoing friendship and relationship-twinning; Ron and Laetitia for welcoming us (and checking out that round apartment!); and Jo and John, for being our Denver family. To Kell & Jen, Leah, Megan, TC, Lisa, Joe, Acacia, Ross, and Parris: all the love.

Thank you to Ander Monson for many years of mentoring, encouragement, and support; to Jim Cook for that "incredible opportunity" to moonlight in the UA visual arts program; and to Adrienne Segall, whose words have made it into two of my books now, and the influence of whose thinking goes far beyond the books.

To my fellow Sierra Nevada University MFA faculty, especially to Sunil Yapa and Pablo Cartaya and Lee Herrick for the conversations at residency (and Pablo, thank you for saying *start it there*). To Brendan Bashem and Camille Dungy for the powerful and inspiring coreadings, and Brian Turner and Suzanne Roberts for your ongoing support.

Immense gratitude to all the wonderful writers/artists/thinkers/humans who participated in and brought your words, thoughts, insights to the autotheory workshops I taught at the University of Arizona Poetry Center and the Bend Writers Workshop and Hugo House, and to Jen Soriano and Shamala Gallagher and others who have helped me develop my thinking about autotheory and autopolitics, which directly informed this writing.

And to Farid, Sohrab, Farah, Fiki, Nouria, Julian, Kailash, Marte, Ali, Dara, Sandile, Tinashe, Themba, Arthur, Joseph, Razan, Fini, Jess, Nash, Uli, Alejandro, Saliou, Juulia, Jimena, Mzwakithi, Justice, and all of the wonderful, amazing students at UWCs around the world, for your vision and idealism and steadfast belief that something better is possible.

To Anna, my love, I owe huge, immense, vast thanks. Most of the thinking in this book is about ten times deeper than it would have been without you—our conversations and your questions and ideas have helped me see my own blind spots, helped me identify what I was really trying to talk about, or helped me name what was at stake beneath the surface of the thing.

I am grateful to the following publications where many of the essays in this book first appeared: *Entropy, Fourth Genre, Witness, Denver Quarterly, Catapult, Southern Review, Tarpaulin Sky*, and *Kenyon Review*. Thanks especially to Emily Nemens for enthusiastically championing portions of this writing, and to Tarpaulin Sky Press and Graywolf Press for your recognition of the full manuscript.

Finally, thank you so, so much to all the folks at the University of Iowa Press who have helped bring this book out into the world—I am so deeply indebted to you for your time, attention, and generosity with it.